Shakespeare and the Institution of Theatre

Palgrave Shakespeare Studies

General Editors: Michael Dobson and Gail Kern Paster

Editorial Advisory Board: Michael Neill, University of Auckland; David Schalkwyk, University of Capetown; Lois D. Potter, University of Delaware; Margreta de Grazia, Queen Mary University of London; Peter Holland, University of Notre Dame

Palgrave Shakespeare Studies takes Shakespeare as its focus but strives to understand the significance of his oeuvre in relation to his contemporaries, subsequent writers and historical and political contexts. By extending the scope of Shakespeare and English Renaissance Studies the series will open up the field to examinations of previously neglected aspects or sources in the period's art and thought. Titles in the *Palgrave Shakespeare Studies* series seek to understand anew both where the literary achievements of the English Renaissance came from and where they have brought us.

Titles include:

Pascale Aebischer, Edward J. Esche and Nigel Wheale (*editors*)
REMAKING SHAKESPEARE
Performance across Media, Genres and Cultures

Mark Thornton Burnett
FILMING SHAKESPEARE IN THE GLOBAL MARKETPLACE

David Hillman
SHAKESPEARE'S ENTRAILS
Belief, Scepticism and the Interior of the Body

Jane Kingsley-Smith
SHAKESPEARE'S DRAMA OF EXILE

Stephen Purcell
POPULAR SHAKESPEARE
Simulation and Subversion on the Modern Stage

Erica Sheen
SHAKESPEARE AND THE INSTITUTION OF THEATRE

Paul Yachin and Jessica Slights
SHAKESPEARE AND CHARACTER
Theory, History, Performance, and Theatrical Persons

Forthcoming titles:

Timothy Billings
GLOSSING SHAKESPEARE

Palgrave Shakespeare Studies
Series Standing Order ISBN 978–1403–911643 (hardback) 978–1403–911650 (paperback)
(*outside North America only*)

You can receive future titles in this series as they are published by placing a standing order. Please contact your bookseller or, in case of difficulty, write to us at the address below with your name and address, the title of the series and the ISBN quoted above.

Customer Services Department, Macmillan Distribution Ltd, Houndmills, Basingstoke, Hampshire RG21 6XS, England

Shakespeare and the Institution of Theatre

'The Best in this Kind'

Erica Sheen

© Erica Sheen 2009

All rights reserved. No reproduction, copy or transmission of this publication may be made without written permission.

No portion of this publication may be reproduced, copied or transmitted save with written permission or in accordance with the provisions of the Copyright, Designs and Patents Act 1988, or under the terms of any licence permitting limited copying issued by the Copyright Licensing Agency, Saffron House, 6–10 Kirby Street, London EC1N 8TS.

Any person who does any unauthorized act in relation to this publication may be liable to criminal prosecution and civil claims for damages.

The author has asserted her right to be identified as the author of this work in accordance with the Copyright, Designs and Patents Act 1988.

First published 2009 by
PALGRAVE MACMILLAN

Palgrave Macmillan in the UK is an imprint of Macmillan Publishers Limited, registered in England, company number 785998, of Houndmills, Basingstoke, Hampshire RG21 6XS.

Palgrave Macmillan in the US is a division of St Martin's Press LLC, 175 Fifth Avenue, New York, NY 10010.

Palgrave Macmillan is the global academic imprint of the above companies and has companies and representatives throughout the world.

Palgrave® and Macmillan® are registered trademarks in the United States, the United Kingdom, Europe and other countries.

ISBN-13: 978–0–230–52480–4   hardback
ISBN-10: 0–230–52480–X   hardback

This book is printed on paper suitable for recycling and made from fully managed and sustained forest sources. Logging, pulping and manufacturing processes are expected to conform to the environmental regulations of the country of origin.

A catalogue record for this book is available from the British Library.

A catalog record for this book is available from the Library of Congress.

10 9 8 7 6 5 4 3 2 1
18 17 16 15 14 13 12 11 10 09

Printed and bound in Great Britain by
CPI Antony Rowe, Chippenham and Eastbourne

'All I have to say is to tell you that the lantern is the moon, I the man i' th' moon, this thorn bush my thorn bush, and this dog my dog.'

A Midsummer Night's Dream 5.1.247–9

Contents

Acknowledgements viii

1. The Institution of Theatre 1
2. Nebuchadnezzar's Tree 19
3. A Pleasure and a Profit: *The Taming of the Shrew* 43
4. Welcome to our Chamber: *The History of Richard III, Sir Thomas More, Richard III* 52
5. Calling Fools into a Circle: *The Woman's Prize, The Two Gentlemen of Verona, The Merchant of Venice, As You Like It* 72
6. The Only Man: *A Midsummer Night's Dream* and *Hamlet* 97
7. A Stranger to My Heart: *King Lear* 112
8. 'Tis Time: *The Alchemist* and *The Tempest* 128

Notes 143

Index 167

Acknowledgements

I am pleased to acknowledge Wolfson College and St. John's College, Oxford for Visiting Scholarships in 1998 and 2006, and the Harry Ransom Center, the University of Texas at Austin for a Fellowship in 2008. The Department of English and Related Literatures at the University of York has provided an almost ideal intellectual environment. I owe a debt of thanks for support and encouragement to colleagues there, including Derek Attridge, David Atwell, Judith Buchanan, Victoria Coulson, Jane Moody, Richard Rowland, Bill Sherman, Geoff Wal, Jocelyn Wogan Brown and particularly to Matt Bevis, for conversations driving to work through dark Yorkshire dawns.

Thanks of various kinds go to colleagues and friends at other institutions: Jonathan Bate, Matt Campbell, Joe Kember, Shirley Foster, Tom Healy, Lorna Hutson, Michelle O'Callaghan and Marcus Nevitt. Tim Armstrong, Alex Houen, David Norbrook, Adam Piette, Sally Shuttleworth and Sue Wiseman have been been particularly generous with all kinds of encouragement and inspiration. Sir John Baker, Mike Braddick, Alan Bryson, Andrew Gurr, David Ibbotson, Neil Jones, Gordon McMullan and John Watts responded to queries, and at Palgrave Macmillan, Paula Kennedy, Steven Hall and my editors Michael Dobson and Gail Kern Paster have seen the manuscript through to publication with patience and perception. I was particularly well served by my readers, who provided extremely helpful suggestions, and generally tried to save me from myself. The extent to which they may have failed is of course my responsibility.

Thanks also to my family, particularly Anne Delnevo, Ian Macro, Mary Turl – and Emma, who always asked me how it was going, even when it wasn't. Invaluable friends have included Martha Campbell, Karen and Peter Goff Leggett and all the Washakies. Dido and Poppy, and now Lily, Plum and Halle supplied chaos and welcome diversion. I should also mention Ecclesall Woods: thanks for being there when I had to think things through.

Finally, a very special acknowledgment to Judy Templeton.

1
The Institution of Theatre

At the beginning of the 1980s the idea of the institution began to transform the traditional boundaries of research in the arts and social sciences.[1] This new paradigm was accompanied by a rejection of formalist and 'totalising' theoretical approaches such as Marxism, deconstruction and psychoanalysis, and by a turn to models of society like that of Michel Foucault, who offered a reading of history in which power is circulated discursively through institutional systems such as the prison, clinic, church or the law. In literary studies, particularly Renaissance studies, it was pioneered by the group of American critics known as the New Historicists, whose work rapidly achieved a level of prestige reflected in its continuing influence today, nearly thirty years later.

Beginning my own academic work around the same time in two unrelated areas – Shakespearean theatre and American cinema – I was struck over and over again by the contrast between the effect, and effectiveness, of institutional approaches in both fields of research. In film studies, they have been instrumental in defining its emergence as a discipline from the disparate range of often incompatible approaches that characterised its early development in academic departments of literature and language across the 1960s and 1970s. In this context, the study of cinema as an institution, and of the institutions of cinema, was attended by the understanding that theories of the institution and the empirical study of particular examples, like the Hollywood studios or production companies, both demanded a place at all levels of education in the field.[2] By contrast, the approach to institutional analysis associated with New Historicism often seemed to add up to little more than secondhand Foucault instilled by a process of intellectual osmosis from other criticism, almost invariably with no extended theoretical discussion, little detailed attention to specific examples and very little apparent agreement about what an institution actually is. As a result, it created more problems than it solved. While much of the most important work of the last two decades has extended and refined the New Historicist position, it has not revisited the question of theory. As a result, when the word 'institution' appears on the surface of a discussion, it almost always reveals the extent to which the underlying intellectual and political tensions that accompanied the emergence of this idea in the 1980s still affect our work. In particular, it limits the extent to which we seem able to combine detailed social and historical accounts of institutional systems like theatre companies and playhouses with a close reading of the individual texts that sustain them. Recent studies present a wealth of contextual analysis, but they have largely confirmed New Historicism's relegation of theoretical exposition and textual hermeneutics to a vestigial position within the discipline as a whole.

To a considerable extent, the dominant characteristic of New Historicist institutional analysis was its attempt to create a reflexive relation between the historical object of its study and its own institutional present. Paradoxically, it is this reflexivity that has been responsible for disabling the application of this potentially transformative intellectual paradigm to the past. In the discussion that follows, I trace the idea of the institution through some of the most important studies of the last thirty years, not to dismiss or belittle work for which I have a great deal of respect, but to show how it maintains a dialogue with principles of criticism that I believe have rendered the idea of the institution ineffective. In the second section of this chapter I suggest that it is to theories of the institution that arose at almost exactly the same time as New Historicism in the 1980s that we might return to reverse this disabling effect.

Back to the future

I begin with a study that made a programmatic statement for what it presented as a new critical agenda: Stephen Greenblatt's article 'Psychoanalysis and Renaissance Culture'.[3] In its account of a French peasant who assumed the identity of the landowner Martin Guerre for four years before his eventual exposure as an impostor, this essay draws on both a materialist approach to property relations and on the Foucauldian model of the disciplinary body to dismiss the adequacy of Freudian psychoanalysis for a description of the historical subject. According to Greenblatt, 'it is only when proprietary rights to the self have been secured ... that the subject of psychoanalysis, both its method and the materials upon which it operates, is made possible'.[4] What guarantees these rights is 'the accumulation of institutional decisions' that surround their contention:[5] 'what matters most in the literary texts, as in the documents that record the case of Martin Guerre, are communally secured property rights to a name and a place in an increasingly mobile social world...'.[6]

So far so good; but here the questions begin. It is not clear whether these two levels of social organisation – institutional decisions and communally secured rights – are assumed to be equivalent: the passive constructions within which both are placed leave all questions of agency obscure. In the event, the question is irrelevant, since within two pages Greenblatt has shifted his ground in a way that radically destabilises both. Observing that psychoanalysis can 'redeem its belatedness only when it historicizes its own procedures',[7] he turns for that redemption neither to Marx nor to Foucault, but to Thomas Hobbes:

> The crucial consideration is ownership: what distinguishes a 'natural' person from an artificial person is that the former is considered to *own* his words and actions. Considered by whom? By authority. But is authority itself then natural or artificial? In a move that is one of the cornerstones of Hobbes' absolutist political philosophy, authority is invested in an artificial person who represents the words and actions of the entire nation. All men therefore are impersonators of themselves, but impersonators whose clear title to identity is secured by an authority irrevocably deeded to an artificial person.[8]

Of course, the attraction of the Hobbesian model is its consonance with Greenblatt's influential notion of self-fashioning,[9] a fact that might prevent us from noticing that, in its shift from an ownership of the self based on proprietary rights institutionally secured in communal decisions to one in which the self is invested in, and by, sovereign authority, his argument appears to have contradicted itself. Its drift from materialism to absolutism suggests that there is more at stake than merely an argument about the past. In the essay that follows in the same collection, 'Towards a Poetics of Culture', Greenblatt gives us a personal insight into the institutional context in which this change of allegiance found its occasion:

> In the 1970s I used to teach courses with names like 'Marxist Aesthetics' on the Berkeley campus. This came to an inglorious end when I was giving such a course – it must have been the mid 1970s – and I remember a student getting very angry with me. Now it's true that

> I tended to like those Marxist figures who were troubled in relation to Marxism – Walter Benjamin, the early rather than late Lukács, and so forth – and I remember someone finally got up and screamed out in class 'You're either a Bolshevik or a Menshevik – make up your fucking mind' and then slammed the door. It was a little unsettling, but I thought about it afterwards and realized that I wasn't sure whether I was a Menshevik, but I certainly wasn't a Bolshevik. After that I started teaching courses with names like 'cultural poetics'.

'It's true', he conceded, 'that I'm still more uneasy with a politics and a literary persepctive that is untouched by Marxist thought, but that doesn't lead me to endorse propositions or embrace a particular philosophy, politics or rhetoric, *faute de mieux*.'[10]

It is impossible to read this without hearing echoes of the so-called 64 thousand-dollar question, 'Are you now or have you ever been a member of the Communist Party of the United States?'[11] Greenblatt's disavowal of Marxism came at a critical time in the American imagination of a post-Cold War global culture. It is crucial for our understanding of the controversial New Historicist anecdote that we see it at work here in its own professional setting, demonstrating the way it mediates personal and institutional contexts with the concept of a proposition-free culture towards which it purportedly aspires.[12] As the essay proceeds we learn what kind of culture that is: one defined by an academic method that attends not to property but to circulation. As Marxist aesthetics conceded to cultural poetics, the study of the institution gave way to that of the market. From Greenblatt's own 'return' to Martin Guerre to his progression 'towards a poetics of culture', there is a shift, in Christopher Prendergast's words, 'from the language of dialectics (rooted ... in the Hegelian–Marxist tradition of explanation) to an openly commercial language of deal-making and exchange'.[13]

Of course, much of the power of Greenblatt's work derived from the fact that he knew this before we did. 'My use of the term *circulation*', he confided in the same essay, 'depends less upon poststructuralist theory than upon the circulatory rhythms of American politics'.[14] Into the 1990s and beyond, it was the pulse of these circulatory rhythms that animated the study of Shakespeare. In *Shakespearean Negotiations: The Circulation of Social Energy in Renaissance England* he gave us an account of Shakespeare's plays as

> intended at once to enhance the power of the theater as an institution and to draw upon the power this institution has already accumulated.

The desire to enhance the general practice of which any particular work is an instance close to the centre of all artistic production, but in the drama this desire is present in a direct, even coarse, sense because of the overwhelming importance and immediacy of material interests. Shakespeare the shareholder was presumably interested not simply in a good return on an individual play but in the health and success of his entire company as it related both to those who helped regulate it and to its audience. Each individual play may be said to make a small contribution to the general store of social energy possessed by the theater and hence to the sustained claim that the theater can make on its real and potential audience.[15]

To a certain extent, the way the idea of the institution works here could be described as Foucauldian: somehow or another, 'theatre as an institution' pre-exists all those agents and agencies – writers, companies and plays – we might have imagined to be responsible for its development. If we wanted a model of analysis that would help us understand how Shakespearean theatre *became* an institution, this would not be it. What exactly is a 'general store of social energy', and how and when has, or did, 'the theater' come to 'possess' it? What exactly is the relationship between this possession and its 'sustained claim' on an audience? Does 'the theater' sustain such a claim *because* it has 'a general store of energy', or does it have a general store of energy because it sustains a claim? As Christopher Pye has suggested, the discourse of 'negotiation', 'liquidity' and 'exchange' has come to articulate an account of the entire social field.[16] Foucault is less to the point here than the more contemporary energies, or rather synergies, of the global media-scape of the 1980s and 1990s,[17] in particular, its preoccupation with movements of return that supplied continuity at a time of massive historical change. As new technologies like video, cable TV and DVD created a multi-media screen culture dominated by the sequel, serialisation and the remake, the Anglo-American academic field responded with theories of pastiche, parody and nostalgia – and with New Historicism, with its intense historical compressions and special relationship with the most cross-marketable of all media commodities, Shakespeare.[18]

If the counterpoint between institution and market, Cold War past and global future, found a formal analogue in Greenblatt's work, it was characteristic of research on Shakespeare throughout the 1980s and 1990s, and the range of variation it generated indicates just how compelling the circulatory rhythms of American politics were. In comparison to the metaphorical intensity of Greenblatt's 'general store of social energy',

Jean-Christophe Agnew's hugely influential *Worlds Apart: The Market and the Theater in Anglo-American Thought 1550–1750* concerned itself with a *durée* that looked back to Greek theatre and forward to the nineteenth and twentieth centuries. Notwithstanding, Renaissance theatre was the focus of its analysis.[19] For Agnew, it articulated a crisis of representation brought about by the historical transformation of the market 'from a place to a process to a principle to a power'.[20] Here, the institutional *durée* in question was not theatre but Bakhtinian carnival: just as metaphorical as 'social energy', but authorised by a body of theory that, particularly in the 1980s, had something of the status of a critical safe house: 'festive misrule no longer served as a periodic ritual designed to throw the commonly accepted boundaries of honour and authority into greater relief. Removed to the theatres of the liberties, carnival had become a permanent institution'.[21] From this perspective, the transition from temporary playing spaces to the custom-built playhouse presents itself as a process of political containment; not, as one might have imagined, professional consolidation or social advancement.

In *Drama and the Market in the Age of Shakespeare*, Douglas Bruster was clearly aware of the potential problems of such an approach.[22] Like Agnew, he saw theatre as '*a priori* a market', and presented the move from temporary playing spaces to the custom-built playhouse as a 'consequence' of 'the historical unfolding' of 'the market system in the west'. But for him, this meant that it was 'part of a complex of centralising institutions'; '[part of] the dawn, in London, of institutionalized capitalism'.[23] However, this analysis produced a more, not less, passive position of creative agency: where Agnew's reading placed the plays within a subversive tradition of popular culture, Bruster located them in what was effectively an Althusserian model of ideology: they 'function' as 'social dreams, collective fantasies ... in which English society worked through issues and anxieties irresolvable by non-ludic means'.[24] In comparison to Greenblatt, who identified Shakespeare as an agent (if primarily an economic one) in the continued development of 'theatre as an institution', both Agnew and Bruster subsumed theatre and the creative labour of those who worked within it into the formal features of another institution,[25] and in doing so begged largely unasked questions about relations between institutional agencies and institutional systems. Can people working in one institutional context really be said to be defined by the interests and values of another? Or is such an assumption more an articulation of the unstable dichotomies of Cold War culture than a structural feature of the institution as a social system?[26]

Emancipating the concept of the institution both from the metaphor of circulation and from a parasitic dependence on the idea of the market, Leeds Barroll's study *Politics, Plague, and Shakespeare's Theater: The Stuart Years* addressed the question of Shakespeare's creative agency decisively,[27] not least in its willingness to identify itself as biography and then to call on biography to rise to the challenge of approaches like cultural poetics:[28]

> These writings have begun to make out a turbulent social and psychological atmosphere in that past time which not only generated mutterings, winds and storms as charged as those today but from which Shakespeare's own dramas emerged as crucial signifiers of cultural trauma.[29]

Yet, as he pointed out (though not with specific reference to them), the attempts of writers like Agnew and Bruster to situate Shakespeare within this turbulence place him in a paradoxically privileged relation to power: we have to 'deconstruct' this position 'if we are to envision this life as consonant with an early modern England so arrestingly refashioned in recent criticism'.[30] His idea of plays as 'signifiers of cultural trauma' may seem to portend a reading similar to Bruster's 'social dreams, collective fantasies', but he avoided this danger by approaching 'theatre as an institution' (Greenblatt's phrase) in a completely different way:

> Thus I consider only the effects of Shakespeare's society and culture on the manner in which the poet was trying to forge a creative career, to wrest a living from a largely untried and new focus of public expression. This focus was the London playhouse, an institution only fourteen years old in 1590.[31]

This perspective is consonant with institutional readings in cinema and media studies, which largely eschew massive generalisations about capitalism in favour of empirical studies of particular production companies or systems of exhibition. But this potentially strong feature of the analysis creates its own problems:

> The crown perceived plague to be a clear and present danger to London as the seat of governance. Closing theaters, gathering places of the multitude, was one measure of preventing this danger. ... Thus Shakespeare's choice of profession led him to work with a social

institution subject to suspension in times perceived as dangerous for any reason at all.[32]

'Clear and present danger': an evocative phrase, and one that does a surprising amount of work. Obviously, it's the fact that Barroll identified his institution as 'the London playhouse' (rather than 'the market system in the west' or 'institutionalized capitalism') that makes it possible even to think of describing it as 'subject to suspension': no one would dream of trying to 'suspend' institutionalised capitalism (although, of course, it may crash of its own accord). But can *any* institution, even one that has only been going for fourteen years, be 'suspended'? Is not the nature of an institution as a social system its capacity to resist such interference? In assuming both that institutions can be subject to external intervention, and that the English crown was an order of authority that could so intervene, Barroll presupposes a level of political threat that would not apply to a relatively routine executive decision, perhaps not even taken by the king himself, simply to close theatres – an action that could easily sustain a radically different reading.[33]

The presence of the phrase 'clear and present danger' is arguably the reason we do not ask these questions. A modification of the term 'imminent danger' from the American Constitution, article 1, section 1, it was famously used by Justice Oliver Wendell Holmes in *Schenck v. United States* (1919), in which Charles T. Schenck, general secretary of the American Socialist Party, and others unsuccessfully appealed against their conviction for espionage on the basis of their First Amendment rights of free speech:

> The most stringent protection of free speech would not protect a man in falsely shouting fire in a theater and causing a panic. ... The question in every case is whether the words used are used in such circumstances and are of such a nature as to create a clear and present danger that they will bring about the substantive evils that Congress has a right to prevent.[34]

Thereafter, the concept of 'clear and present danger' became the basis of the so-called Holmes-Brandeis immediacy test, and it recurs across the twentieth century in a series of cases against radical activists, notably in the Smith Act trials of the early Cold War period. In 1989, two years before Barroll's book, the expression was popularised by Thomas Clancy as the title of a novel (and then, three years later, a film featuring Harrison Ford)[35] about the ethics of American military intervention in Latin America, anticipating the extension of the Cold War across the globalising 1980s into the new military arenas of the 1990s. To read Barroll's phrase into this fraught contemporary history may seem an overreaction to what could be taken simply as a casual figure of speech, but the fact is that the phrase carries the full weight of his argument. It is only if we see Shakespeare's political distance from 'the crown' as in some fundamental way 'like' the relation between a radical activist and the US government that Barroll's argument about his social vulnerability works.[36] And the fact that Holmes' evocative metaphor of 'shouting fire in a theatre' underpins the phrase, if only subliminally, brings a political edge to the relation between 'governance' and 'the multitude' that an institutional reading of Shakespearean theatre might not wish to endorse.

Paradoxically, it is because Barroll scrupulously avoids buttressing theatre with another institutional system that this problem arises. In *The Culture of Playgoing in Shakespeare's England*, Paul Yachnin and Anthony B. Dawson provide a powerful illustration of what happens when the doubleness of the New Historicist institution is brought to the forefront of an analysis.[37] To begin, they assert that they share common ground in 'the most influential account of the cultural position of the theatre': 'new historicist theory and its appropriation of cultural anthropology' – a statement that alerts us to the possibility that they will agree about very little.[38] Like Bruster, they argue that New Historicism 'obscures the relation of the theatre to a central social institution' by positioning it as marginal.[39] But they disagree about what, in Bruster's phrase, the 'centralising' institution is: the Church for Dawson, the market for Yachnin. What results from their subsequent efforts to 'trace the filiations of various discourses and practices as they flow to and from the theatre' is an account of a 'quasi-unified institutional culture emerging for both playmakers and playgoers'.[40] But what *is* a 'quasi-unified' institutional culture? For Dawson, 'the theatre was a powerfully, even greedily appropriative institution, ingesting and transforming a whole range of cultural phenomena and making them its own'.[41] For Yachnin, an institutional account opens up a 'richer topical reading' that 'localizes the politics of the play [Middleton's *The Witch*] in terms of the entertainment market and the trade in cultural goods'.[42] Of course, the difference between these two approaches, one centripetal, the other centrifugal, is the point of the book, and very engaging it is. But can the contrast between them really mean either that 'theatre is an institution in and of itself, engaged in practices specific to itself' or that they agree that it is, as Dawson suggests they do?[43] Is this not, rather, a fundamental theoretical disagreement about what institutions are and how they work that needs to be resolved at a fundamental theoretical level?[44]

In fact, both writers were later to express reservations about the model of analysis advanced in this study. As Yachnin puts it:

> I still believe that this account is substantially right, but I no longer think that it does justice to the social situation and social identity of Shakespeare and his fellows. I now think that the drama's critical dimension is more than an automatic effect of the structure of relations or the theatrical practice of imitation. It comes also from an artisanal ethos that I suggest was a persistent feature of Shakespeare's working life and remains also a persistent if less visible feature of his writing.[45]

I agree completely with his interest in 'the value of theatrical labor',[46] but the direction in which he takes it, towards the notion of a 'cultural market' 'involved with developing new ways of forging communities and workable values'[47] seems to me simply to reinscribe the problem at a higher level of description. This move was characteristic of the so-called 'cultural turn' that Annabel Patterson detected in Renaissance research at the turn of the millenium,[48] and it is characteristic of the ambitious and wide-ranging project with which Yachnin's work is now associated, McGill University's 'Making Publics 1500–1700: Media, Markets and Association in Early Modern Europe' project. The online introduction describes the project's origins in 'a vigorous set of partnerships with leading research institutions in Canada, the USA, and Europe'. Despite this, however, the idea of the institution that appears in the project itself is regressive and repressive:

> We have coined the word 'publics' to refer to the open-membership groups that coalesced around certain practices, areas of interest, and forms of publication and/or performance. Publics differed from traditional groupings such as guilds, universities, or parliaments, which were characteristically exclusive, institutionalized, highly credentialized, and hierarchical in their internal workings. Publics were loosely organized, more or less egalitarian in their internal workings, and open to anyone that had the interest, competence, money, and time to participate. They fostered and were fostered by new technologies of representation and dissemination – the printing press, new pictorial forms, new sites for and styles of theatrical and musical performance.

They were encouraged by the development of a market in works of art and/or printed works such as plays, paintings, musical compositions, sermons, news pamphlets, maps, histories, and scientific reports.[49]

The concept of the institution, it would seem, is incompatible with any form of human association that is democratic and egalitarian, while the market appears to be virtually its guarantor. Do we really believe that universities are less open and creative than Wall Street or the City? While the role of the market in the creation of publics is identified as one of its research questions – 'are market conditions always necessary for the formation of a public?' – it also repeatedly appears as part of the answer; in particular, to questions about how the past links to the future that becomes our present, and how that present creates the terms on which we give value to the past.[50]

At this point I can imagine a reader coming to the conclusion that the force of this English writer's argument is simply that I find the work I have been discussing here just too *American*. Even if that were the case, I would not be the only person to suggest it: Christopher Prendergast found Greenblatt's 'Towards a Poetics of Culture' 'overwhelmingly Amerocentric'; Michael Bristol, himself a member of the McGill project, has considered the 'Americanization' of Shakespeare.[51] However, my concern here has been less with individual research, or with American history or society in general, than with the fate of an idea in the particular tradition of scholarship within which that idea has so far been allowed to express itself. It is only when we look at the range of often incompatible arguments about the nature of theatre as an institution; at the correlation between these arguments and the contemporary transition from Cold War to global market (and back again); and at the way this correlation is back-projected onto early modern and Shakespearean theatre, that we begin to see what that fate was and why it might be doing both Shakespeare and contemporary Shakespeare studies a disservice. Interestingly enough, the 1980s also saw the rise of a fully developed theory of the institution in the context of a political philosophy that sought to redefine social democracy for a post-Cold War and globalised era. The fact that the work of Anthony Giddens is associated with the European New Left probably explains its relative lack of uptake in the US. This is not to say that he has been completely ignored: he is frequently glanced at, but never fully engaged.[52] In the next section my aim is to introduce Giddens' theory of structuration by way of preparation for the textual readings that follow in an effort to review and renew the application of the concept of the institution to the study of Shakespearean theatre.

Towards an institution of theatre

Giddens describes the theory of structuration as arising from the 'lack of a theory of action in the social sciences', and it is precisely that – agency rather than discourse – which his work helps us to describe.[53] He approaches 'social systems' as 'regularized patterns of interactions involving individuals and groups'[54] and describes the outcome of these regularised practices as 'the sustaining of a legitimated series of prerogatives over occupied social space'.[55] This useful equation recurs in the chapters that follow, where my aim is to identify the way its individual terms – sustaining, legitimation, prerogative; the occupation of space – perform in plays written at a series of chronological points in Shakespeare's career. 'Sustaining' is perhaps the operative word: when 'regularized patterns of interaction' are 'deeply layered' in time and space, Giddens describes them as 'institutions'. John Thompson has extended this analysis with a further distinction between 'specific' institutions and 'generic' or 'sedimented' institutions,[56] a formulation that will enable us to differentiate between the particular company, working in a particular playhouse with particular writers and performers, and 'the institution of theatre' as a concept of structure reflexively engaged in this process of deep layering.

As these formulations suggest, structuration theory uses the term 'structure' to refer not to abstractions functioning as external determinants, as in structuralism, but to dynamic systems that are 'both medium and outcome of the reproduction of practices'. This principle, which Giddens calls 'the duality of structure', is its central perception:[57] 'structure enters simultaneously into the constitution of the agent and social practices, and "exists" in the generating moments of this constitution'.[58] It is thus 'enabling as well as constraining'.[59] This idea is one of the most attractive things about the theory: it encourages us to recognise institutionalisation as fundamentally a creative process.

It also encourages us to approach the question of intentionality in a more nuanced way than is characteristically associated with literary authorship. Giddens sees intentions not as 'discrete mental events' – the characteristic preoccupation of convential literary models of authorship – but as 'a chronic feature of the reflexive monitoring of action',[60] where 'reflexive' refers to the practical understanding of social systems, and not to discursive representations. These distinctions will be useful in my readings of early plays like *The Taming of the Shrew* and *Richard the Third*, both of which were written before Shakespeare was permanently associated with a particular company or playhouse, but are demonstrably already concerned with the sustaining of legitimated professional prerogatives and the occupation of a theatrical social space. From this perspective, Greenblatt's idea of a Shakespeare 'presumably interested not simply in a good return on an individual play but in the health and success of his entire company' reveals its limitations, since the idea of 'company' we associate with the establishment of the Chamberlain's Men in 1594 might most appropriately be seen as an unintended consequence of an intentional act, not the act itself. And since both intentions and their unintended consequences operate 'in conjunction with unacknowledged conditions and outcomes of action',[61] we can discuss the intermittent closure of the theatres without seeing it either as the suspension of an institution or as a source of social vulnerability. Indeed, we can now also see that Barroll's thesis assumes that Shakespeare would have *expected* playhouses to stay open; an idea that presupposes a level of institutionalisation that can arguably only be associated with the stage in his career when he was already beginning to withdraw from the company.

The value of an institutionally nuanced model of intentionality proves itself more in the formative decade of the 1590s than in the Stuart years, when – however you read Shakespeare's relation to the crown – the King's Men's relationship with the court was assured. The circumstances facing the professional player and writer in the early and mid-1590s were altogether more precarious. A general decline in the material support provided by patronage was associated with a literary culture that was prepared to let its artists make their own way without significant economic assistance.[62] This attitude explains why the decade was characterised *both* by the establishment of the Chamberlain's Men and the Admiral's Men as a duopoly playing in the Theatre and the Rose; *and* by the support in 1597 of Chamberlain's Men's patron George Carey for a Privy Council bill *against* his own company's move to the new Blackfriars theatre, when the lease on the Theatre was about to expire.[63] The unintended consequences of this financially induced autonomy included the priority given by the companies themselves to popular performance, a suggestion that counterbalances approaches that link popular performance to a politicized concept of popular culture;[64] decisions to release play scripts into publication, which counterbalances approaches that link the publication of playbooks to concepts either of popular culture or a public sphere;[65] and a willingness to take legal and financial risks, like those involved in the Burbages' often unscrupulous efforts to retain control of the Theatre (which I discuss in Chapter 2) and its eventual demolition and reassembly as the Globe. Shakespeare's plays in the 1590s chart the transformation of prestigious but unsupportive patronage into profitable popularity. *A Midsummer Night's Dream* was written in 1595–6 for the Chamberlain's Men then resident at the Theatre but under the threat of dispossession from the very outset. It is deeply marked by the need to pay lip service to the dynamics of patronage while progressively distancing itself from its social terms of reference.

This may seem a surprising assertion. After all, the Mechanicals' performance for Theseus's wedding celebrations is an act of service, and we are shown the mechanisms by which it is presented in some detail: the event which provides the occasion for performance; the range of contrasting forms it takes, the process by which a selection is made and the rationale for that selection. But there is already within the play the beginning of a separation of courtly taste and that 'practical understanding' referred to above as 'a chronic feature of the reflexive monitoring of action'. In the alignment of the play itself – Shakespeare's play – with supernatural agencies to which the diegetic audience has no visual or even imaginative access, this play, in its active, even aggressive, role in sustaining the legitimated prerogatives that enabled this company to continue occupying the social space of theatre, might be said to conceive an institution of theatre that decisively reverses the political, economic, even arguably the symbolic, relations of priority between theatre and court. By the time of *Hamlet*, written in 1600–1 for performance at the Globe, such a conception stands structurally and aesthetically at the heart of the play. The Tragedians of the City come unbidden to Elsinore, where the Danish court receives them and welcomes the opportunity for their performance, but is not the occasion of it: the players' arrival is *not* associated with the royal wedding feast, but with what is presented to both diegetic and extra-diegetic audiences as a familiar structural feature of a self-contained, reflexive continuum of professional life. The court finds a political use for the performance, but that use is accidental and, unlike the performance itself, split by opposing intentions from which the performers remain resolutely aloof. The performances the company offers at Elsinore are drawn from their repertoire in ways that stress their independence from exploitation by any courtly political interest, including Hamlet's.

The notion of a theatrical agency free from political accountability will be central to the concept of an institution I put forward in this study. Taking the example of the Ford Company, John B. Thompson points out that individuals who, in their everyday productive activities, reproduce the institutions of the Ford Motor Company may also be said to reproduce the conditions in virtue of which those institutions are capitalistic. But it is not difficult to imagine circumstances in which individuals may effectively transform those institutions *without* transforming their structural conditions. Every act of production and reproduction may also be a potential act of transformation, as Giddens insists; but the extent to which an action transforms an institution does *not* coincide with the extent to which social structure is thereby transformed.[66]

In a political context in which post-feudal power structures were still relatively unstable, social systems we would now describe as institutions were frequently characterised by behaviour New Historicist criticism tends to describe as subversive, but was in fact more simply and directly creative of institutional *durée*.[67] This is the way I approach Shakespearean theatre in this study: as an ensemble of practices that sought to sustain legitimated prerogatives over occupied social space, but *not* to transform the structural conditions within this institutional system subsisted – not least because its sustainability would only be threatened by such a transformation. Like the Earl of Essex, whose commissioning of a performance of *Richard II* from the Chamberlain's Men early in the same year preceded his own fatal rebellion,[68] Hamlet's personal actions may eventually transform the social structure of the Danish court, but those of the players and their writers are insistently and systematically separated from such an effect.

As this discussion suggests, it may be necessary to distinguish between different kinds of institutions, but also to recognise that such distinctions are not always easy to make. According to Giddens, all processes of structuration involve three dimensions: domination, the exercise of power, which is either political (concerned with authorisation, or 'command over persons') or economic (concerned with allocation or 'command over objects or other material phenomena'); legitimation, the judgement of conduct; and signification, the communication of meaning. In presenting an account in which all institutional systems are held to contain all these dimensions in different configurations, this approach suggests that it may not be easy, or even desirable, to decide what *kind* of institution any given institution is. It also helps us to think in more complex terms about those chiasmic formulations we considered earlier. If we consider the Chamberlain's Men from the standpoint of the company's relations to its aristocratic patrons, we may decide that what we are looking at is an aspect of the long-term development of a political institution (though one that would differ materially from the abstract *durée* of Agnew's 'permanent institution of carnival' or Bruster's 'institutionalized capitalism'). If we focus on the players themselves, we would probably want to approach it as the early stages of a new economic institution (though one that would create difficulties for Barroll's formulation of 'the London playhouse', as opposed to 'The Theatre', as a fourteen-year-old institution). The point that needs to be made is that, as a 'specific' institution, it would be all of these things at the same time. It would only be at the point in its development at which we could approach it generically, not as 'an institution' but as 'an' or 'the' institution of theatre that we could refer to it, with Dawson and Yachnin, as an institution 'in and of itself, engaged in practices specific to itself'. Curiously, one thing we might have real difficulty in deciding, at any stage of development, is the basis on which we might describe this social system as a symbolic institution. As both *Hamlet* and the Essex affair show, while it clearly *is* engaged in 'the communication of meaning', it is not easy to decide who is doing the communicating. In fact, we may be more likely to decide that theatre as an institution is engaged in the communication of meaning if we see it as a political institution operating in the interests of the court than if we see it as an economic institution operating in the interests of the players since, as *Hamlet* demonstrates, this is likely to be a situation in which the communication of meaning is systematically disavowed.

All of which suggests that any account of an institution of theatre will depend on its capacity to identify those practices by which it really could be said to operate in the interests of those who work there. John Thompson has noted that the distinction between authoritative and allocative resources gave Giddens 'a critical purchase on those forms of Marxism which tend to associate domination with the ownership or control of property and which give insufficient attention to forms of authority'.[69] One can easily see why, in the 1980s, social scientists – like literary critics – would seek conceptual parameters that could rise to the challenge of a post-Marxist intellectual ethos. But one of the virtues of this model, at least for the present study, is that, in formulating a framework that makes it possible to conceive of social systems that are not grounded in ownership and the control of property, it also makes it possible to recognise the distinctiveness of those that *are*. As all theatre historians agree, the Chamberlain's/King's Men were unique in precisely this respect (though curiously the significance of their role as owners of their own playhouse plays little part in any of the studies I discussed earlier). In the chapters that follow, I pursue questions of property and ownership as a far more complex factor in that institutional sustaining of legitimated prerogatives over occupied social space than can be addressed by generalisations about capitalism. I take as my starting point particular historical developments in the laws of property that opened up the duty circle of property rights to people like Shakespeare and the Burbages. In Chapter 2 I introduce the historical background to the principle of beneficial ownership and then apply it to the litigation surrounding the ownership of the Theatre as the context within which we can approach their own understanding of the playhouse as a form of property. This is followed by a series of textual readings in which I follow Shakespeare's creative adaptation of legal principles of ownership to the individual plays by which that property was maintained throughout his career.

I begin with a reading of *The Taming of the Shrew*, which I approach as a play that inaugurates Shakespeare's institutional aspirations in its treatment of contemporary arguments about the creation of property by industry, establishing a monopolistic conception of theatre even before he could be identified with a particular company or playhouse. I then discuss a linked series of texts – Thomas More's *History of Richard the Third*, the collaborative play *Sir Thomas More* and *Richard the Third* – in order to show how Shakespeare emerges from an environment of professional collaboration to anticipate the formation of both a dedicated space of performance and the quasi-legal bond between player and spectator that sustains their mutual occupation of it. After that, I consider three comedies covering the period from the pre-Theatre years through to the Chamberlain's Men's residence at the Theatre, and finally the move to the Globe: *The Two Gentlemen of Verona*, *The Merchant of Venice* and *As You Like It*. I argue that these plays display an innovative principle of dramatic action based on the idea of beneficiary or third party interest and show how it underpins the development of the Shakespearean woman's part and of its relation to what was becoming an identifiably Shakespearean audience. While all these readings suggest that his work sustained a continuing dynamic of institutionalisation across the whole decade, each play demonstrably 'enables' a particular set of institutional circumstances; circumstances that will often require strongly contrasting modes of critical, historical and theoretical description. In the discussion of *Hamlet* that follows, I argue that the pre-eminence that coincided with the company's move to the Globe engaged wider social and political questions of prerogative raised by the monopoly crisis of 1601 and the anticipation of Elizabeth's death, and I ask whether such an engagement should be construed in terms of a Habermasian concept of the public sphere, or more simply as a transition from a specific to a generic mode of institutionalisation.

In the last two chapters I ask whether this status is consolidated or diminished by changes in Shakespeare's work associated with the accession of James I. In a discussion of *King Lear* I consider Shakespeare's autobiographical reworking of the Elizabethan three daughters stories which provide the 'sources' for this play, including a text by Greene not hitherto associated with it, and suggest that the differences between his own variant readings of the narrative can be attributed to an ambiguous personal and professional rapprochement with the contractualist principles of Jacobean power. *The Tempest* suggests that that rapprochement was temporary: with the reopening of the Blackfriars, Shakespeare increasingly began to distance himself from the Jonsonian aesthetics associated with the new space of performance and its audiences. I conclude with a reading of the 'face-off' between Shakespeare and Jonson in *The Alchemist* and *The Tempest* and of the affirmation of the Shakespearean institution of theatre that accompanied his withdrawal from London and return to Stratford.

2
Nebuchadnezzar's Tree

Until 1290, the only way for a feudal tenant to transfer an interest in an estate in land to another person was by subinfeudation, a process by which a new tenure was simply embedded within the existing chain of obligations. But the statute of *Quia emptores terrarum* (18 Edw. 1, 1290) made it possible to alienate land without a landowner's consent and without paying feudal incidents. The direct consequence of this development was the rising popularity of forms of conveyance that made it possible for landowners to retain both the title to the land and the income they could derive from allowing someone else to occupy it, usually for a specified period of time. By the mid-fifteenth century the separation of a title to land into possession and 'use' had come to dominate English conveyancing practices. This separation took a range of forms, including the freehold use and the non-freehold lease for term of years. I do not pursue the distinction between freehold and non-freehold estates here: the complex historical relation between use and lease is well illustrated in the 25-year litigation for the ownership of the Theatre, which I discuss in the second section of this chapter.[1] My more immediate concern is with the overall category of beneficial ownership and its transformational role in the conceptualisation of modern English property. It would, I think, be true to say that without this distinctive 'imagination' of property there would have been no such thing as the custom-built playhouse, let alone an institution of theatre.

An English custom of property

According to John Guy, a use was a device that 'allowed shrewd property owners to treat the land as their own while escaping the penalties and obligations associated with legal title'.[2] A use was set up when a title-holder entered into an agreement to allow another person to occupy his property on the understanding that she, he or a third party (referred to as the *cestuy que use*), should retain the beneficial interest, or 'enjoyment', of the land. Since the common law saw the *cestuy que use* as a 'stranger', the use was recognised as an estate in equity only, a situation that ensured the rise of the courts of Chancery to handle the resulting tide of litigation. Third party or beneficiary actions became a 'path to privity' for those traditionally excluded from the duty circle of proprietary rights and obligations.[3] J. H. Baker's account of the 'terminology of trusteeship' that haunts these arrangements is instructive because it draws our attention to the presence within the Elizabethan exploitation of beneficial ownership on the one hand of ideas of feudal service as a trust-based relationship, and on the other of anxieties about beneficial owners as self-interested outsiders.[4]

The gradual acceptance of the use into the common law took its cue from Richard III's Statute of Uses of 1484 (1 Ric 3, c.1):

> Since so much land was vested in people who had no visible connection with it, third parties could be at a considerable disadvantage in conveyancing. To protect those who purchased from beneficiaries in possession, the statute provided that the beneficiary could pass a title good against his own feoffors. This remarkable measure enabled the beneficiary to convey something he did not in law have; he was treated by fiction as if he were the legal owner for the purpose of conveying title.... The beneficiary's interest was in this way assimilated to legal property concepts; it could be seen as a thing, a thing which descended to heirs on an intestacy, a thing which could be bought and sold and settled on a succession of beneficiaries. Nevertheless, the new kind of ownership was inherently foreign to the common law because it conflicted with the feudal system.[5]

Throughout the sixteenth century, 1 Ric 3, c.1 recurs as the point of reference for Tudor defences of the use against Henry VIII's attempts to contain the impact of this 'new kind of ownership'. One of the most notable was Christopher St German's 'Second Dialogue' of *Doctor and Student*, which I quote at length because I return to it in my discussion of *King Lear* in Chapter 7:

> Uses were reserued by a secondary conclusion of the lawe of reason in thys maner/when the generall custome of propertye wherby euery man knew hys owne good fro hys neyghboures was brought

in amonge the people it followed of reason that suche landes and goodes as a man had ought not to be taken fro hym but by hys assent or by order of a lawe/and than syth yt ys soo that euery man that hath landes hathe therby two thynges in hym/that ys to say/the possessyon of the lande whiche after the lawe of Englande ys called the franke tenement or the free holde and the other ys authorytye to take therby the profytes of the lande/wherfore it foloweth that he that hath lande and intendeth to gyue onely the possessyon and freeholde thereof to a nother/and to kepe the profytes to hym selfe ought in reason and conscyence to haue the profytes/seynge there ys no lawe made to prohybyt/but that in conscyence suche reseruacyon may be made.[6]

The idea that 'profit' could combine public good with private interest is an important nuance within this defence, and the main reason why Henry was determined to do away with it. In the assault on the use led by Thomas Audley during the 1520s and 1530s, we begin to note what had already become a distinctive feature of its rhetorical register: the description of it as an 'imagination'. In his 'Reading on Uses' in 1526, Audley asserted that the use had been 'imagined and compassed' in order to defraud the king of his feudal dues, such as wardship.[7] The phrase 'imagined *and compassed*' has precise legal connotations: it is the form of words established in 25 Edw 3, st. 5 c.2 for indictments for treason. The use was routinely described as a 'subversion' of the common law in the purely technical sense that it overturned feudal customs of inheritance, but the application to it of the wording of the treason statute pushes the notion of subversion into a political domain. In his own Statute of Uses the following year, Henry took decisive action: by 27 Hen 8 c. 10 the *cestuy que use* became title-holder of the legal estate, thereby collapsing the separation of possession and use:

Where by the common laws of this realm, lands, tenements and hereditaments be not devisable by testament, nor ought to be transferred from one to the other but by solemn livery and seisin, matter of record [or] writing sufficient, made bona fide without covin or fraud, yet nevertheless divers and sundry imaginations, subtle inventions and practices have been used whereby the hereditaments of this reall have been conveyed from one to another by fraudulent enfeoffments, fines, recoveries and other assurances craftily made to secret uses, intents and trusts, and also by wills and testaments sometimes made by nude parols and words, sometimes by signs and tokens, sometimes by writing ... and many other inconveniences have happened and daily do increase among the king's subjects, to their great trouble and inquietness, and to the utter subversion of the ancient common laws of this realm ...[8]

Henry's efforts were in vain. Against all legal attempts to close the use down, its popularity grew across the sixteenth century precisely because it offered remarkable opportunities for 'subtle invention' at a time when the laws of property were subject to immense pressure of change.

If there is one single case that illustrates this, it is the extraordinary *Corbett v Corbett* (1600).[9] As the case goes, in April 1598, Christopher Corbett of Stockerston, Leicestershire, enfeoffed his estate to his own use and that of his male heirs for life, after his death to the use of his older son Roland and his heirs, in default of which the estate passed to the use of Arthur (the younger son) and his heirs. According to Arthur, there was a proviso that if Roland or his heirs should attempt a common recovery (a device to convert an entailed estate into a fee simple), the estate would pass to the next person. Roland however later denied that such a proviso had been made. On their father's death, Roland entered (that is, staked his claim to the estate) as tenant in tail. Since he had no heir, he attempted a recovery. At this point, Arthur entered, Roland demurred (admitted the facts of the case but denied that they were such as to entitle the plaintiff to legal relief, thus arresting the action) and the case went to Common Pleas, where it was heard by Chief Justice Sir Edmund Anderson. There, a surprising revelation was made. William Burton, subsequently author of 'The Description of Leicester Shire' and then a student at the bar, takes up the story:

> [Stockerston] is memorable for that great case of perpetuities between Corbet and Corbet.... The truth is, never any Corbet was lord of this manor, neither was that a true case as between those two Corbets, but a feigned case in names caused by Sir Anthony Mildmay of Apethorpe in the county of Northampton, knight, whose lands being perpetuated in the same manner, and having only one daughter ... to whom he intended to pass all his inheritance, was desirous to be ascertained of the law in this case.... But Sir Edmund Anderson ... at first not being made privy to the business, but after understanding of it, being then upon the bench at Westminster, that in a fury he flung out the Hall, saying he came not thither to argue any counterfeit cases.... But after, being better qualified, he argued the case and gave judgement against perpetuities.[10]

Many things about this extraordinary case fascinate, not least the fact that Anthony Mildmay, son of the Chancellor of the Exchequer Sir Walter Mildmay, used this 'feigned case' about a struggle for inheritance between older and younger brothers (one of which is called Roland) to create a 'path to privity' for a daughter.[11] With its striking points of contact with Shakespeare's *As You Like It* (written 1599–1600 for performance at the Globe), it provides a context for our understanding of the relation between contemporary ideas about third party agency and the theatrical woman's part, which I develop in Chapter 5. Despite the discomfort caused by his unwitting participation in this 'phantasicall conceit',[12] Sir Edmund recognised the importance of the principle it enacted. Arguing against the 'execution of the use' by 27 Hen 8 c. 10, he asserted that

> if the law was as the greater part of the judges held it, divers houses of noble persons and others of great living would be destroyed, which by this means of giving power and prerogative to the uses would be continued, and their heirs and lands preserved in dangerous times of civil dissension; and to destroy these uses is unfitting, and tends to destroy Nebuchadnezzar's tree, whereon rests the fowls of the air, and in the shade whereof lie the beasts of the earth ... for it would be mischievous, since the poor and common sort of people lie down beneath this tree and rest upon the branches.[13]

'Nebuchadnezzar's tree' provides a compelling metaphor for a society in which the framework of property rights that supported the great estates also provided a structure (in that 'enabling' sense discussed in Chapter 1) for those lower down the social order. In a note from Chancery around 1600, we learn that

> Two things do principally and properly entitle the Chancery to all causes: equity in the cause and inequality between the persons, as where the plaintiff is a mean man and the defendant a great man in his country, so as there is no hope of indifferency in trial.[14]

But we also learn from the entry immediately preceding this in the same manuscript that there might be some types of cause and person from whom such entitlement might be withheld:

> My lord keeper [Sir Thomas Egerton] says he never did relieve him that exhibits his bill concerning any playhouse, dining house, bowling alley, band house, or such like. He says that the constable of the ward is fit to hear their causes.[15]

We cannot conclusively say that this particular note alludes to the litigation that surrounded the dismantling of the Theatre and subsequent construction of the Globe, but it seems likely. As a member of Privy Council, Thomas Egerton would have been directly involved in the decision against the opening of the Blackfriars in 1597, and subsequently also in a complaint about the Burbages which came to Star Chamber in 1601 (discussed later in this chapter). Another note from Chancery, dating from about the same time, refers to 'Burbage' directly, and apparently displays the same anti-theatrical prejudice:

> Barbege exhibited a bill in equity concerning the interest he had on a theatre, which was a playhouse. The court dismissed the cause and would not relieve such [an] unprofitable matter.[16]

So what kind of cause *did* Egerton consider suitable for equitable relief? In 1612, some years after his elevation to Chancellor, he noted that 'clothiers, mariners and such like good members of the public good should be greatly favoured...'.[17] Apparently, the concern of the courts of equity with the common weal predisposed an assumption that the particular form of profit to be found in a playhouse was not in the interests of the 'public good'.

This negative evaluation of the social status of playing is hardly a new perception. What is less well established is a sense of its implications for our understanding of the custom-built theatre as property. We are faced here with a significant paradox. One might have thought that a playhouse would be exactly the kind of property that should have been able to look to the equitable jurisdictions to defend its owner's right of possession. As W. H. Bryson explains,

> In some situations, the common law solution to a breach of contract, compensation by the payment of money, is an inadequate remedy. Where the object of the contract of sale is a unique item or a specific piece of land, the plaintiff cannot take the money received as damages and buy the equivalent object or land from another person.... No farm is like any other one, and thus the disappointed buyer cannot go and buy another farm to replace the lost bargain, as can the purchaser of a ton of gravel. In agricultural England, the specific enforcement of land sales contracts became so much the normal remedy that all land is now considered unique as a matter of law, and the remedy of specific performance is always available no matter how indistinguishable one unit of condominium may be from another.[18]

In the 1580s and 1590s, what unit of condominium was more 'specific' than a playhouse? The fact, however, as Bryson makes clear, is that the principles of tenure that underpinned sixteenth-century property law were still fundamentally agrarian, and that made it hard to evaluate the new forms of property that were coming to characterise town and city life: a custom-built theatre had yet to become customary. Just as the common lawyers saw the 'crafty inventions' of sixteenth-century conveyancing as an utter subversion of the common law, so Egerton and the lawyers of Chancery, in adjudicating the attempts by the poor and common sort to rest on the branches of what had become a rather precarious tree, began to discriminate between those 'good members of the public good' whose matter was 'profitable' for the common weal, and those who created only trouble and inquietness. Reading the litigation that surrounds the ownership of the Theatre, we may well come to the conclusion that the ownership of a theatre falls into the latter category.

Troublesome tenants

> But true it is the said James Burbage & his wife & his son Rychard Burbage did w^t violence thrust this depo^t and the said Margaret and Robert Myles awey from the said do^r ... Burbage & his mother fell upon the said Robert Myles and beat hym w^t A broom staffe calling him murdering knave ...[19]

The history of the litigation surrounding the Theatre began with events that continued to be the subject of legal argument long after its timbers had been taken down and carried away: the events surrounding the original ownership of the Holywell site on which it was built. Like many of the properties on which the new London playhouses would subsequently be built, Holywell was a dissolved ecclesiastical property, granted in 1544 to Henry Webb, a gentleman usher to Queen Katharine Parr. It passed in a marriage contract to the Peckhams; the Peckhams sold it to the Bumpsteads, and they in turn mortgaged it to Christopher Allen and his son Giles in 1555. In 1562 the Allens withheld the final payment of the mortgage on the basis that the property was not worth what they had been asked, Bumpstead counter-suited, and the case remained unresolved, leaving the final conveyance of the property to the Allens incomplete. Notwithstanding, Giles Allen leased the property to James Burbage in 1576 for a conventional term of 21 years, with a series of considerations guaranteeing renewal, including the proviso that 200 pounds be spent improving the existing buildings.

What followed was 25 years of litigation in which James Burbage, and then his sons Richard and Cuthbert, fought – sometimes physically – to retain ownership of the playhouse. This litigation divides chronologically into two phases. The first covers Burbage's partnership with John Brayne, Brayne's death in 1586 and Brayne's widow Margaret's subsequent attempts to benefit from her husband's interest in the property, culminating in her death in 1593. This phase precedes the formation of the Lord Chamberlain's Men, Shakespeare's membership of the company and their residency at the Theatre, so commentary on it has characteristically situated it in at best an oblique relation to Shakespeare's work.[20] Nonetheless, it provides the context we need to understand if we are to approach Shakespeare's own understanding of the custom-built theatre as property, and the way that understanding was extended into the professional activities that sustained it, like the writing and performing of plays.

The second, much shorter phase of Theatre litigation begins around 1596 with the Burbages' attempts to negotiate a renewal of the lease, leading to the dismantling of the Theatre in 1598, its reconstruction in Southwark as the Globe in 1599 and the subsequent litigation against this action by Allen. This phase follows the establishment in 1594 of the Chamberlain's Men at the Theatre and parallels their consolidation as the most successful company in London, which includes Shakespeare's rise as their most successful dramatist. Because of this it has received far more critical attention, but rarely in the context of a commentary on the preceding phase of litigation. Without that first phase, the temptation to apply an inappropriate teleology – for instance, to assume that the Chamberlain's Men's success was underpinned by increased security of possession – is almost irresistible, whereas the fact is that that status coincided with a period of extreme insecurity, articulated in the radical separability of possession and use spectacularly enacted in the demolition of the Theatre and its reconstruction as the Globe.

Burbage did not have the money to build and finance the playhouse on his own, so he entered into a partnership with John Brayne, a grocer married to his wife's sister. Since we only have documents relating to the subsequent collapse of this relationship, we have to reconstruct what must initially have been a hopeful enterprise from its later adversarial representation by the participants themselves. Certainly, the fact that the childless Braynes initially proposed to leave their share of the Theatre to the Burbages' children suggests that the partnership began in a spirit of amity. Burbage later recorded that Brayne 'practised to obteyn some interest therin',[21] but according to Robert Miles, a soap maker who was to become intimately involved in the Braynes' personal and financial affairs, Brayne was a wealthy man who had been subject to 'swete and contynuall persuasions' by Burbage.[22] He had already built a public playhouse, the Red Lion, in 1576, so he was experienced in this kind of venture. Burbage, a joiner who had become a player, was known as 'a po^r man ... of small credit ... suche as nether merchant nor Artificer wold gyve him Credit ... unless his brother Braynes wold join w^t him'.[23] This opinion of the relative economic status of these two men appears to have been held by everyone except the Burbages. One way or another, Brayne was receptive to Burbage's argument that the enterprise 'wold grow to ther contynuall profit & commodytie through the Playes that shuld be used there everye weke'.[24] According to one of his fellow grocers, he 'begann to slack his own trade and gave him self to the building therof ... his affecion was given so greatlie to the finishing therof in hope of great welth and profitt during ther lease'.[25]

Brayne's position in relation to the lease was the source of all his subsequent troubles, and it is at least arguable that Burbage was instrumental in ensuring that this position remained unclear. The terms used to describe their partnership vary: Burbage describes it as a 'bond'; Margaret refers to 'an agreement'.[26] Robert Miles later asserts that Brayne told him he had been advised 'to suffer the said Burbage to take the said lease in his owne name and he to convey over to him the said Braynes ... the moytie and halfe of all the profittes ... least yf the said lease had come in both ther names the Survyvo^r shuld go away wth all'.[27] The most reliable account is given by William Nicoll, the notary who drew up the agreement:

> Though the lease was taken in the name only of the said Burbage yet it was meant to be for both their uses, and therefore he the said James Burbage was willing to assure the one moytie of the premises to the said John Brayne ... W^{ch} lease so engrossed this Deponent thinketh ... was not sealed by the said James Burbage for that the originall lease made to him by the said Giles Allyn and Sara his wife was then at pawn for money wch was borrowed for the building of the said Theatre. And therefore the said John Brayne afterwards ... did require this deponent to draw an obligation wherein the said James Burbage should be bound to the said John Brayne in four hundred poundes for the making unto the said John Brayne ... a good and lawful lease graunt and other assuraunce of the moitie ... and afterwardes the said James Burbage did seale and delyver as his dede the said obligacion ...[28]

Despite this assurance (a legal term we shall have cause to consider at greater length in Chapter 3) the relationship between the two men began to founder. Brayne suspected Burbage of 'indyrect dealing' (Burbage allegedly had a collection box with a hidden compartment in which he concealed a proportion of the takings, thus enabling him to lie about how much he ought to give to someone entitled to a share) so they came back to Nicoll for 'bondes of arbitrement'. Brayne claimed that he had put more money into the building of the Theatre than had Burbage; Burbage hit him, 'and so they went together by the eares in somuch that this deponent could herdly part them'.[29] This is the first of many occasions on which this legal dispute shades into a breach of the peace. The dispute went to arbitration, and an arbitrement was made agreeing to an equal division of the profits.

Nicoll's suggestion that the lease was already 'at pawn' probably refers to a mortgage on the property taken out with John Hyde, also a grocer. There is some uncertainty, strategic or otherwise, about whether this mortgage was taken out by Brayne or Burbage; evidence taken from Hyde on behalf of Burbage implies that it was taken out by Brayne, but with payments made by Burbage. It is at this point that Brayne begins to be represented, by Burbage, as someone whose financial difficulties are becoming a burden. For Hyde's greater security an additional bond of 200 pounds was jointly made to Hyde by Brayne and Burbage. Predictably, the mortgage was not repaid in full within the specified time, so 'not only the said lease but the said James Burbage the Def[endant] his title therin was absolutely forfeited and lost to him'.[30] At this point, Hyde threatened to put Burbage out of possession and set an arrest in motion, but Burbage came to his house, paid Hyde's wife 20 pounds, and subsequently gave Hyde new bonds and a surety for the remaining sum. According to Burbage, Brayne made none of the agreed payments, so, in the light of his 'right title and interest', Hyde sent a servant to 'chargd the said Brayne not to deale ay further wth ay thing concerning the said Theatre, except he wold deliver unto hym this dp^t [deponent] the money he received'.[31]

Thus, by 1580, Brayne's position had declined from a man of known considerable means – 'wo^{r}th one thowsand pundes at the least'[32] – to one close to destitution and systematically excluded from any kind of property rights in the Theatre. For men as poor as Burbage, the scale of the risk involved in seeing the enterprise through from 'sweet persuasion' to 'great wealth and profit' gives us some insight into this conversion of amity into enmity – a consequence that common lawyers saw as the almost inevitable result of this kind of conveyance.[33] John Griggs, a fellow carpenter, later referred to Burbage's 'unhonest parciall dealing',[34] Giles Allen to his 'covetous humor', 'whoe respected more his owne Commoditie then the good reporte and Creditt either of the Defend^t or himself'.[35] But Burbage may not have been wholly the cause of his brother-in-law's undoing. Brayne was involved in other financial risks, notably with Robert Miles. If Nicoll's deposition suggests a careful man trying to keep a grip on a slippery situation, witnesses suggest that in his final years he became reckless: in a scenario reminiscent of Mel Brooks' *The Producers*, he tried to raise money by making repeated deeds of gift of his goods, including the contested moiety in the Theatre.[36] According to Henry Bett, he 'semed to be careless of the same lease, the rather, for that yt was mortgaged; and would often tymes confesse, that yf the said lease might not be redeemed wth the profittes therof, that yt should never be redeemed for him, and made careless and inconvenient bargaines ...'.[37]

After Brayne's death, his widow Margaret sought to secure her husband's interest in the Theatre as her rightful inheritance. Were it not for a dubious relationship with Robert Miles, her cause would be unquestionable. She had initially blamed Miles for her husband's death, but we soon find Miles acting energetically on her behalf, and the fact that, after years in a childless marriage, she had given birth to a posthumous daughter, Katherine, was met with unguarded suspicion, particularly by the Burbages. However, we have to remember that, if Margaret's claim had been recognised, the existence of a child would threaten Brayne's original stated intention, sedulously recorded by Burbage, to leave his interest in the Theatre to Burbage's children, Richard and Cuthbert. As Margaret's attempts to enforce the arbitrement became increasingly urgent, the Burbages became more and more confrontational. John Allen, an inn holder, and Miles' 22-year-old son, Ralph, testified separately to his response to their efforts to claim a share of the profits on her behalf: 'he then did answere hang her ho^r [*whore*] qd he she getteth nothing here lett her wyn it at the Commen lawe'; 'revyling the comp^l [complainant] w^t termes of Murdering ho ^{r} & otherwise and chardged her and her companye to get out of his grounde'.[38] This section of the testimony is highly suggestive, its evocation of face-to-face encounters, complete with 'dramatic' direct speech, indicative both of the theatrical context of its staging and its potential status as evidence in court. As the now almost totally destabilised relation between possession and use degenerates into unmanageable aggression, Burbage's occupation of the Theatre begins to acquire almost military overtones. On one occasion Margaret, Robert and Ralph go to the Theatre upon A playe daye to stand at the do^r that goeth uppe to the galleries of the said Theater to take & Receyve for the use of the said Margaret half the money that shuld be given to come uppe into the said Gallaries at that do^r according to the foresaid Award & an order made therupon by the co^{r}t of Chauncerye ... But true it is the said James Burbage & his wife & his son Rychard Burbage did w^t violence thrust this depo^t and the said Margaret and Robert Myles awey from the said do^r ... Burbage & his mother fell upon the said Robert Myles and beat hym w^t A broom staffe calling him murdering knave ... at wch tyme the said James Burbage told the said Robert Myles that he had but wch he might wype his tale w^t and rather then he wold lose his possession he wold commit xx contemp$^{tes'}$.[39]

From this point on, Margaret and Miles take every opportunity to present Burbage's behaviour as contempt of court (for breaking the agreement established in the arbitrement). A week later, they threaten him with the combined force of the Chancellor's displeasure and a complaint to the Lord Admiral (one of the patrons of the combined Lord Strange's and Lord Admiral's Men, which played at the Theatre) and duly report his response: 'I care not for three of the best lordes of them all',[40] a claim 'uttered by him in the Attyring house or place where the players make them readye',[41] the implication of such an act of information being, presumably, that this combination of violence and contempt, so publicly displayed, verges on something much worse than breach of peace – something more like sedition, perhaps.

Throughout the 1580s James Burbage had to fight many attempts to take possession of the playhouse, and by 1589 he appears to have exhausted his resources. At this stage Cuthbert's employer, Sir Walter Cope, wrote to John Hyde, who later deposed that

m^r Walter Cope being Attendaunt upon the Lord Treasaurer did write his letteres to hym this dp^t thereby intreating hym that he wold sell to his the same m^r Copes Servaunte Cuthber burbage his title and interest of the said lease the rather for that he might help discharg his father (meaning the def) out on may [*i.e. many*] troubles ...[42]

Hyde agreed, and the lease was transferred to Cuthbert.

Clearly, this intervention was crucial. What is less clear is how we should understand it. In Chapter 1 I suggested a contrast between a service-based system of theatrical patronage and an economically independent theatre grounded in the practical understanding of professional men. Where would we place Cope's intervention within such an analysis? It looks like the former, but behaves more like the latter. Cope does not engage any significant issues of power: he does not enforce or authorise, his approach is described as an entreaty and his stated reason is to 'help discharge [*Cuthbert's*] father'. Hyde agrees, but there is no suggestion that he stood to lose anything had he refused, and there is no apparent context in which a refusal could have been subject to discipline or punishment. It is important to recognise this, not least because it helps us evaluate the fact that no comparable intervention was made to facilitate the renewal of the lease a few years later, when the Chamberlain's Men were both more obviously central to Elizabethan court culture and more obviously in danger of losing their livelihood. One way or another, with the conveyance of the lease to Cuthbert, the first part of this litigation was effectively over. Margaret died in 1593, leaving her estate, and Katherine, to the care of Miles. The little girl too died within a year. Miles continued to claim the Braynes' moiety until the year after James Burbage's death, but made no further progress. By this time, however, the question of the renewal of the lease had already reared its head, and the second phase of the litigation begins.

Burbage's original lease had stipulated that the lease might conditionally be renewed after ten years, but when that point came in 1585 Allen refused, as he did again when the term approached completion in 1595. We might recall that Allen had his own problems with the title, but there is no indication that his refusal had anything to do with this, even though Cuthbert would later claim that this 'variaunce and controversie' had prevented his father from 'enjoying' his possession:[43] according to Cuthbert, James had been 'verie much troubled and often Chardged to finde men to keepe the possession of the said premises from the said Edmond Peckham'.[44] When his father died, Cuthbert continued to negotiate, and all indications are that Allen was willing to proceed. However, for reasons which remain unclear, they could not agree on terms. Allen insisted that Burbage had not paid the 200 pounds originally stated as given in consideration for the renewal; he also insisted that he was owed back-rent and that he wanted to convert the Theatre to residential property within five years. At one point the Burbages, who by now no longer had the prospect of the Blackfriars as an alternative venue, appear to have been willing to accept all his conditions, but the renewal date passed without a firm agreement. Allen allowed them to continue to occupy on a year-by-year basis, but in 1598 they entered the site with the carpenter Peter Street and dismantled the Theatre.

This action was not in itself illegal: the right to remove specified fixtures and fittings was a standard feature of the lease, which stated that

> it should be lawful ... in consideration of the employing and bestowing of the foresaid sum of £200 in form aforesaid ... to take down and carry away to his [*i.e. Burbage's*] and their own proper use all such buildings and other things as should be builded ... either for a theatre or playing place or any other lawful use.[45]

Since Allen had stated his intention to return the site to residential use, one might have imagined that he would have been glad to be rid of a structure that would have been impossible to convert. It has been suggested that Allen wished to 'gain a playhouse' in order to start profiting from it himself, but there is no evidence to support the idea that this old man, living quietly in the country, had any interest whatsoever in getting involved in the theatre business.[46] However, I do not think we need to go that far to understand why the title-holder of a piece of land containing a unique, irreplaceable unit of condominium would have baulked at their actions: Allen would have realised that this fixture was now part of the property's value. He claimed that the Burbages had no right to dismantle the Theatre because the lease had expired, and sued at King's Bench for trespass. Cuthbert claimed he had the right in conscience because Allen should have renewed, and countersued in Chancery. Amazingly, Chancery supported Burbage, and Allen took the case to Star Chamber, where he finally lost. He briefly tried the court's patience by 'calling the same matter againe into question, and in labouringe to have the said cause, after such iudicciall sentence and decree past against the said Complayn^t in the said honorable Courte ...', and was instructed to 'surcease and staye and noe further prosecute or proceede at the Common lawe in the said accion ...'.[47] Cuthbert was instructed to 'be at libertie to take his remedie,' and awarded 'reasonable costes'.[48] The rest, as they say, is history.

But what *kind* of history? The answer to this question is to some extent determined by the form imposed on these documents in publication. Because they are voluminous, confusing and make no mention of Shakespeare whatsoever, they are usually excerpted, with the result that they have largely been used to provide points of information about theatre history, notably questions of the Theatre's physical construction and of the personalities of those involved, particularly James Burbage.[49] William Ingram provides a full account of the documentation, but believes that its 'larger narrative' may well be best served simply by 'laying out the ingredients'.[50] Theodor Leinwand is more ambitious, but to a certain extent illustrates the value of Ingram's caution. His account of Burbage's 'affective adaptation to indebtedness' offers a Foucauldian epistemic model for the history of the custom-built theatre, but, as Scott Cutler Shershow has argued, gets little further than a problematic concept of 'temperament'.[51] Carol Chillington Rutter and Andrew Gurr are more straightforward. Rutter sees James Burbage's manoeuvres as manipulative but heroic, even Herculean: he 'holds absolute sway over his Theater'; 'keeps his creditors at bay with a series of fiendishly complicated lawsuits'; when he attacks Miles and Margaret with a broomhandle he is 'flanked by his cubs'. She refers to his 'style'.[52] Andrew Gurr appropriately emphasises Burbage's professional experience and his role as a member of a team, but his vocabulary is oddly contemporary – perhaps influenced by the commercial rhetoric of New Historicism. His Burbage is 'self-assured', his thinking 'progressive and adventurous'; his actions are described as 'policy', a 'plan' and a 'vision'.[53] Gurr identifies him as a 'key creative force' alongside Shakespeare, though the emphasis here is on Burbage's role, in the last few years of his life, in moving towards the possession of two theatres and thus of a year-round schedule of performance: 'if Carey and Burbage had got their plan through in 1596 the Globe might never have been built, and London playing would have moved indoors far earlier than it did'.[54]

One might observe that, if Burbage's 'vision' had been realised, the company would have moved from the Theatre to the Blackfriars, Shakespeare would not have become a co-owner of the Globe and his interest in the company (in every sense) may have taken an entirely different direction. Much virtue in 'if': compelling as Rutter's and Gurr's accounts are, they are embedded in Great Man theory, the implications of which for institutional analysis have been well examined in film studies by Edward Buscombe.[55] An almost inevitable effect of this approach is a simplification of the range of agencies at work in a history of this kind, and in this case that definitely includes Margaret Brayne and her daughter Katherine. Since a primary contributory factor to the success of Shakespeare's plays was their sensitivity to contemporary amplifications of the social, and particularly legal, status of women, both should be of considerably more interest to contemporary scholarship than they have been. Margaret's claim for recognition as a beneficial owner, and the Burbages' refusal of it, must be seen, not as individual positions between which we might discriminate according to competing scholarly affiliations (Marxist aesthetics; cultural poetics) but as contributory elements to an institutional sustaining of legitimated prerogatives over occupied social space. Although the 'law's delay' has become notorious as a strategy by which lawyers keep lucrative cases going without regard to their client's interest, it is hard to avoid the conclusion when reading these documents that, even as this litigation contests and destabilises the categories of title, possession and use, it actually constitutes the continuum of experience within which these categories can be said to apply. In other words, if across the 1590s the Theatre and the Chamberlain's Men achieved institutional *durée*, then this litigation is the basis on which it can be described in such terms, not the obstacle to doing so.

If we are to understand this we need also to understand the way this documentation adapts the idea of beneficial ownership across a wide range of types of property, some already recognised by law, some not. While the word 'use' is not etymologically linked to the English verb 'to use', and J. H. Baker considers that there is no connection between the two senses of the word,[56] this litigation suggests that such a connection developed – or better, was actively *created* – by people like the Burbages. In its first phase, the phrase 'to the use of' emerges over and over again as a way of trying to make sense of the problematic Burbage–Brayne partnership, and it does so in a way that traverses the full range of properties to which the term 'use' might be applied, from freehold to the term of years, taking in what might now be seen as emergent concepts of intellectual property on the way. Thus in an interrogatory on behalf of Burbage, Giles Allen is asked whether the lease was intended to be 'in trust to the same Burbage to his the said Braines use'.[57] He rejects this description, but we then see the idea emerging in discussions of John Hyde's mortgage: crucial, since that mortgage was the medium through which the Burbage–Brayne partnership was dissolved and replaced by the single ownership of Cuthbert, which was itself the medium through which ownership of the Theatre was replaced by that of the Globe in the 'tripartite indenture' of 1599. In a deposition in Michaelmas 1590, Hyde responded to a series of interrogatories in which the question of the relation between title and possession, legal and beneficial ownership, circles like a flock of unsettled birds. In Item 1, Hyde is asked, 'was not the said Lease and other bondes made by Giles Allen, for the enjoying Therof, Delivered into yor handes and possession [*by Burbage and Brayne*]?'[58] In Item 2 he is asked whether, following the default of the mortgage he considered himself 'therby Rightfull owner of the said Lease and title of this defend^t James Burbage'.[59] And in Item 4 he is asked to confirm the fact that, when he threatened to put Burbage out of the Theatre, Burbage came to his house and made a payment to his wife 'to yor use',[60] so that what Neil Jones refers to as 'the broad sense of the use' – an action for money had and received[61] – is called on to buttress a position in which Hyde is presented as a *cestuy que use* in a situation in which Burbage continues to occupy the property.

But the inherent instability of the idea makes it equally available to the other side of the argument. Thus, to Burbage's recollection, when Robert Miles seeks to represent Margaret Brayne's interests following the arbitrament, he claimed that 'the said Award the moytie of the Theatre and the Rent therof are to be had and Recyved by & to the use of the said comp^l',[62] which refers to both the lease and a money claim, and suggests that Margaret saw her status as that of a beneficial owner, and/or that Burbage's argument stresses her separation from legal title. It is thus not surprising that Giles Allen is asked directly whether or not Brayne's status in the original agreement entitles him to be seen as a beneficial owner:

> And whither did John Brayne at the ensealinge of the said Lease or at any tyme before, make sute or require of yo^u to be ioyned with the said Burbage in the said Lease. Or to make the same in trust to the same Burbege to his the said Braines use?[63]

Allen replies in the negative to both questions – invaluable testimony for Burbage, because it displaces Brayne from both legal *and* beneficial ownership. But claims for Brayne's status as a beneficial owner of the lease and of the moneys received continue to emerge, particularly after the Chancery arbitration. For instance, Ralph Miles deposed that, after the mortgage had been redeemed, 'the said Jo. Brayne his executors & assignes shuld take have and enjoy to his owne use all the profittes of the said Theatre till he were satisfied of such some of money as the said James Burbage was owing unto him';[64] in 1592, Item 3 of the interrogatories on behalf of Margaret asked whether the lease was 'taken at Allyns handes only in the name of Burbadge, but not wthstanding to the use of bothe', and in response, John Griggs deposed that it was 'crediblye reported' that this was the case.[65]

The adversarial potential embodied within the separation of legal and beneficial ownership, so clearly a pervasive feature of Elizabethan society at large, is fully articulated within this litigation. Perhaps the most significant example is the fact that when Robert Miles gives his account of Cuthbert's purchase of the lease from Hyde, the resulting title is initially described as a use, but then the word is deleted: 'true it is the said James Burbage ... did so labo^r him ... and speciallye by letters from one Mr Cope one of the lord Treasorers gentlemen that he shuld make over his interest & claime of & in the said lease to Cuthbert Burbage ... [to the use of him the same James Burbage (stricken out)]'.[66] This is intriguing. Miles's accusation might well confirm the suggestion, made earlier, that Cope's intervention was persuasive rather than powerful. But in that case why would Miles – or more probably the Chancery lawyer taking the deposition – have reservations about this particular wording? Because, while the accusation is illuminating on the discursive level at which the idea of the use circulates throughout this litigation, here Miles comes dangerously close to implicating the influential Sir Walter in an accusation of fraudulent conveyance. The fact that Miles backs away from the term 'use' at this point makes a strong statement about what it is allowed to imply elsewhere.[67]

In some of the examples cited above it is clear that there is also an overlap between 'use' in the legal sense of 'to the benefit of' and 'use' in the everyday sense of 'the act of employing a thing for any (esp. a profitable) purpose; the fact, state or condition of being so used; utilization or employment for or with some aim or purpose; application or conversion to some (esp. good or useful) end'.[68] For instance, at p. 62 – 'the said Award the moytie of the Theatre and the Rent therof are to be had and Recyved by & *to the use of the said comp^{lt}*' – it is arguable that both senses are present simultaneously in the discussion of the rent. In the later stages of this documentation, this semantic overlap begins to appear in contexts hovering between concepts of real and intellectual property. When the question of renewal arises, Allen proposes that 'the Theatre there erected should continue for a playinge place by the space of five yeares onelye, and that it should be converted to some other use for the benefitt of the Comp ^{lte} Duringe his terme [Burbage], and after for the benefitt of the Defend^t [Allen]'.[69] A deposition on the same matter from Robert Vigerous says that the two parties had agreed to 'converte the said Theatre to his [*i.e. Burbage's*] best benefit for the residue of the said terme then to come; and that afterward it should remaine to the onelye use of the Defendte'.[70] When Allen appeals to Star Chamber, he refers to his intention to pull down the Theatre and 'convert the wood and timber therof to some better use'.[71] And Robert Miles refers to 'the Plays that shuld be used there everye weke'[72] and to 'the proffittes that shuld Ryse by the said Playes there to be used'.[73] Across this discussion, the ideas of the Theatre as a 'use', and of the 'use' of the plays within the Theatre, come together as the basis on which its occupation is profitable. Episodes in the litigation as a whole thus identify 'plays' in an institutional sense as a schedule of performance that brings in 'great somes of money gathered & had of the repairers therunto'.[74] Over and over again, those who consider themselves to have a claim to this profit – the Burbages, the Braynes, Robert Miles, John Hyde, Giles Allen – come to the Theatre, enter its premises and participate directly in the profit-making process. And the litigation as a whole constitutes an attempt to obtain and retain the right to occupy the Theatre and to continue to put on plays on those terms.[75] On this basis, there is a direct equivalence between the troubling, troublesome *durée* of the litigation and the professional aspiration towards the day-by-day, week-by-week pattern of exhibition that would convert this contested legal 'term of years' into the deeply layered institutional temporality of theatrical performance: 'But that's all one, our play is done, And we'll strive to please you everyday'.[76]

Thus the word recurs, mapping the seemingly endless circulation of claims to title and possession across all the contested positions in the negotiation. The extraordinary narrative of the Theatre litigation gives us a very good example of the way the concept of beneficial ownership extends full participation in the duty circle of property rights to parties conventionally excluded by estate or lack of means. In particular, it helps us understand the basis on which the trouble and inquietness of this competitive dynamic of contested property rights converted into the 'quiet possession' of the efficient, effective professional group who established their ownership of the Globe.

'Quiet possession' was an equitable right frequently contested across the sixteenth century. Significantly for the history of the custom-built playhouse, three of the four petitions for injunctions for quiet possession recorded by Bryson relate to disputes over dissolved ecclesiastical properties.[77] James Burbage drew on this notion from the very start: in his first bill to Chancery in 1588 he made the claim that the Braynes' legal machinations 'troublethe yor Orator & his tenantes in the^r peacable possession'.[78] A request for an injunction for quiet possession was one way of getting property cases into Chancery: as J. H. Baker has noted, 'although the Chancery could not in theory interfere with legal title, it could decree possession and ensure that a successful party was put in possession.... [I]t could also make decrees to 'quiet' possession, either to protect the party in possession or to restore possession wrested by force.'[79] Although Burbage's bill is not a petition for quiet possession as such, a decree of this kind would not have been impossible, and Burbage must have been hoping for this kind of outcome, effectively a confirmation of his ownership. Despite the degree of inquietness that arose from his own defence of his occupation, and the fact that Allen repeatedly asserted that Burbage was himself a 'troublesome tenant',[80] this was an argument to which the Burbages continually returned. According to Cuthbert in 1600, a year after moving into the Globe, his father had been 'verie muche troubled' by the 'controversie' about title between Peckham and Allen: 'and often Chardged to finde men to keepe the possession ... from the said Edmond Peckham neyther could this Comp^ltes said father enjoy the said premisses according^e to the lease to him'.[81] In these later stages of the litigation, the institutional implications of this position become clearer when several witnesses suggest that 'm^r James Burbadge was muche disturbed and trobled in his possession of the Theater and Could not Quietlye and peacablie enjoy the same. And therefore the players forsooke the said Theater to his great losse'.[82] It is perhaps significant that this particular claim only emerges in the litigation retrospectively, after the successful development of the Chamberlain's Men in the mid-1590s and is therefore made from a position in which the Burbages' enjoyment of the property is plausibly linked not just to the profitability of their profession, but to the fact that that profitability had by then been recognised as an aspect of the public good.

This shift is significant. After all, if early modern theatre really had been as subversive as some New Historicist and cultural materialist critics have urged,[83] Allen's petition to Star Chamber gave Elizabeth's government the perfect opportunity to deal with it. As the climax of 25 years' unbroken litigation, it focuses very precisely the nuances of the repertoire of legal discourses brought to bear on the very idea of theatre as property. As the case shifts from the Court of Requests to Star Chamber, its linguistic register shifts discernibly from that of equity to civil disorder. Allen's complaint in Star Chamber described Burbage's action as 'riotous assembly'; the everyday carpenter's tools used to dismantle the Theatre are represented as offensive weapons: 'with divers and manye unlawfull and offensive weapons, as namelye, swords daggers billes axes and such like ... and there armed as aforesayd in very riotous outrageous and forcible manner and contrary to the lawes of your highness Realme attempted to pulle downe the sayd Theatre'.[84] The 'greate vyolence' that results is said to have a 'terrefyeing' effect not only on those who tried 'in peaceable manner' to resist, but also on 'divers others of your ma:^ties loving subjects there neere inhabitinge'. 'Terrefyeing' is a strong word, one clearly directed at Star Chamber's distinctive niche in civil jurisdiction. Far more significant than modern critical discussions of a politically subversive theatre is the fact that its contemporaries were prepared to describe it on such terms in courts of law, not to seek to contain or expose its subversion, but to contest entitlement to its rights of interest as a property. Baker further notes that allegations of misdemeanour at Star Chamber 'were often fictitious or exaggerated, and the council was being asked in reality to try title',[85] and that is the case here, but there is a striking consonance between the wording of this bill and the idea, expressed in Thomas Egerton's comment cited earlier in this chapter, to the effect that the very idea of owning a playhouse appears to have an in-built association with 'disturbing the peace'. From this perspective we might have expected Egerton to act in Allen's favour. I pointed out above that he was a member of the Privy Council from April 1596, the year the petition against the Blackfriars was upheld, and he would also have sat on Star Chamber when Allen's bill was presented in November 1601. By then, this famously irascible man had been given more than enough encouragement to decide that theatre litigation was at best a waste of the court's time.[86] He had been drawn into the Essex's abortive coup in February that year. Having gone in person to see Essex on the day of the uprising to try to calm things down, he was forcibly held at Essex House, an imposition that resulted in his implacable involvement against Devereux in the subsequent trial for treason – a trial that implicated the Chamberlain's Men for their specially commissioned performance of *Richard II*. In August, Elizabeth had her famous discussion with the antiquarian William Lambarde about Essex's 'wicked imagination' – a phrase that comfortably encompasses both the theatrical and treasonous senses of the word 'imagination'.[87] And here, only two months later, was Allen in Star Chamber providing the court with an opportunity to do something about it. But they did not take it. In fact, the outcome of the case was a recognition that, if anyone, it was Allen that was troublingly inquiet: 'calling the same matter againe into question, and in labouringe to have the said cause, after such iudicciall sentence and decree past against the said Complayn^t in the said honorable Courte ...'. As we have seen, Cuthbert was instructed to 'be at libertie' – another very strong term – 'to take his remedie'. Thus, despite Egerton's own comments to the contrary, what we see happening in this period is a transition from a position in which a petition from 'him that exhibits his bill concerning any playhouse' would be dismissed as intrinsically unprofitable, to one in which, within two more years at most, the Chamberlain's Men would receive James I's patent investing the Globe with customary status and protecting the company's activities on that basis.

How do we understand this? How exactly did the Shakespeare company's ownership of their own theatres make this striking transition from trouble and inquietness to an equitable right to quiet possession? The answer supplied by many contemporary commentators would, of course, be 'patronage'. But even if we continue to apply this term to an ensemble of social and economic relations that were increasingly articulated in terms of professionalism and friendship rather than power and service, it would have to be understood as an explanation after the fact. What precedes it is, quite simply, a day-by-day contest for the sustaining of a legitimate series of prerogatives over occupied social space that has nothing to do with these external interventions, and which itself serves to legitimate those interventions. To begin with, we have to accept the fact that a 'quiet possession' is intrinsically a shifting, unstable, antagonistic dynamic: it is by definition something you have to go to court to obtain. The fact that the Theatre litigation is underpinned by a rhetoric of violent confrontation informs our understanding of the extent to which institutionally constitutive practices – even relatively simple ones like standing at the door and taking the money – take shape not just as relations of property, but as competitive ones.

The reason this documentation is supremely useful to an understanding of 'Shakespearean theatre' is that it helps us focus the role of Shakespeare's plays in the transition from the contested possession of the Theatre to the secure ownership of the Globe. We can do this by reading the Theatre litigation in which general statements about 'playes that shuld be used there everye weke' are made, first as the basis of an inducement to finance the Theatre, and later in arguments about who should benefit from it, against the document in which the man by then recognised as the leading writer of those plays is named as a party to the lease for the site on which the Globe was built. If the Theatre litigation displays all the dangers anticipated by Anderson and Popham – an under-financed speculation by people of the poorer or common sort; a duty circle based on kinship; a chaotic proliferation of competing claims – then the Globe indenture of 1599, a tripartite agreement between Nicholas Brend, the carpenter from whom the site was leased, the Burbage brothers and then Shakespeare, Augustine Phillips, Thomas Pope, John Hemings and William Kempe, creates a duty circle in which the parties are experienced theatre professionals with highly developed and institutionally complementary skills. It is thus an agreement in which the 'path to privity' is *not* 'natural love',[88] but skill or expertise, and the trust and confidence reposed in all parties is a recognition of and reliance on this expertise. Thus, although the Globe lease, like the Theatre lease, is still a lease for term of years, the *durée* it institutes is qualitatively transformed. For Shakespeare and his fellows, it is a period of time with a secure future – as secure as an Elizabethan future could be, perhaps.

The Theatre litigation is a painstaking, often painful, undignified, insecure process by which the idea, not so much of the play, as of an institution of theatre, is kept active against a complex range of resistances. It is in this complex range of resistances that we should look for the dynamics which we would describe as the basis of the institutional development of Shakespearean theatre in this period, and it is in that institutional development that we find the basis of the confirmation of their virtual monopoly in the theatre culture of London in the patent issued to the now King's Men at James's accession in 1603.[89] This document is usually understood as a statement of patronage. But, like Walter Cope's intervention with John Hyde, it is not an operation of power: it does not instigate or change anything; it does not even legitimate. It acknowledges, and arguably even exploits on behalf of the monarchy, the position of professional pre-eminence achieved with limited court intervention, by the combined agencies of the company members themselves across the last decade of Elizabeth's reign. Certain significant turns of phrase may well be taken as landmarks in the history of theatre, but they are not changes of condition created by the king on their behalf. The company is licensed 'to show and exercise publicly to their best commodity' and we note the complementary ideas of 'showing publicly' – in comparison with the hitherto pervasive notions of trouble and inquietness – and 'to their best commodity'. There is now an explicit recognition that 'showing publicly' is associated with the competitive capacity to excel, and to do so 'within their *now usual* house called the Globe within our County of Surrey', retrospectively imposing on the structure the customary status it so clearly lacked before the end of the 1590s. Significantly, this recognition has the effect of extending their prerogative over occupied social space to some from which they had hitherto been excluded: 'any town halls or moot halls or other convenient places within the liberties and freedom of any other city, university, town or borough whatsoever within our said realms and dominions'. Henceforth, when a travelling group of players come, as in *Hamlet*, to a public place to perform, they come to a space in which their rights of occupation had priority over those of its titleholders.

If we read on, we might conclude that this patent is in some sense more of an equitable injunction for quiet possession than a licence. Echoing the standard wording of bills to the courts of equity requesting injunctions for quiet possession,[90] James enjoins 'every of you' not only to permit and suffer them herein, *without any your lets, hindrances* or molestations during our said pleasure, but also to be aiding and assisting to them if any wrong be to them offered, and to allow them such former courtesies as hath been given to men of their place and quality.

James's inclusive 'every of you' confirms the now accepting 'public' identified in the former section as a receptive culture of spectatorship: a quiet possession of theatre.

3
A Pleasure and a Profit: *The Taming of the Shrew*

> *Lucentio*: Here is a wonder, if you talk of wonders.
> *Hortensio*: And so it is. I wonder what it bodes.
> *Petruchio*: Marry, peace it bodes, and love, and a quiet life.
> *The Taming of the Shrew* 5.2.110–12[1]

Although it is generally agreed to have been produced around 1590–1, *The Taming of the Shrew* has been dated as early as 1589.[2] Written before his work was associated with any specific company or playhouse, this play draws on arguments about the creation of property by industry which suggest Shakespeare saw his relationship with the professional theatre in institutional terms as potentially one of quiet possession from the very outset.

Things of pleasure

> If a lord beats his villain, or a husband his wife, or someone beats an outlaw, traitor or heathen: these people shall have no action, because they are unable to sue. But here he has taken my dog, and although it is a thing of pleasure, I still have property in it. At the beginning of the world all beasts were obedient to our first father Adam, and all the four elements were obedient to him; but after he broke the command of our lord God all beasts began to rebel and be wild, and this was punishment for his crime. And now they are in common, *et occupanti conceduntur*: as fowls in the air, fishes in the sea, and beasts upon the land. And when I have taken a fowl, and by my industry I have made it tame by restraint of its liberty, now I have a special property in it,[3] inasmuch as it is made obedient by my own labour, and then it is not legal for anyone to take it.
>
> *Fyllol v Assheleygh* (1520)[4]

Fyllol v Assheleygh came to the Court of Common Pleas in Trinity Term 1520. It was one of a number of cases from 1520–3 which were the first sixteenth-century reports to be printed, apparently because they illustrate changes in the form of pleading associated with demurrer and as such anticipate the equitable principles on which Edmund Plowden would base the selection of cases for his influential *Reports*.[5] Part of its modernity lay in the way it used ideas about animals to test new principles of property and ownership, in this case the increasingly important question of the distinction between profit and pleasure.[6] Before the sixteenth century, the conventional position on 'things of pleasure' had been that they were purely personal and could be revoked without substantial loss. *Fyllol* marks the emergence of a position in which pleasure itself came to be seen as a form of profit, and those 'things' that give pleasure protected on that basis. Other texts from this period mark a similar argument: this case worked through questions surprisingly similar to those that concerned Sir Thomas More in *Utopia*, first published in 1518. (As we shall see in the next chapter, More's humanist commitment to the pursuit of pleasure gave him something of a mythical status in London's professional theatre in the early 1590s.) For More, the ownership of things was in some sense always competitive, usually destructively so: owning something was fundamentally a case of preventing someone else from doing so. While the commodities of life are *materia voluptatis*, the matter of pleasure, their unfair division constitutes a violation of the public good: they are 'nothing but a certain conspiracy of rich men, procuring their own commodities under the name and title of the commonwealth'.[7] What was distinctive about *Fyllol v Assheleygh* and crucial to any attempt to understand the process by which the 'unprofitable matter' of theatrical entertainment achieved customary status as a form of property was the fact that it arrived at a position where 'things of pleasures', and their ownership, were protected by law.

The case was an action of trespass brought by Sir William Fyllol of Dorset (father-in-law of Edward Seymour, 1st Duke of Somerset, the then future protector) against a neighbour, Henry Assheleygh. According to Sir William, Assheleygh had beaten one of his servants and taken away a bloodhound. In response to this allegation, Assheleygh entered a demurrer: first, that Fyllol had not demonstrated that he was legally entitled to own a bloodhound, and second, that because a dog is a 'thing of pleasure', and therefore has no value, it cannot be stolen. The Year Book report records the debate about legal principles that followed. The first of the two issues, the question of entitlement to ownership, was the more controversial. According to the provisions of the Game

Act 1389 (13 R2 stat 1 c. 13), the statutory qualification for keeping a hound was the capacity to spend 40 shillings a year. According to Justices Fitzherbert, Roo and Elyot, Sir William had not demonstrated this capacity in his count and therefore could not bring the action. However, Justices Newport and Newdigate asserted that he did not need to prove his entitlement since it was for the defendant to prove otherwise. This counterargument is illustrated with reference, not to the Game Act, but to the Statute of Apparel, 7 Hen 8 c. 6: 'if someone brings an action against me for taking his velvet robe or golden chain, he does not have to show in his count that he can spend so much value in land according to the statute, since it is for the defendant to show this by a plea in bar'.[8]

I shall pursue the implications of this cross-referencing of the Acts of Gaming and Apparel in due course. In the context of this case, the argument simply addressed the question of whether Sir William's proposed action lay on a statute. As Baker points out, 'this was not a very strong argument, since the statute only created a criminal offence and was not material to the cause of action': it was obviously intended simply as a insult. What *was* material was the question of what value a dog had and whether it could be stolen. Fitzherbert and Elyot acknowledge the traditional position: 'no action lies for a dog, for no one shall have an action for something of no value or profit, and a dog is of no value but is a thing kept for pleasure':

> If someone takes my dog, I am not much damaged by it. If my horse or ox wanders off into another county, and a stranger takes it, I shall have an action of trespass against him; but if my dog runs away into another county and someone takes it, I shall not have an action for it, for when it is out of my possession, I have no property in it.[9]

Speaking in favour of the action, Brudenell argues that a dog counts as property because of the labour and cost involved in ensuring that this does not happen:

> I agree that one shall not have replevin or detinue for such things [as dogs] because they are of no price: and one shall not say 'of the price' (*precii*) and shall not say '*his* wild beasts (*feras suas*) as it appears in 3 Hen VI... But when I have tamed such beasts by my labour, and at my cost, the property in them is changed and the nature is altered, and then if anyone takes them I can certainly have an action: not because he has broken my close, for perhaps he took them in the common street or outside my house, or took my sparrowhawk from its perch without trampling on my grass or breaking my close, and yet because

I have a property in it and it is for my benefit I shall have an action against the person who took it.... Likewise, if I have a tame otter, or a tame hind and someone takes them, I shall have an action, because the property is now in me by reason of the nature being changed through my industry, and because I have a pleasure and a profit from it. If my hound strays, however, and someone takes him, I shall not have an action. But if my hound follows me (or is with my servant) and someone takes him, I shall have a good action, because he was in my possession.[10]

Reading this case, one might be struck by the odd illogic of its argument, or perhaps by the rationality of a society capable of making it. If the Acts of Gaming and Apparel stipulate the economic status of someone entitled to own a bloodhound, and you cannot bring a case for the theft of a dog unless you demonstrate that status, how is it possible to argue that the animal has no value? This is not an anachronistic question: it is implicit in the case itself, a fact that gives weight to a suggestion that this illogic is not only what is interesting about the case now, but also what seems to have been available from it for transmission, by whatever cultural mechanism that may be, into Shakespeare's play.

The contradictory relationship between these arguments about value creates a complex fabric of thought, compellingly dramatised in form of the legal debate about the nature of pleasure and its value. To begin with, any attempt to establish a figure for that value is problematic. Brudenell asserts that 'dogs are of no price' ('one shall not say "of the price" [*precii*]'), but agrees that they count as property because of the labour that goes into taming them and the cost of that labour. Notwithstanding, the Latin record of the case that follows specifies a price: it describes the dog as '*unum canem vocatum "a bludhownd" ... precii decem marcarum*':[11] 'price ten marks' (£6 13s 4d), an extraordinarily high figure and far in excess of contemporary records of what a dog like this would actually cost to obtain. From the household records of the Manners family at Belvoir Castle, we learn that in 1536 Thomas, Earl of Rutland paid 3s 2d to Sir John Markham's servant for bringing him a brace of greyhounds; in September 1549, Henry, 2nd Earl of Rutland, paid one pound 'to a Ducheman that gave [him] a dogge', but the payments there may apply to the service involved in supplying the animal, rather than something we might, again with the benefit of hindsight, describe as its use or exchange value.[12] *Fyllol v Assheleygh* led to an award to Sir William of 40 shillings, described as 'damages by reason of the taking and leading away of the aforesaid dog'.[13] Forty shillings is more in keeping with the kind of sums mentioned above than 10 marks; but it is not in any simple sense a valuation of the animal. In fact, this indeterminacy of value is not a problem; it is precisely the point. In a situation in which the 'thing of pleasure' is coming to be seen as 'profitable', attempts to value it are characterised by the *imaginative disproportion* between, first, what something costs to acquire and second, what, in Hector's words from *Troilus and Cressida*, it 'doth cost the holding' (2.2.50–1). And of course 'holding', as Troilus finds to *his* 'cost', is where the question arises of whether or not a thing of pleasure 'follows me' or runs off into another county.

Characteristic of attempts to evoke this 'imaginative disproportion' is a discursive interplay between a complementary range of 'things'. Pollard's argument opens up as naturally to questions of clothing as it does to dogs:

> For instance, if I give my robe to a tailor to repair, and he will not give it back... these cannot be called felony, and yet I shall have a remedy or else it would be against reason. Likewise in this case my hound is my treasure, for he catches game for my pleasure. Moreover, even though my sparrowhawk is wild by nature (*ferae naturae*) yet I have changed its nature by cost, labour and diligence, and although it was previously common I now have property in it; for if I allow my sparrowhawk to fly at a bird, and someone else takes it, I shall have an action, inasmuch as it is still in my possession.[14]

Robes, tailors, hounds and falcons are not merely interchangeable examples of property; they are metonymically generative of each other's presence in the text in a way that anticipates the cultural and theatrical space of *The Taming of the Shrew*, particularly that of the Induction and of Petruchio's house. It is a space created by the act of occupation: in *Fyllol* it emerged in due course that what was actually at stake was not the dogs, but property rights over the land in which they were being used to hunt. But the interesting thing about it is the fact that the question of property rights was suppressed in favour of an argument about the intrinsic value of the thing being occupied. Hector's assertion that 'value dwells not in particular will. It holds its estimate and dignity As well wherein 'tis precious of itself As in the prizer' (2.2.53–5) suggests the extent to which this imaginative disproportion, which we shall encounter again in *The Taming of the Shrew*, could be said to anticipate an *a priori* concept of aesthetic value, and to apply it to the idea of theatre.

A special property in theatre

We might note in passing that the relation between the very English Induction of *The Shrew* and the Italianate play that follows it is in certain respects curiously like the framing relation between the law French report of the *Fyllol v Assheleygh* demurrer, and the subsequent Latin record of the case itself. Earlier, I was noncommittal about the 'cultural mechanism' by which the ideas in *Fyllol* might 'transmit' into Shakespeare's play. I want to suggest that this relation might best be seen, not as that of a 'source', but as a mode of paratextuality. Indeed, I would want to generalise this idea by suggesting that the notion of paratextuality may be our best point of departure for thinking about the way, in Shakespeare's plays, legal thinking opens an intellectual threshold for the creation of a special property in theatre.[15] The Induction begins with an argument between 'the Lord' and his huntsman about the exemplary performance, and (therefore) imaginatively disproportionate value of his hounds. Of Silver, who 'made it good At the hedge corner, in the coldest fault', we hear that 'I would not lose the dog for twenty pound' (Induction 15–17) – an extraordinary figure about three times as much as Sir William Fyllol's already remarkable 10 marks. The Lord's compelling synthesis of profit and pleasure provides a rationale for his intention, expressed at end of this exchange, to hunt again the very next day:

> If Echo were as fleet
> I would esteem him worth a dozen such.
> But sup them well and look unto them all:
> Tomorrow I intend to hunt again.
>
> 22–5

That 'tomorrow' is indicative: in 1591, Sir Thomas Cokayne advised that 'this disport of hunting bee vsed by you only as a recreation to enable both your bodies and minds thereby to better exercises, & not as an occupation to spend therein daies, moneths, and yeres'.[16] Here, there is an immediate slippage from the idea of hunting as a repetition to that of the play as an 'occupation' for the time that intervenes between the end of one hunt and the beginning of the next; a repetition that anticipates the iterative concept of performance that emerges in the idea of Shakespearean theatre that consolidates across the 1590s ('our play is done, and we'll strive to please you every day').[17] The Lord's disport with Sly begins as something like a hunt - he is discovered as a 'monstrous beast' lying 'like a swine' (30) – but it evolves rapidly into a play with 'parts' (65). As in *Fyllol*, there is a curious intermeddling of questions of gaming and apparel. The 'practise' (32) the Lord proposes is to dress Sly up in the kind of 'excess of array' referred to by 7 Hen 8 c. 6, the point of the exercise being the pleasure he would derive from seeing Sly 'forget himself' (37) in a 'flattr'ing dream' (40).

What we would now see as a distinctively Shakespearean ontology of theatre is thus, at this early stage of its development, based on a creative manipulation of the relation we see in *Fyllol* between the idea of the thing of pleasure and the subversion of statutory limitations on the 'show of apparel' and the right to recreation:[18] 'Someone be ready with a costly suit, And ask him what apparel he will wear. Another tell him of his hounds and horse...' (55–7). Sly's unexpected skill in imagining himself into this position provides the opportunity for a comparable response from the rest of the company, a response that complicates the fact that, at an obvious level, the 'play' they start to perform constitutes an act of service. For it is at this point that those engaged in this 'pastime' begin to identify their activities both as theatre - 'we will play our part...' – and as an 'industry' in which, regardless of their status as servants, they demonstrably have a special property: 'as he shall think *by our true diligence* He is no less *than what we say he is*' (65–7). At this point, still only 70 lines into the play, Shakespeare has himself laboured industriously to create an action that moves, with a swiftness equalled only by Silver himself, from the exemplary performance of the Lord's dogs, to the 'duty' offered by a group of servants who are transforming themselves into players before our eyes. Not surprisingly, it is also at this point that a troupe of professional players arrives. The performance that follows, in which a company of common players is employed by a lord to perform for a vagrant who believes he is a lord watching his own company, presents a dialectical image of theatre looking back at its origins in service and forward to its status as a profession that would, within a very few years, create its own special property in theatre.[19]

The legal framework that Shakespeare uses to assert his ownership of this special property is provided by the 'assurance'. *The Shrew* uses the terms 'assure' and 'assurance' more often than all his other plays put together, so it is hard to miss the possibility that it is doing something interesting with it. An assurance is 'the securing of a title to property; the conveyance of lands or tenements by deed'.[20] In *The Shrew*, a distinction between the acquisition of property by conveyance and the creation of property by industry parallels a distinction between arranged marriage and marriage based on love. Initially, Kate's and Bianca's courtships are negotiated in terms of the assurance. But the difference between them becomes apparent when, responding to Petruchio's offer to

> assure her of
> Her widowhood, be it that she survives me,
> In all my lands and leases whatsoever.
> Let specialties be drawn between us
> That covenants may be kept on either hand.
>
> 2.1.121–5

Baptista substitutes the idea of the 'specialty' – a sealed contract – with the more open-ended (indeed, potentially indefinitely so) negotiation of 'that special thing':

> Ay, when that special thing is well obtained
> That is her love, for that is all in all.
>
> 126–7

The suggestion is, of course, that he is going to have to work very hard to get it, and that unless he gets possession, it will not matter whether he has a title to her or not.

Although the actions that follow preposterously invert the order of events stipulated by the proviso, the contrast between love as industry and marriage as conveyance prevails within the play and in the conception of 'pleasant comedy' it puts forward. Paradoxically, because Bianca is seen as so much more obviously desirable, the question of *her* 'special thing' does not arise. Whilst Kate's value to her prospective husband is clear-cut – he simply offers all he has[21] – there is an extremely imaginative disproportion in Bianca's value to her competing suitors:

> *Gremio:* What, have I choked you with an argosy?
> *Tranio:* Gremio, 'tis known my father hath no less
> Than three great argosies, besides two galliases
> And twelve tight galleys. These I will assure her,
> And twice as much whate'er thou off'rest next.
>
> 368–72

But Kate's value begins to be industriously renegotiated when she returns with Petruchio to his house. When she contradicts Petruchio's insistence on the wrong time of day, she too uses the idea of assurance, though here in the transferred sense of 'to guarantee...to promise as a thing that may be depended on':[22] 'I dare assure you, sir, 'tis almost two' (4.4.183). Petruchio's response aligns his labour directly with that of the players of the Induction; in fact, he *echoes* them: 'we will play our part As he shall think by our true diligence He is no less *than what we say he is'*; 'I will not go today, and, ere I do *It shall be what o'clock I say it is*' (4.4.188–90). If in the Induction, dressing Sly in finery shows how connections between questions of gaming and apparel feed into an emergent 'idea of the play', the sustained engagement in the play itself with the contrast between assurance and industry sets up an equivalent distinction between a false theatre and a true one. The scene in which Tranio dresses a complete stranger as his father in order to provide the assurance required for marriage to Bianca immediately precedes the episode in which Petruchio destroys Kate's new gown, and then insists on going to her father's house in 'honest, mean habiliments... For 'tis the mind that makes the body rich' (4.3.164; 166).

The values at stake here are finally put to the test in the last scene, notably in Petruchio's challenge to 'Sir Assurance' at 5.2.66. Here it becomes clear that, despite the apparent disproportion of Bianca's value in 2.1, it is Kate whom we can now confidently identify both as the thing of pleasure and as the exemplary performer: 'What's the wager? Twenty crowns. Twenty crowns? I'll venture so much of my hawk or hound But twenty times so much upon my wife. A hundred then' (5.2.71–7). The outcome of the wager tops all previous estimates:

> The wager thou hast won, and I will add
> Unto their losses twenty thousand crowns
> Another dowry to another daughter
> For she is changed as she had never been.
>
> (5.2.116–19)

For Petruchio, Kate's value is demonstrated, not by the complex indeterminacy of price or cost, but by her capacity to outperform the rest of the pack. The wager of obedience is thus a direct formal balance to the Lord and his Huntsman's debate about which is the better dog, and what kind of value can be placed on outstanding performance. The play is aware of the extent to which the hunt that frames its action defines its frames of reference. Tranio points out to Petruchio, '"tis well, sir, that you hunted for yourself.' He acknowledges that 'Lucentio slipped me like his greyhound Which runs himself and catches for his master' (5.2.54–6), thus confirming the distinction set up in the Induction between an idea of performance that owns the value of its own labour and one that is a merely a form of service to a master. From this perspective we should understand Kate's willingness to 'follow' Petruchio in 5.2. not as female submission, but as the profitable transformation of a wild thing into a thing of pleasure, and thus as the embodiment of a brand-new form of industry: a play by Shakespeare.

4
Welcome to our Chamber: *The History of Richard III*, Sir Thomas More, *Richard III*

> And as for the politic and wholesome laws that were enacted in his time, they were interpreted to be but the brocage of an usurper, thereby to woo and win the hearts of the people, as being conscious to himself, that the true obligations to sovereignty in him failed and were wanting.[1]

Pace Sir Francis Bacon, the approach to land management enshrined in Richard III's Statute of Uses was one of the great triumphs of the Yorkist dynasty. In 1467, Edward IV announced his intention to finance the king's household from his private estates rather than by imposing charges on his subjects. Driven by the conviction that the king's lands were part of the fisc of the realm,[2] the Yorkist land revenue experiment took its cue from contemporary techniques of estate management.[3] In practical terms, it meant that royal revenues would be administered not by the Exchequer but by *camera regis*, the 'king's chamber'. Under Richard, the transition to a chamber system was complete. With twenty years' experience of administering his own lands and advising his brother, he was so successful that in his admittedly brief reign "'no receiver of the king's lands made any appearance at the exchequer'".[4] At first, Henry VII allowed the system to fall into decay, but within a decade he began to rediscover its benefits. Under Henry VII and Henry VIII, the king's chamber became the basis of the Tudor reinvention of prerogative rights: hence 27 Hen 8 c. 10.

In a postwar period presided over by G. R. Elton's *The Tudor Revolution in Government* and *England under the Tudors*, Richard III's 'true obligations to sovereignty' were largely unappreciated.[5] But if a re-evaluation has begun in the discipline of history, it has yet to make its mark on Shakespeare studies. From the arguments I put forward in Chapter 2 it is hard to avoid the conclusion that Tudor (mis)representations of Richard constituted at some level an attack on his changes to the laws of property. Kathy Eden has pointed out that classical and humanist traditions define the tyrant as one who treats his subjects, and their possessions, as his own private property: "'he who looks to the common good is a king; he who looks to his own good is a tyrant'".[6] Given that the aim of 27 Hen 8 c. 10 was to return to Henry feudal rights over property effectively redistributed by 1 Ric 3 c. 1, which was the king and which the tyrant?

Curiously, Sir Thomas More is our primary source for both the Tudor myth of Richard and for sixteenth-century critiques of Henry VIII's increasingly tyrannical conception of kingship. As far as its transmission into Shakespeare's play is concerned, the relationship between these conflicting readings has typically been approached via rhetorical traditions of the dilemma or paradox.[7] In this chapter I consider the possibility that *The Tragedy of King Richard III* draws more directly on the intellectual legacy of Richard's reign. As Shakespeare began to establish himself in the London theatrical scene, Richard and his 'new kind of ownership' provided him with the terms for a special property in theatre that was soon to be realised in the formation of the Chamberlain's Men and their residence in the Theatre.[8]

I am not suggesting that Shakespeare was in any simple sense a 'Yorkist', though the idea may be at least as relevant to an understanding of his work as the more fashionable question of whether he was Roman Catholic.[9] But I do want to suggest that he was well aware that features of the Yorkist legacy advanced his professional interests more than Tudor governmentality, and that he was capable of adapting them to his own purposes. Reading More's *The History of Richard III* it cannot have escaped his attention that More had done something very similar.[10] Most critics agree that *The History*, written around 1518 at about the same time as *Utopia*, is 'a moral drama about the evils of tyranny', but most also agree that the tyrant More had in mind was Henry, not Richard,[11] and that the complex narrative structure that resulted from this oblique act of counsel is one that intermittently allowed Richard's historical virtues to slip out from beneath the elaborate mask of defamation. More's work was reproduced throughout the sixteenth century in pro-Tudor histories like Hardyng, Hall, Holinshed and Stow, but it also underpinned a parallel tradition of resistant readings. These include the text now commonly referred to as the *Encomium of Richard III*, probably of early Tudor authorship but circulated in manuscript in Elizabeth's reign, possibly by members of Essex's circle in the late 1590s.[12] The *Encomium* was published in 1616 as one of William Cornwallis's *Essayes of certaine paradoxes*, but it was already known to Sir George Buc while writing two explicitly Yorkist texts, *Daphnis Polystephanos, An Eclog treating of Crownes and Garlandes and to whom of right they appertaine* (1605) and *History of the Life and Reigne of Richard III* (not published until 1642). Buc was associated with the group of scholars who founded the Antiquarian Society in the 1580s: John Stowe, Sir Edward Coke, William Camden, Robert Cotton and John Selden. In true antiquarian style, his Yorkist sympathies were articulated in a generational account of his 'ancientry', in which he recalls his great-grandfather Sir John, Richard's Controller of the Household, beheaded by Henry VII, and the Bucs' subsequent alliance to the Yorkist Howards, who maintained and advanced the family after the White Rose had, as he put it, 'withered'.[13]

Family connections, or connectivity, may well be our best approach to Tudor nostalgia for a Yorkist past, including Shakespeare's. More himself came from a Yorkist background. His father was fiercely loyal to Edward IV, and as 'son Roper' famously recorded, he was himself fiercely loyal to his father. Shakespeare acknowledges this loyalty in one of the two episodes (referred to as Addition III) attributed to him in the suppressed collaboration *Sir Thomas More*, where it is given direct bearing on More's rejection of political corruption, and subsequent refusal of Henry VIII's Articles:

> Good God, good God,
> That I from such an humble bench of birth
> Should step as 'twere up to my country's head
> And give the law out there; ay, in my father's life
> To take prerogative and tithe of knees
> From elder kinsmen, and him bind by my place
> To give the smooth and dexter way to me
> That owe it him by nature! Sure these things,
> Not physicked by respect, might turn our blood
> To much corruption.[14]

The fact that a similar critique of the moral and political consequences of the elevation of son above father emerges in the Fool's confrontation with Lear in the Folio *The Tragedy of King Lear*, where it is usually taken to allude to Shakespeare's elevation above his own father ('he has a mad yeoman that sees his son a gentleman before him' [3.6.11]) suggests the possibility that Shakespeare's thinking about history drew on a generational dynamic in which usurpation, like the use, had come to be seen less as an abuse of traditional principles of succession than as the historical condition for their performance. In an article of 1976, William Huse Dunham and Charles Wood put forward a reading of the period from the death of Edward II in 1327 to that of Richard III in 1485 as a sequence of depositions that 'led Englishmen better to understand the circumstances under which a king could lose his right to rule'.[15] According to Dunham and Wood, the debates that attended these depositions, particularly in the deposer's address to the people for consent, came to constitute a 'doctrine of restraint' that acknowledged the authority of the estates of the realm, and ultimately of parliament itself.[16] They argued that this process culminated in the process of 'consultation' undertaken by Richard before his succession: 'no king of England did so much – on paper – as did Richard III to raise parliament's position in the frame of government'.[17] Dunham and Wood's paper must now be placed in an American tradition of historiography that celebrated the birth and export of liberty, particularly in the context of the Cold War: their emphasis on deposition and popular election has given way in more recent work to an interest in the constitutionalist tradition associated with Sir John Fortescue and rule by council.[18] But the debate as a whole alerts us to the possibility that the significant shared feature of More's *History* and Shakespeare's *Richard III* is not a simple exposure of Richard's evil, but a far more complex engagement with Richard's address to mechanisms of popular consensus in general, and theatre in particular.

More's distinctive narrative technique – what Elizabeth Story Donno refers to as 'the invoking of "common knowledge"'[19] – has been the subject of much commentary on his *History*. One or two examples will establish the features of this technique for the purposes of this discussion. In the account of young Edward's situation in Wales at his father's death, we are told that Edward is under the 'governaunce and ordering' of his mother's brother, Sir Anthony Woodville, Lord Rivers:

> Adioyned wer there vnto him other of the same partie, and in effect euery one as he was nerest of kin vnto the Quene, so was planted next about the prince. That drift by the Quene not vnwisely deuised, whereby her bloode mighte of youth be rooted in the princes fauor, the Duke of Gloucester turned vnto their destruccion, & vpon that grounde set the foundacion of all his vnhappy building. For whom soeuer he perceiued, either at variaunce with them, or bearing himself their fauor, hee brake vnto them, som by mouth, som by writing & secret messengers, that it neyther was reason nor in any wise to be

suffered, that the yong king their master and kinsmanne, should bee in the handes and suctodye of his mothers kindred, sequestered in maner from theyr compani & attendance, of which eueri one ought him as faithful seruice as they, and many of them far more honourable part of kin then his mothers side: whose blood (quod he) (8).[20]

More creates a complex structure of historical consciousness that modulates from third person narration, with internal inflections of point of view facilitated by latinate inversions – 'that drift by the Quene not vnwisely deuised...the Duke of Gloucester turned vnto their destruccion' – to indirect free style representing multiple voices – 'som by mouth, som by writing & secret messengers' – and direct speech: '(quod he)'.

Commentators have described this as a 'dramatic' technique, which makes it easy for us to see why More's work might have appealed to Shakespeare.[21] But this would, I think, be a shortcut to just what it was about this text that made it so attractive to him when he was writing *Richard III*. If we look at the passage again, we note the range of media assimilated into this complex speech act, together with the scepticism it expresses about their capacity to advance the interests of 'the people'. This preoccupation recurs. When Richard sets about the task of getting himself 'elected' by the commons, we learn that, while he and Buckingham were to all appearances involved in setting up young Edward's coronation, 'as fast were they in an other place contryuyng the contrary, & and to make the protectour kyng':

To which counsel, albeit there were adhibit very few, & they very secret: yet began there here & there about, some maner of muttering amonge the people, as though al should not long be wel, though they neither wist what thei feared nor wherefore: were it that before such great thynges, mens hartes of a secret instinct of nature misgueth them. As the sea without wind swelleth of himself sometime before a tempest: or were it that some one man happely somewhat perceiuing, filled mani men with suspicion, though he shewed few men what he knew...Thus many thinges comming togither p[a]rtly by chaunce, partly of purpose, caused at length, not comen people that wauve with the winde, but wise men also & soe lordes, yeke to marke the mater and muse theron: so ferforth that the lord Stanly, that was after Erle of Darbie, wisely mistrusted it, & saied vnto the lord Hastings, that he much misliked these two seuerall counsels. For while we (quod he)

talke of one matter in the tone place, little wote we wherof they talk
in the tother place. My lord (quod the lord Hastinges)...

(26)

More's account of 'many thinges comming togither p[a]rtly by chaunce,
partly of purpose' presents a temporal dynamic marked by multiple
agencies and contrasting motivations. His primary concern with this
complex, fractured collectivity is with its implications for acts of political
address. This becomes particularly significant in Richard's manipulation
of the people in his election, where there is a crucial ambiguity in his
representation of the range of media involved in Richard's exploitation of
mechanisms of consensus (the proclamation about Hastings; Dr Shaw's
sermon at St Paul's; Buckingham's oration; Richard's election; his public speech when he accepts the crown). On the one hand, he asserts that
Richard is dissimulating and therefore abusing these media; on the other,
he draws Tudor attention to the fact that they were being used.

As this implies, More obviously had some surprisingly contemporary
reservations about the role of media in public life. These surface in the
famous metaphor that appears at the climactic point in his argument:

And in a stage play, all the people know right wel, that he that playeth
the sowdayne is percase a sowter. Yet if one should can so lyttle good
to shewe out of seasonne what acquaintance he hath with him, and
calle him by his owne name whyle he standeth in his magestie, one
of his tormentors might hap to break his head, and worthy for the
marring of the play. And so they said that these matters bee Kynges
games, as it were stage playes, and for the more part plaied upon
scafoldes. In which pore men be but the lokers on. And thei that wise
be, wil medle no farther. For they that sometime step vp and playe
with them, when they cannot play their partes, they disorder the play
& do themselves no good.

(47)

This episode was brought into the critical limelight by Stephen Greenblatt, who put it at the heart of his account of the theatricality of power
in *Renaissance Self-Fashioning*.[22] This influential study overshadowed the
more cautious position adopted by Antony Hammond in his Arden
edition of *Richard III*, published the following year. But Hammond's
approach was in certain ways potentially more illuminating. Quoting this passage in his introductory discussion of the historiographical

tradition on which Shakespeare drew in this play, Hammond explains he had chosen it

> partly because Shakespeare did not elect to use it... partly because in it More shows his fondness for the theatrical metaphor (which Shakespeare must have found entertaining and profitable) and partly for its dry irony, concluding with a pun so good it is surprising that Shakespeare made only limited use of it.[23]

As I suggested in Chapter 3, the juxtaposition of entertainment and profitability seems to me exactly what interested both More and Shakespeare. Richard's election is presented in three stages: his appearance at St Paul's Cross towards the end of Dr Shaw's famously disastrous sermon; Buckingham's oration at the Guildhall to the 'commons of the citie' and supplication to Richard before 'the people' at Baynard's Castle. Buckingham's speeches are a *tour de force*. More describes him as 'of nature marveilouslye well spoken' (39), but is concerned to balance the presentation of his rhetorical skills with an account of their manipulative effect on uneducated people. The episode sustains the weighty part of More's critique of Tudor tyranny, and it does so by invoking the concept of *camera regis*, the king's chamber, referred to in the text and annotated in the margin.

We might begin now to see how the idea of Richard carries forward a vestigial recognition of the more successful aspects of Yorkist governance:

> And yet bee ye the people whom he had as singuler cause wel and kyndly to entreat, as any part of his realme, not onely for that the prince by this noble citye, as his special chamber & the speciall wel renoumed citye of his realme, much honourable fame receiueth among all other nacions: but also for that ye not without your great coste and sundry perils and iopardies in all his warres, bare euer your specyall fauoure to his part...
>
> (41)

Buckingham associates the potential 'profit' of Richard's kingship with the particular economic mode of public good associated with London as the commercial centre of the realm:

> to no part of the realm more profitable, then to you citizens of this noble citie. For why, that thing that we wote well ye haue long time lacked and sore longed for, that ye would haue geuen great good for,

that ye woulde haue gone farre to fetch, that thynge wee bee comme hither to bringe you, withoute youre labour, payne, coste, aduenture or iopardie. What thynge is that? Certes the suretye of your owne bodyes...

To profit from Richard's succession, the citizens have only to become party to a profitable agreement with him:

> if ye the worsshipfull citizens of this the chief citie of this realme ioyne with vs the nobles in our said request. Which for your owne weale we doubte not but ye will, and natheles I hartelye praye you so to doe, wherby you shall doe gret profite to all this realme beside in chosing them so good a king, and vnto yourselfe speciall commodite...
>
> (42/3)

The idea of 'being party' emerges explicitly in the final stages of Buckingham's argument. Frustrated at the common's failure to respond, he resorts to the manipulations of the mountebank: 'we woulde not gladly do withoute you, that thing in which to bee partners is your weale & honour'. Here we note the combined legal and theatrical connotations of these terms 'part', 'party' and 'partner': 'one who has a share or part with another or others... one who is associated with another or others in some business, the expenses, profits and losses of which he proportionately shares.'[24] Despite this apparently unbeatable offer, Buckingham does not get the answer he wants: 'the people began to whisper among themselves secretly'. This collective position may suggest a capacity for political resistance, but for More it was evidence of a vulnerable passivity: their whispering is 'neyther loud or distincke, but as it were the sounde of a swarm of bees'. Buckingham misrepresents the indeterminacy of their response as assent – 'euery man with one voice no manne saying nay' – and the next day he presents a 'peticion' to Richard 'on behalf of them all' (45; 54).

The commons are then left to reflect on this situation in a passage in which More moves from the idea of the part as a form of contract to that of theatrical part:

> the lordes went up to the kyng (for so he was from that called) and the people departed, talking diuersely of the matter euery man as his fantasye gaue hym. But muche they talked and marueiled of the maner of this dealing, that the matter was on both partes made so straunge, as though neither had euer communed with other thereof

before, when that themself wel wist there was no man so dul that heard them, but he perceived wel inough, yt all the mater was made between them. Howbeit somme excused that agayne, and sayd all must be done in good order though. And menne must sommetime for the manner sake not bee a knowen what they knowe. For at the consecration of a bishop, every man woteth well by the paying for his bulles, yt he purposeth to be one, & though he paye for nothing elles. And yet must he bee twise asked whyther he will be bishop or no, and he muste twyse say naye, and at the third tyme take it as compelled there unto by his owne wyll. As in a stage play...

(46)

What we are presented with here, superbly realised, is a kind of cinematic long take, like the famous staircase scene in *The Magnificent Ambersons*: a sustained sweep through a crowd that picks up here and there its 'diverse talk' and individual 'fantasye'.[25] But even though we now 'hear' these voices distinctly, what they are saying affirms their vulnerability:

And so they said that these matters be Kynges games, as it were stage playes, and for the more part plaied vpon scafoldes. In which pore men be but the lokers on. And thei that wise be, wil medle no farther. For they that sometime step vp and playe with them, when they cannot play their partes, they disorder the play & do themselves no good.

(47)

Clearly, More recognised quite sophisticated skills of spectatorship, but did not see them as the basis of a social or political empowerment. It is precisely because Buckingham addresses his audience as 'partners' that they recognise this 'play' as something less than a partnership.

More's doubts about the profitability of partnership were obviously of considerable interest to dramatists of the early 1590s. Unfortunately, we do not know the exact form of the partnership that subsequently produced the collaborative play *Sir Thomas More*. We know it was written around 1592-3 by Anthony Munday, Henry Chettle and possibly a third writer; that it was revised after the Master of the Revels, Edmund Tilney, demanded substantial cuts; and that the writers involved in the revisions include Chettle, Thomas Dekker, Thomas Heywood and Shakespeare. There remains differences of opinion on whether the revisions were made immediately after its first censorship in 1593 or later, around 1603. Scott McMillin has argued that the revisions were made at the later date, but that Shakespeare's contributions were part of the original collaboration.[26] Gary Taylor confirms Shakespeare's participation, but insists on the later date. There is a difference of opinion too on both the company for which it was written and the reasons why it was not subsequently performed. For some, the part of More was written for Edward Alleyn and the Admiral's Men; for others, it was written for Richard Burbage and Strange's Men at the Rose, and passed thence into the hands of the Chamberlain's Men at the Theatre in 1594. For yet others, it was written for Pembroke's Men, a company which toured in 1592–3 and was associated with Shakespeare's *The First Part of the Contention ... twixt the Houses of York and Lancaster* and *The True Tragedy of Richard Duke of York* (the plays that carry the early development of the Richard character).[27] Most commentators agree that the performance of *Sir Thomas* was prevented by the closure of the theatres, but Giorgio Melchiori believes it was vetoed a second time by Tilney and then abandoned because of the 'radical reorganisation of theatre companies in 1594–5'.[28]

How do we deal with this level of uncertainty? Happily, it is only a problem in conventional models of authorship.[29] If we approach this complex field of interaction from an institutional perspective, the uncertainty itself becomes informative because it tells us a lot about that 'reflexive monitoring of action' associated with 'practical understanding' I noted in Chapter 1. We know that 1592–3 was a point in Shakespeare's career when the institutional aspirations articulated in *The Taming of the Shrew* had already attracted attention, not least that of Robert Greene in the famous insult in *Greenes Groats-worth of Wit*: '[F]or there is an upstart Crow, beautified with our feathers, that with his *Tygers heart wrapt in a Players hide*, supposes he is as well able to bombast out a blanke verse as the best of you and being an absolute *Iohannes fac totum*, is in his owne conceit the only Shake-scene in a countrie.'[30] We also know that Chettle, Greene's publisher and co-author of *Sir Thomas More*, met Shakespeare soon after *Groats-worth* was released, at almost exactly the time *Sir Thomas* was being written, and that he issued an apology for his role in the dissemination of the insult that suggests he recently had cause to evaluate Shakespeare's abilities in more flattering terms: '[M]y selfe haue seene his demeanor no lesse ciuill than he exelent in the qualitie he professes: Besides, diuers of worship haue reported, his vprightnes of dealing, which argues his honesty, and his facetious grace in writting, that aprooues his Art.'[31] From this we might conclude both that Chettle had recently worked with Shakespeare and – perhaps surprisingly – that the skills required for successful collaboration are the same as those that underpin the competitive capacity to excel. Interestingly enough, this idea turns out to be one of the prevailing themes of *Sir Thomas More* itself.

The historical More's concern with the profitability of Richard III's succession for the citizens of London provides us with a direct context for the play's symbolic identification between the city and 'More' as a dramatic character. As a consequence, we might fairly expect a specific engagement with More's metaphor of theatre, and we get it. The action of the play begins roughly around 1517, the point immediately before More entered into Henry VIII's service, when he was a sheriff in London and writing both *Utopia* and *The History*. It demonstrates the extent to which, in the early 1590s, he retained his status as a symbol, almost a personification, of London as a 'speciall wel renoumed citye', particularly of the political independence acknowledged by More's Buckingham and Richard in their pursuit of the citizens' approval. As 'More' himself expresses it to the Lord Mayor, 'it is not state That can our love from London separate' (4.1).[32] In the course of the play, More becomes a courtier, but remains at heart a citizen, and it is that, and not the particular characteristics of his religious belief, that is seen as the defining element in his audience's response to his subsequent martyrdom. Commentary on this play identifies its important scenes as his quelling of the May Day insurrection,[33] which include the section attributed to Shakespeare and referred to as Addition II.D, and the speeches on the scaffold before his execution. But I would argue that the heart of the play is his encounter with a company of players: not one of Shakespeare's scenes, but the episode that most conspicuously draws the overall sense of London's political autonomy into a deliberate revision of the historical More's negative assessment of theatre as a mechanism of consensus. I would also argue, *pace* John Jones, that Shakespeare knew this scene and responded to it in *Richard III* and in later plays.

The character More's imaginative exploitation of ideas about 'playing' creates the most important source of continuity within the play's loosely episodic structure. In an early scene, he exposes an opinionated Justice by staging the theft of his purse; in a scene that anticipates Olivia's reception of Cesario in *Twelfth Night* 1.5, he makes a servant stand in for him when he meets Erasmus for the first time. There is, of course, a 'theme' here, as the great humanist himself appropriately observes: 'Your honor's merry humor is best physic Unto your able body: for we learn Where melancholy chokes the passages Of blood and breath The erected spirit still Lengthens our days with sportful exercise' (3.2). The play maps this image of More's 'able body' onto the image of London itself, where issues of public order are presented in terms of freedom of passage through its streets. More himself, however, is arguably as sceptical about the 'justice' of theatre as he is in *The History*, and there is some sense of a degree of conflict between the two. At the beginning of 4.1 he receives a troupe of players and asks them to perform for his guests. Like Theseus in *A Midsummer Nights Dream* written a few years later, he is given a choice of available entertainments, and selects one that reflects the meaning of his own role in the play of which he is himself a 'part', 'The Marriage of Wit and Wisdom': 'The Marriage of Wit and Wisdom! that, my lads; I'll none but that!' When the character playing Good Counsel is unable to make his entrance because he has forgotten to bring the necessary beard, More 'steps up' and plays with them.

What follows makes three important things clear. First, this scene is unquestionably a direct engagement with the historical More's discussion of 'stageplays' in *The History*. As if to confirm 'his' own analysis, in 'his' own words, the character More insists that he has 'marred' the play, 'which through the fellow's absence, and by me Instead of helping hath been hindered... Thus fools oft times do help to mar the play'. But (second and third) it presents an idea of theatre which transforms More's analysis, offering an extremely positive identification between the rising culture of professional theatre and precisely those episodes of collective action for which the play was censored by Tilney. As the players wait for the banquet to finish, their discussion touches briefly on the possibility that there might be political danger in blurring the boundaries between political and theatrical protocols, reminding us once again of the precise wording of More's account. The Vice-character Inclination says,

> Would not my lord make a rare player? O he would uphold a company beyond all hope, better than Mason among the king's players! Did ye mark how extemprically he fell to the matter, and spake Lugginses part almost as it is in the very book set down?

Wit reprimands him, wittily speaking More's part almost as in the very book set down: 'Peace; do ye know what ye say? My lord a player! Let us not meddle with any such matters' (*'thei that wise be* wil medle no further'). Despite this, the issues raised by More's intervention bear almost exclusively on questions relating to standards of performance. In a phrase used by Shakespeare in a similar context when Puck disorders 'the play' by putting love juice on the wrong eyes,[34] Wit accuses Luggins, 'this is your negligence'. This legal commonplace introduces into the theatrical transaction a notion of obligation to perform which significantly adjusts More's idea of theatre. In accusations of negligence, the defendant was alleged to have undertaken a task with want of care or skill, and with resulting harm. In contrast to More, whose concern about the dangers of 'stepping up' revolve around personal risk, the players are clear what the harm is in this case: they would have been unable to finish their performance, with resulting 'disgrace', 'discommendation' and obvious implications for their continued profitability. In this context, More's skills as a spectator, and the opportunity they provide to cross the boundary between audience and stage, constitute a qualification, not a risk, and they do so at a time when being a professional player came with no guarantees: 'he would uphold a company beyond all hope'. We should note the implications of the fact that the character who suggests this is the Vice-character, Inclination. In this play, as later in *Hamlet*, the idea that the protagonist might escape his appointment with destiny by joining a fellowship of players is indeed a temptation – a temptation strongly at odds with the typological framework that offers the presiding hermeneutic for its interpretation. If the episode pays lip service to More's account of the personal danger of getting drawn into 'kinges games' (it marks the point at which his own fortunes begin to fall, since his fatal confrontation with Henry begins in the very next scene), it also makes it clear that the stage play occupies a position of relative autonomy from affairs of state. The point at which More 'steps up' is not merely an allegory of More's own exemplary life. It is a point of exit and entrance from one cultural space into another. In Deleuzean terms, 'becoming player' is now a possibility with real historical potential.[35]

If the character More transforms the passivity of the historical More's citizen spectator into an active practice of participation, he nonetheless remains a privileged figure. It is to *Richard III* that we must look if we want to see the development of a practice of critical spectatorship in audiences in which the 'lokers on' are the 'pore men' of More's own metaphor. John Manningham's famous anecdote records the establishment of a highly developed agency of participation based on a 'fantasye' of crossover from audience to stage:

> Upon a tyme when Burbidge played Rich[ard] 3. there was a Citizen grewe soe farre in liking with him, that before shee went from the play shee appointed him to come that night unto hir by the name of Ri[chard] the 3. Shakespeare, overhearing their conclusion, went before, was intertained, and at his game ere Burbidge came. Then message being brought that Richard the 3d. was at the dore, Shakespeare caused returne to be made that William the Conquerour was before Rich[arde] the 3. Shakespeare's name was William. (Mr. Touse).[36]

The anecdote is unspecific as to date: 'upon a time'. Since it was written in March 1602, it might be said to record the conditions of performance associated with a revival rather than a first performance, but that does not mean it cannot tell us anything about the play at the point at which it was first produced. As an anecdote that had clearly been in circulation for some time, it records precisely the 'sustaining of legitimated prerogatives of occupied social space' to which *Richard III* decisively contributed. Unlike either More's citizens, or More himself in *Sir Thomas*, Manningham's Citizen – a woman acting from the space of performance in a way that apparently calls for no further account of her personal or domestic circumstances – seems on the one hand not to share More's citizens' reservations about 'stepping up', and on the other to respond fully and without reservation to the opportunity of its temptation. There seems no danger whatsoever of her 'disordering' the play by calling Burbage 'by his owne name whyle he standeth in his magestie'; indeed, she specifically directs him to *maintain* this 'magestie' when he 'comes' to her in the night. By extending the fiction of the play beyond the boundaries of the individual performance, her response not only does not 'mar' the play, it constitutes the basis on which it would become profitable and entertaining in a rapidly increasing range of media. After such a great night out, how could she resist a commemorative copy of one of the three bad Quarto editions already available by 1602?[37]

On the evidence of Manningham's anecdote, we might conclude that *Richard III* offered its spectators a position of reception which was *precisely* the profitable and entertaining 'partnership' Buckingham offered the citizens of London if they 'chose' Richard as king. This may seem an unpromising suggestion: *Richard III* is one of Shakespeare's most popular plays in performance, but it is actually one of the least likely to generate new readings. Postwar interpretations have been dominated by two recurrent but fundamentally incompatible critical approaches: providentialist readings of the play as an articulation of Tudor myth, and 'theatre historical' readings of the play's relation to conventions of performance, notably those of the morality play.[38] As Alexander Leggatt has demonstrated, the Vice character began to display the affiliation to the economic interests of theatre represented by Inclination in *Sir Thomas More* as early as the mid-fifteenth century;[39] by 1580 he had attained the status of a 'star part'.[40] This being the case, Hammond's suggestion that the attractions he offered could reach the point where an audience would respond to a providentialist 'fall' with 'a sigh of relief' is surely wrong:[41] Manningham's Citizen alone is evidence of this. The difficulty arises from a misrecognition of the textual level at which the play's providentialism is articulated. The New Cambridge editor Janis Lull has suggested that 'there is no question that this interpretation is available within the play,[42] and that is precisely the point (although it is not exactly hers). The providentialism of *Richard III* is an interpretative activity engaged *by its characters* as a demonstration of the gap between their understanding of the plot and Richard's. It works diegetically to organise the spectators' understanding, not of 'history', but of the duration of the performance, and to use that understanding to create an exclusive bond between Richard and his spectators for their occupation of the space of the theatre. The distinctive technique of word-for-word citation which Shakespeare associates with it creates a mechanism of memory in which the recall of individual parts across the gap of intervening scenes simulates the skills of the player himself: watching this play is 'like' knowing the lines.[43]

I suggested above that, in *Sir Thomas More*, a Deleuzean dynamic of 'becoming-player' is presented as a possibility with real historical potential. In *Richard III*, the spectator is offered an 'imagination' of what might be involved in realising that potential, not at the clownish level of *Sir Thomas*, but at the height of top-class professional performance. In the collaborative play, there is a certain political subservience in the players' admiration of More's rather unremarkable 'extemprical' participation (four lines of undistinguished verse). *Richard III* initiates a direction in Shakespeare's work that leads directly to the players' scene in *Hamlet* 2.2, where, in the subsumption of the spectator Hamlet's imperfect memory into the First Player's effortless professional recall, both the 'skills hierarchy' of *Sir Thomas*, and the relation of priority between the king's game and the stage are decisively reversed.[44] Recent commentators have been interested in the ways in which sixteenth-century dramatists achieved effects of inwardness. Many have associated this with the rise of the equitable jurisdictions and the questions of intention that informed their judgements.[45] From an institutional perspective, Richard's importance has little to do with either. He embodies a principle of action – not subjectivity – that defines the theatre as a temporally defined space of occupation. This principle of action has its own verb: to bustle. Although it *feels* as if this word is everywhere, it is used just twice, and only by Richard: once at the beginning of his 'plot' – 'God take King Edward to his mercy And leave the world for me to bustle in. For then I'll marry Warwick's youngest daughter' (1.1.151-3, followed immediately by his precipitous courtship of Anne in 1.2) – and again at the end: 'Come, bustle, bustle! Caparison my horse' (5.6.19, followed immediately by the final reported image of him on the battlefield enacting 'more wonders than a man'). 'Bustling' thus marks the exact equivalence between *Richard's* 'plot' and the duration of the play.

It also serves to place Richard as an inhabitant both of theatre and of London. With the exception of the final battle scenes and the short execution scene at Pomfret (3.3) *Richard III* is set wholly in London. It is the only Shakespeare play of which that is the case. If the effects of distanciation characteristic of Shakespeare's later work for the Theatre and the Globe exploit the opportunity to 'transport' its audience to a new time-space – 'Can this cock-pit hold The vasty fields of France?'[46] – *Richard III* performs the institutionally prerequisite task of bringing the people of London together *as* an audience, and configuring their participation in Richard's show as spectatorship, in much the same way that More's Richard configures the people of London's participation in his show as an 'election'. Although it makes use of formal public spaces in its court scenes, its continuity derives from its use of what Marc Augé has called '*non-lieux*': streets, passageways, thresholds, points of transit.[47] Richard's incessant movement through them, and the 'accidental' meetings he creates within them, turn them into a spatio-temporal continuum, notably in the tightly plotted sequence of scenes that make up Act III, leading from young Edward's arrival in London for coronation (3.1) to Richard's 'election' in 3.7 and subsequent coronation at the beginning of Act IV.

It is at the beginning of this sequence that the idea of *camera regis*, the king's special chamber, surfaces in Shakespeare's play.[48] Where More places it at the heart of Buckingham's speech in praise of Richard, Shakespeare uses it to welcome young Edward to London in general, and to the Tower in particular: 'welcome, sweet prince, to London, to your chamber' (3.1.1). Since it operates pervasively within the play as an orientational device, the Tower's emergence within the narrative at this point comes as no surprise. It is frequently the space from which people have come and to which they go; conversations, particularly in Act III, stage-direct their characters towards it ('Go you towards the Tower?' [3.2.119]). The mesh of intersecting spaces over which it presides becomes the location of competing paradigms of kingship and theatre, and of their embodiment both in Richard and in his performance. It becomes, in short, the chamber to which spectators like Manningham's Citizen would increasingly be welcomed in the years to come, and thus the basis of an institutional conception of theatre that may well be associated with performance at the Theatre, but demonstrably precedes the formation of the Chamberlain's Men. It is at the beginning of Act III that Richard's 'plot' to occupy it can for the first time be identified as a deposition or usurpation, but it is also here that we begin to become aware of the range of roles he takes on to achieve this goal. Richard is not in any simple sense a single part: he is, rather, an embodiment of the concept of the part as the organising principle of professional performance.[49] He identifies himself as a Vice-character at 3.1.75, and commentators tend to assume that this is what he remains all the way through the play. But he assumes different parts at different points in the action, and these parts combine to create a complexly nuanced structure of theatrical duration. Across Acts I and II, he is identified, by himself and by others, as the villain, the lover, the devil. At the beginning of Act III, he begins the phase of bustling that culminates in his emergence as the deep tragedian who performs in 3.7 for the citizens of London. As 'the deep tragedian', he takes on 'the maid's part' (3.7.51), followed in Act IV by 'the tyrant', then the tyrant himself playing 'the lover', and finally in Act V by the soldier, 'enacting wonders' in his last, reported, act in the play.

Editors have seen 'the maid's part' as a bawdy reference, but it brings into our evaluation of Richard's skills precisely the area of formal innovation I discuss in the next chapter: the performance of women by men. For the present, its implications lie in the way its inclusivity – glancing knowingly at the woman's part in a way the *The Taming of the Shrew* does not – serves to anticipate the relationship between the part and the idea of consummate professional performance we would come to associate with plays written for the Theatre and the Globe: 'all the world's a stage...one man in his time plays many parts'.[50] In *A Midsummer Nights Dream*, written for the Theatre in 1595–6, Bottom, like Richard, wants to play everything: the lover, the maid, even the lion. Like Richard, his 'chief humour' is 'for a tyrant' (1.2.22).[51] Happily, Quince succeeds in limiting him to the lover, largely by convincing him that Pyramus would be more attractive to his female spectators. Like Richard, his performance marks out a progression from comedy to something 'deeper', at least in the eyes of one of his female spectators, Titania, and it is a progression that is similarly associated with the formal identification within the play of a theatrical 'chamber' that frames the space-time of performance and identifies it as the location of a bond between player and spectator. Like Manningham's Citizen, Titania 'steps up' quite forcibly to relocate the action of the play from its improvised stage to her bedchamber. We should note Shakespeare's insistence on the combination of skill and seduction that underpins this bond. Waiting for Bottom's return, Quince describes him, in terms that identify what the audience already knows but Quince does not, as 'a very paramour for a sweet voice'. Flute fastidiously corrects him: 'you must say paragon. A paramour is, God bless us, a thing of nought' (4.2.12–13).

Richard's embodiment of this concept of exemplary performance similarly rewards a comprehensive framework of critical skills. At the point when he identifies himself as the Vice, he gives his spectator precise instructions on how to use the information: 'Thus like the formal Vice, Iniquity, I moralise two meanings in one word' (3.1.83). Across Act III this conventional device is raised from local semantic effect to a sophisticated dynamic of textual organisation. In the scenes leading up to his performance for the citizens of London in 3.7, the disabled Richard's occupation of London's streets and passageways, a counterpart to that of the able-bodied Thomas More, is mirrored by a sequence of characters who consistently fail to read the textual complexity of the action in which they are implicated, thus emphasising the privilege of intimacy with Richard now enjoyed by the spectator. We noted that Anthony Hammond found it 'surprising' that Shakespeare made 'only limited use' of More's metaphor of theatre. We are, I think, now in a position to conclude that this *use* is not only far from limited, but extremely beneficial. As Richard's performance to the citizens of London in 3.7 begins, More's passive vulnerable citizens and *Sir Thomas More*'s enthusiastic amateur have both been superseded by a star performer and skilful, active spectators. If, like Hammond, we now note the absence from Shakespeare's play of More's account of the passive but sceptical citizens of London walking away from Richard's 'stageplay', 'talking diuersely of the matter euery man as his fantasye gaue hym', we can also now see why the 'diversity' of Shakespeare's audience functions not as a marker of division and vulnerability but as the guarantee of profitable and entertaining popular spectatorship.

If Thomas More's *History* and *Sir Thomas More* present the bond between player and spectator as a political risk, Shakespeare presents that risk both as its terms and conditions and as the source of its pleasure. Richard presents his 'deep intents' as a series of bets: 'And yet to win her, *all the world to nothing*? Ha!' (1.2.225); '*My dukedom to a beggarly denier*, I do mistake my person all this while' (239); 'Slave, I have set my life upon a cast And I will stand the hazard of the die' (5.7.9–10). His vigorous imagination is far more easily identifiable as that of the scheming younger son of city comedy – or perhaps someone trying to cheat his partner out a playhouse – than a peer of the realm. When he first introduces the idea of 'bustling', it is embedded in exactly the kind of register More's Buckingham uses to make the citizens of London feel he is talking their language: 'but yet I run before my horse to market.'

(1.2.157–60). Given the importance of this transaction, it is not surprising that we meet Richard's horse again, and that it is associated with the same acquisitive energy: 'Come, bustle! bustle! Caparison my horse' (5.6.19); 'A horse! A horse! My kingdom for a horse! (5.7.13).

These lines have been the subject of considerable editorial commentary, focusing mainly on the question whether they precede or follow similar lines in the anonymous *The True Tragedie of Richard III* and George Peele's *Battle of Alcazar*, both published in 1594.[52] There is, however, a level of reference in Shakespeare's version of these lines (which adds the famous offer) that has hitherto escaped notice. In 1484, the Year Books record a case in which the defendant claimed to have given satisfaction for a debt of 100 shillings by payment of a horse, and the plea was accepted.[53] In an entry for Hilary Term 1494, the idea emerges in a discussion of diversity, a legal principle that addresses to the possibility of differing conditions for satisfaction of a bond and which clearly informs the notion of critical diversity discussed above: whether you can settle for less than the agreed amount, before or after the specified day, in a place other than that originally agreed; whether a third party can settle on your behalf.[54] As we saw in chapter 2, the principle of specific performance makes it clear that you cannot simply substitute one similar property for another: 'if I am held in a bond on the condition that I enfeoff you with the manor of Dale by such and such a date, and then I enfeoff you with the manor of Sale, my bond is forfeit, because the condition is changed into another nature'.[55] However, offering a horse in satisfaction for an incommensurate sum was apparently not contentious: 'if I am bound to you on the condition that I pay you £10 by a such and such a date, and then I give you a horse for the said £10, and you receive it, I am excused and discharged'.[56]

By 1496, this argument had become a fully functional precedent:

And the defendant said that he paid 20s each Easter, except the previous Easter. And he said that before that Easter he had leased to him the vesture of an acre of land for one year for his 20s. *Keble:* That is not a plea: for the lease of an acre of land cannot be intended as a payment. *Jay:* Why isn't that as good as a horse? You won't deny that if the condition of an obligation is that I pay 20s, it is a good plea to say I paid you a horse in the name of the 20s, and you received it.[57]

How are we to understand this? Glossing a case that hung on the question of whether 'payment and acceptance of part before the day in satisfaction of the whole shall be a good satisfaction in respect of the circumstance of time', Edward Coke recorded the decision that 'by no possibility can a lesser sum be satisfaction to the plaintiff for a greater sum', but noted that

> [T]he gift of a horse, sparrowhawk or robe, and so forth, in satisfaction is good: for it shall be presumed that a horse, sparrowhawk or robe will be more beneficial to the plaintiff than the money, in respect of some circumstances, or else the plaintiff would not have accepted it in satisfaction.[58]

So, a horse can be accepted as satisfaction precisely because it *is* a different kind of property, and can therefore have more value than another example of the same kind of property in circumstances in which a horse might actually turn out to be more beneficial than an estate of land. We can, I think, see how this illuminates our understanding of the end of Shakespeare's play. In respect of the particular circumstance in which Richard now finds himself, a horse would clearly have been more beneficial than a kingdom. His famous last words might be said to confirm Francis Bacon's suggestion that, as a usurper, he was ready to disregard the true obligations of kingship, but for Shakespeare, it was an offer he could not refuse. Richard's horse survives his master as the figure for a bond between player and spectator that not only offered diverse conditions for satisfaction in the play itself, but also provided a precedent for plays to come. In the next chapter I show how the principle of beneficial ownership provided the basis of a fully fledged principle of dramatic action in *The Two Gentlemen of Verona*, *The Merchant of Venice* and *As You Like It*.

5
Calling Fools into a Circle: *The Woman's Prize, The Two Gentlemen of Verona, The Merchant of Venice, As You Like It*

I suggested in Chapter 4 that *Richard III* satisfies its spectator's participation in the performance by converting the 'term' of theatrical occupation into a habit of critical spectatorship. A feature of this satisfaction is the fact that, as the play moves towards its conclusion, it offers opportunities to renegotiate terms even more beneficial than those of the bond with Richard sustained across the central part of the play. What results is a shift from a position of reception that could be seen as a kind of coverture ('man and wife is one flesh')[1] to something more like Elizabeth Woodville, the widow who, in 4.4, emerges from passivity to a powerful position in the negotiation of the Tudor succession. For Richard, his courtship of Elizabeth, both mother and daughter, merely repeats his successful seduction of Anne in 1.2. For the audience, it is the end of one special relationship and the beginning of another. In a superb piece of theatrical timing, in which the crucial information is provided as an afterthought to a greeting sent by the elder Stanley to his son ('Well, hie thee to thy lord ... Tell him the Queen hath heartily consented He should espouse Elizabeth ...' [4.5.16–18]), the scenes that follow are the first in which the spectator's grasp of the plot exceeds Richard's. This shift creates an effect of generic redirection that affiliates the action with the open-ended temporality of the courtship plot of Shakespearean comedy, and with the conception of female agency which would come to be associated with it. Elizabeth's negotiations of a marriage settlement for her daughter introduce into the partnership between player and spectator an element of meaning that would have had a very contemporary force: the fact that the decisive interest in this action is in a third party. Of course, young Elizabeth makes no independent demands on the plot; indeed, she does not even appear in the play. She might thus be described as a very pure form of third party agency, one that is maintained and advanced by others on her behalf. But even on these terms she holds the key to our understanding of the Shakespearean woman's part as it develops in the comedies across the 1590s.

I suggested in Chapter 4 that recent commentators have associated the innovative characterisations of Renaissance drama in general and Shakespeare in particular with effects of subjectivity that derive from contemporary explorations of contractual intention. In this context, there has been considerable interest in the rise of consideration, a quid pro quo principle that was increasingly used to test the enforceability of promises. As A. W. B Simpson explains, 'the actionability of informal promises is made to turn upon an analysis of the motivating reasons which induced the promissor to make the promise'.[2] The case almost invariably cited in these discussions is *Slade v Morley* (1602), an action for assumpsit following non-payment for a harvest of corn in 1595.[3] Slade's Case has long been viewed as a 'watershed decision';[4] 'a crucial step in ... the transition from a status to a contract society'.[5] As such formulations indicate, it has carried a heavy burden of historical explanation. For David Harris Sacks, 'the decision ... reinforced the performative and internalist view of selfhood that underpinned it'; for Luke Wilson, 'it heralded a new self-consciousness in social actors, who were forced to leave their customary, unreflective ways of operating, and to engage in vigilant self-inspection in order to monitor the intentions with which the law now presumed them always to act'.[6] If you take the measure of the 1590s by Slade, you might indeed come to such a conclusion, because the reason it became a leading case is also the reason it remained difficult to apply for another 100 years: the principle did not easily apply to cases concerned with the kind of obligations that arise from what Thomas Popham referred to as 'natural love', particularly those associated with marriage settlements.[7]

It is to such cases that we must look if we wish to consider the interests at stake in the comedies with which Shakespeare consolidated his occupation of the London theatrical scene across the 1590s. There, we almost invariably find both that consideration was not upheld as a privity limitation against third party interests and that there was a broad and complex debate on the subject, a situation that in itself argues against a single view of 'selfhood' or 'consciousness'. Thus, in *Levett v Hawes* (1599):

> it was found ... that the plaintiff had agreed with the defendant that the plaintiff's son John should marry one Constance, a kinswoman of the defendant, and that in consideration that the plaintiff agreed

to assure lands of a certain value to Constance for her jointure, the defendant promised the plaintiff that he would pay £200 to the son in marriage with Constance. The marriage took place, and the land was assured, but the money was not paid. The plaintiff brought assumpsit and failed, it being held that the action should have been brought by the son.[8]

This case clearly indicates the extent to which late sixteenth-century thinking about what it was to be 'party to an action' remained guided by an open-ended principle of interest rather than the privity-limited position increasingly associated with the rise of consideration. In the process, it counsels against approaches to sixteenth-century legal culture that base their reading on a single law case, or even on a single position within the judgment on a single case. The fullest account of *Levett v Hawes* is provided by Croke's Elizabethan Reports, compiled 1582–1603. The case itself began in Michaelmas Term 1598:

> A father cannot maintain *assumpsit* on a promise made to him to pay so much to his son, in consideration of his son's marrying the defendant's kinswoman. Ante, 63. Post. 652. 849. 1 Salk. 29. Cowp. 294.

> *Assumpsit.* And declares, in consideration that the plaintiff agreed with the defendant that J. Levet, son and heir of the plainitiff, should espouse Constance, the defendant's kinswoman; and in consideration that the plaintiff agreed to assure to the said Constance lands of 10 l. per annum for her jointure, the defendant assumed to the plaintiff to give to J. Levet the son in marriage with the said Constance 200 l. and alledgeth *in facto* that the marriage took effect; and that the plainitiff had assured such lands for the jointure; and that the defendant had not payed to his son the 200 l. whereupon the father brought the action. Upon non assumpsit the issue was found for the plaintiff. It was moved in arrest of judgement that the action ought not to have been brought by the father; for the son only is to have the advantage thereof. But it was said on the other side, that the promise is only made with the father, and all the considerations arise on his part, and the son is a stranger thereto; and therefore the son cannot maintain the action, but the father. But the Court doubted thereof. *Et adjournatur.*[9]

After adjournment, the case was moved again in Hilary Term 1599, and at this point Popham prevailed with the decision that, because the case successfully demonstrates that the son had the interest, he should also have had the action. Our now familiar formulation of the use comes into focus as the rationale for the decision – here, crucially, as a description not of the property itself but of the promise to convey it:

> And Popham was of opinion, that the action ought to have been brought by the son, and not by the father; for the promise is made to the son's use, and the ordinary covenants of marriage are with the father to stand seised to the son's use, and the use shall be changed and transferred to the son as if it were a covenant with himself; and the damage for non-performance thereof is to the son. And of that opinion was Fenner. Clench J. doubted. Gawdy was absent.[10]

Even then the decision was by no means clear-cut: as we see here, it was annotated with continuing opinions against. We should also note the fluidity within these reports of the exact status of 'the said Constance'. Croke refers to her as the 'defendant's kinswoman', but in every other report she appears as his daughter: in Moore, for instance, the adversaries are presented as 'pere le fits' and 'pere le file'.[11] In fact, Constance appears as a daughter in the *citation* of Croke that appears in Taunton's account of *Bowen v Morris*:

> [T]he Plaintiff declared in assumpsit, that in consideration that he would assure lands of the annual value of 10 l. for the jointure of his daughter upon her marriage with the Defendant's son, the Defendant undertook to give 200l.; and it was moved in arrest of judgement that the action ought to have been brought by the son, who was to have the benefit, not by the father: the court gave judgement for the Defendant, and overruled a case there cited of *Cardinal v Lewis*, in which it had been held that the father might sue. *Rippon v Norton*, Cro. Eliz 884, 849[12]

It is almost as if there is a gravitational pull within these accounts towards the *idea* of the daughter as the role in which a woman becomes visible as a social actor by virtue of actions taken by other parties in her behalf; a role which therefore contrasts with that of *feme covert*, where precisely the same situation makes her conventionally invisible.

This idea has considerable bearing on Shakespeare's consistent interest in plots that focus the transition between the two roles, and it will become important again in my discussion of *King Lear* in Chapter 8. Here, in a discussion of the comic woman's part of the 1590s, much of my interest lies in the extent to which the daughter role embodies a third party position that is interchangeably male and female – a situation I began to consider in my discussion of the 'feigned case' of *Corbett v Corbett* in Chapter 2. In Hetley, the decision that the interest lay in a male third party precipitated the citation of a precedent in which the party 'who should have the action' was female:

> An action on the case was brought, that in consideration the plaintiff would consent that his son should marry the daughter of the defendant, and that after the coverture, upon request of the defendant, the plaintiff shall make a joynture of 20 l. to the wife, that the defendant should give 200 l. to the son in marriage, they are married, the money is not payed the father of the son brings this action, and shews how he is indamaged by it, because that he is constreined to give more to the son and his wife for to allow them maintenance then otherwise, with an averment, that he is forced to make that joynture, if the other will make the request. Richardson, This action should have been more properly brought by the son, for he is the person in whom the interest is. And he put the case *22 Eliz*. A man had a license to transport herrings to Spain, and the daughter one of the parties had a license. And a stranger comes to the father, and says to him, procure me that license, and I'll give you 100 l. and 100 l. to your daughter. It was held that the daughter should have the action for the one 100 l. for more specially it concerns her.[13]

Richardson's (unidentified) precedent '22 Eliz' is evocative because here the ownership in question concerns an interest in a licensed industry, and, as in *The Taming of the Shrew*, the citation suggests equivalence between that and a marriage settlement. In fact, *Levett v Hawes* (by which I mean the discursive field that accumulates across these complementary readings) could be read as a 'what-happened-next' scenario for the *The Shrew*. As such, it illuminates the relationship between Shakespeare's play and John Fletcher's sequel, *The Woman's Prize or the Tamer Tamed*,[14] which I discuss here by way of preparation for the textual readings of Shakespearean comedy that follow.

The daughter should have the action

Written for Shakespeare's company around 1611, Fletcher's play looks back across the years between *The Taming of the Shrew* and his own play. Maria approaches her marriage to Petruchio in terms that make it clear that she has learned everything Shakespeare's comedies could teach her. Remembering Kate (or rather, acting as a voice for an audience that remembers her), she commits herself to the position of the party 'who should have the action' from the outset: 'Let her be nam'd Mongst those that wish for things but dare not do 'em' (1.2.288–9). One of the play's textual cruxes sustains a legal allusion so oblique that it can only have as its purpose the 'seeding' into the play of the idea of Maria as a third party, apparently in order that she can have the pleasure of insisting that she should pursue her own interests. In an otherwise puzzling reference, Fletcher implies that Petruchio, whose assurance in Shakespeare's play of 'all my lands and leases whatsoever' to Baptista preceded his acquisition of 'the special thing ... that is her love', has entered into a settlement – something like a trust for Maria's use, not with her father, but with a friend:[15]

> *Soph.* Pray you tell me one thing truly; [1650]
> Do you love her?
> *Petru.* I would I did not, upon that condition
> I past thee halfe my Land.
>
> (3.3)

There *were* precedents for this kind of arrangement, usually in cases where a woman did not have a father to assure her future: in *Johnson v Smythe* (1586), the defendants are named 'as friends in trust to take a bond of £1000 for the assurance of a jointure'.[16] But since Maria's father is still alive, the point of the reference seems simply to make it more obvious that Maria insists on an agency which is separable from her role as either daughter or wife.

As if to emphasise this, Fletcher makes her use the argument that as *feme covert* she is no longer obliged to obey her father as paradoxical justification for a refusal to submit to her husband. He is also careful to make her insist that she *already* loves Petruchio, thus distinguishing her situation from the preposterous relation between marriage and the creation of property by industry explored in Shakespeare's play. When Maria asserts that she loves Petruchio, and would take him 'in's shirt, with one ten Groats to pay the Priest Before the best man living, or the ablest ones' (1.3/555–6), Petruchio replies, 'let your love confirme it' (562). Her response, 'that bargain's yet to make' (563), is accompanied by the expression of an intention to demolish Petruchio's house and rebuild it more to her own personal taste – also a demolition and rebuilding of *The Shrew*'s central scenes. Petruchio's question, 'is there no keeping A wife to one mans use? no wintering These cattell without straying?' (3.3/1833–5) is typically read as an imputation that her refusal to consummate is a form of sexual promiscuity, but – with its glance at arguments about animals familiar from *Fyllol v Assheleygh* – it is more appropriately seen as a reminder to the audience of Kate's role as the early embodiment of theatrical property and hence of the institutional ground covered by the development of the woman's part in the intervening years. The idea that the duty circle Maria insists on entering is something her audience would recognise as that of Shakespearean theatre is marked by a striking ventriloquism:

> For I am he am born to tame you, Kate ...
>
> (*The Shrew* 2.1.268)

> You have been famous for a woman tamer,
> And beare the fear'd name of a brave wife-breaker:
> A woman now shall take those honours off,
> And tame you; nay, never look so bigge, she shall, beleeve me,
> And I am she ...
>
> (*The Woman's Prize* 1.3/683–7)

It might be tempting to see Shakespeare's play as the 'source' for this reference, but the relation between the two is more subtle than that. If Shakespeare's early plays welcome his audiences to a theatrical 'chamber', Fletcher's play might be described as an echo chamber. In 1611, an audience that can 'hear' his substitution of Petruchio's 'I am he' with Maria's 'I am she' as precisely a substitution (as Fletcher clearly expects they can), will also hear the theatrical conjugation that gathered into the duty circle of Shakespearean comedy across in the intervening years: 'a sister: you are she'.[17]

Vying with *The Comedy of Errors* and *The Taming of the Shrew* for identification as Shakespeare's first play, *The Two Gentlemen of Verona* was possibly written at the end of 1580s; like them, at a time when we are uncertain where he was or what he was doing. I place it here, at the beginning of a discussion of a group of comedies that covers the period from the early years to the opening of the Globe, because, like *Richard III*, it lays the foundations for a conception of a property in theatre that would become characteristic of the plays we associate with the formation of the Lord Chamberlain's Men. But if *Richard III* is associated with the establishment of a theatrical chamber, the comedies are concerned with an idea that would structure the shifting, unstable dynamics of the company's occupation of that chamber across the 1590s: the idea of theatre as a duty circle.

Myself am one made privy to the plot

> A modern legal dictionary ... indicates that while privity originally meant 'knowledge', it now denotes in a secondary sense 'a peculiar relation in which a person stands either to a transaction or to some other person'. This transition suggest that privity *the fact* became a source of obligations when legal meaning was attached to the personal bond or 'inward relation' resulting from knowledge and familiarity. Contracts, for example, have a recurrent factual basis in the privacy of meetings, discussions, and personal dealings. The word covenant still indicates this original basis. Well before it came to signify a promise or an action at common law, covenant meant a convening, as assembly, or a 'coming together,' and those who were not there could not know nor perhaps accurately relate what had transpired. From the fact of close relationship would follow the concept of the closed circle. Outside the circle are strangers who can neither be benefited nor burdened by the rights or duties concerned. The number of these circles is almost infinite, but duties and relationships are kept quite distinct. A's debt to his friend B places them together in the duty circle, but B would be a stranger towards A with respect to A's dealings with someone else. The size of the circle and the number of privies within it would vary, depending on the scope of the duty and its real and personal nature.[18]

In *The Two Gentlemen of Verona*, duty circles open and close repeatedly, rippling across the action of the play like the competing and overlapping circles of obligation I observed in the Theatre litigation in Chapter 2. Each character changes duty circle in a way that their position as 'privy' to one switches to that of 'stranger' in the next. The play is careful to provide us with an embodiment of performance that guides our interpretation of this potentially open-ended process: the dog Crab. Crab's failure to weep at his master Lance's parting from his family when they go to Milan in the service of Proteus produces a dynamic of substitution that parodies the way first and third party interests jockey for position on the path to theatrical privity ('I/you am/are he/she'): 'This hat is Nan our maid. I am the dog. No, the dog is himself and I am the dog. O, the dog is me, and I am myself. Ay, so, so' (2.3.18–20). Proteus's actions have a similarly destabilising effect on those inside his circle. Named as the principle of change, his entry into the 'world' of Milan sets this restless substitutive energy in motion in a way that leads inexorably to the final unlikely reconstitution of that world in the last scene. Following his switch from Julia to Silvia (which turns Julia into the 'stranger' who enters his service as a man after discovering that she has been abandoned as a woman), Proteus breaks what he himself identifies as the 'law of friendship' (3.1.5) in favour of a feigned duty to Silvia's father as duke when he reveals Valentine's plans to elope with Silvia: 'myself am one made privy to the plot' (12).

As with Julia, the effect of Proteus's 'privity' within Valentine's 'plot', in which Valentine himself is progressively relegated to the position of stranger, is to embody Valentine as a 'one' whose world is that of theatre, not the fictional society from which he has been excluded. Of all the characters in the play, Valentine is the least visibly inscribed within a family circle. He is on his way 'abroad' as soon as the play begins, and his destination is always beyond the point at which he rests within the action at any given point. He arrives at Milan, but his direction is an unspecified and unrealised imperial court that continues to be projected beyond Milan throughout the play (even by the duke). He thus embodies a set of obligations which do not simply switch from one duty circle to another, like Proteus, but are embedded in an idealisation that culminates, paradoxically, in his membership of and isolation within a group of outlaws in the forest at the beginning of 5.4.

The idea of the world associated with Valentine thus cannot be stably identified as a specific location in the way that London can be identified with Richard in *Richard III*. It is, rather, a movement away.[19] His movement away from Verona to an imperial court, temporarily arrested in Milan, is immediately substituted by the planned flight from Milan with Silvia, which is already underway by the time Proteus arrives. It is indicative of Silvia's role in this dynamic that he characterises her as a *'principality* Sovereign to all creatures on the earth' (2.4.145–6). Editors gloss 'principality' as 'angel',[20] but in the 1590s the term also referred both to 'the rule or government of the prince of a small or dependent state' and to 'the territory ruled or governed by a prince'.[21] From this perspective, Valentine's energy identifies itself as a principle of reterritorialisation which relates to the dynamic of becoming-player I proposed in Chapter 4.[22] In response to Proteus's advice that he 'let her alone', he replies, 'not for the world' (2.4.160–1). The outcome of this decision places him outside 'the world' in the everyday sense, but inside a theatrical world that is rapidly acquiring ontological status on the basis of precisely this distinction.

The soliloquy at the beginning of the last scene articulates this position in a particularly striking way. Just as Silvia is presented as a synthesis of both prince and state, so here Valentine is both person and place. It is worth looking in some detail at the complex structure of thought in this remarkable speech:

> How use doth breed a habit in a man!
> This shadowy desert, unfrequented woods
> I better brook than flourishing peopled towns
> Here can I sit alone, unseen of any,
> And to the nightingale's complaining notes
> Tune my distresses and record my woes.
> O thou that doth inhabit in my breast,
> Leave not the mansion so long tenantless
> Lest, growing ruinous, the building fall
> And leave no memory of what it was.
> Repair me with thy presence, Silvia.
>
> (5.4.1–11)

The New Cambridge editor Kurt Schlueter glosses 'mansion' in l.8, 'refers to himself, or more specifically, to his body'; the Norton editor adds, 'referring to his body as Silvia's home'.[23] The ambiguity sustained between the two readings – that the building in question might be either his or hers – is relevant (as it will later be relevant in *The Merchant of Venice*). At the point at which the solo performer emerges, in soliloquy, from the play's competing and overlapping duty circles, it does so in an embodiment of ownership as a contested relation of title and possession. In an obvious way, the ideas of 'use' and 'habit' in the first line draw into a general conception of custom. But since, within the plot, the notion of custom is not easily associated with 'sitting alone' in 'unfrequented woods' as a member of a group of outlaws, Valentine's situation is a *break* with habit, or perhaps rather an establishment of what we are invited to see as a new kind of habit: 'sitting-alone-unseen-of-any' as the phenomenology of the professional player. In line 7, the potentially contradictory relation between 'habit' and 'use' becomes coherent within the notion of performance that is both person and property – 'O thou that dost inhabit in my breast' – where 'tenantless mansion' provides what is immediately identifiable as the correct semantic environment for the idea of the use. Its connotations as a mode of ownership are indispensable for our understanding of what follows. Valentine retains the title to his person ('my breast'), but Silvia has the possession, and she is described here as *not* taking up her interest in the property. Valentine's invocation 'repair me with thy presence' enjoins her to do just that.

The collocation of ideas in this speech, glancing as they do towards the social dilemma encapsulated in a legal action of waste, produces a striking anticipation of the nature of Shylock's 'interest' in Antonio in *The Merchant of Venice*, which I discuss shortly. Here, we should simply observe that it provides all the information we need *not* to make the mistake of evaluating Silvia's silence in the remainder of the play in the negative terms associated with certain types of feminist criticism.[24] When Valentine witnesses Proteus's attempt to 'force' Silvia, the alienation articulated in his soliloquy is given a strong statement of intent in the subsequent dialogue with his former friend. But where we might have expected him to respond to this betrayal by asserting *his* position as stranger to the world, what he actually says is the opposite: 'I am sorry I must never trust thee more But *count the world a stranger* for thy sake' (5.4.69–70). What we see here is an idea of theatrical personality that is, once again, emphatically not a question of 'inwardness' but rather the mutually constitutive relation of occupation between body and space. It is only if we understand this that we can see what happens next, when Proteus, once again, changes his mind. Valentine's renewed promise of friendship – 'And that my love may appear plain and free All that was mine in Silvia I give thee' (82–3) – has almost invariably been interpreted as meaning that he 'gives' Silvia to Proteus in a way that contemporary criticism characterises as 'uncongenial' and 'immature'.[25] But the play is far more acute in its understanding of the emergent property relations of Shakespearean theatre than its critics. Valentine's property 'in' Silvia is one of the interest, not title, and it arises in a situation in which we have already been told that Silvia has a similar interest 'in' Valentine. This mesh of reciprocal third party interests precipitates in the play a display of the mechanisms by which the play integrates these conceptions of ownership into ideas of performance and spectatorship. As Valentine gives his 'all-that-was-mine-in . . .' to Proteus, Julia collapses. On recovery she 'mistakenly' offers the ring by which Proteus gave *his* 'all-that-was-mine-in' to *her*, thus exposing *herself* as the third party – 'Julia' - that now demonstrably holds that interest. Looking at 'Sebastian', Proteus is the first to recognise this claim and renew the earlier agreement: '*What is in Silvia's face but I may spy More fresh in Julia's, with a constant eye*'.

The space created by this action – hitherto apparently outside the 'world' – thus comes to function as a court where such obligations are tested and upheld.

The reason it is easy to overlook the property base of this emergent theatrical world is that *Two Gentlemen* does not materialise questions of property in its action in the way that later plays do. But this disavowal is itself a structural feature of the imagination of a special property in theatre that begins in earnest in these early plays. Despite the fact that Julia lives at home with her parents, she apparently already has the kind of property a later play might tempt us to describe as some kind of woman's separate estate.[26] Notwithstanding, when she leaves Verona she makes no attempt to take any of it with her (where a later play would make it clear that she does), leaving it instead under the stewardship of a maidservant, Lucetta: 'all that is mine I leave at thy dispose, My goods, my lands, my reputation' (2.7.86–7). It is important not to ask irrelevant questions about whether or not this is a realistic representation of sixteenth-century women and property. There is a direct correlation between this state of contrived dispossession and her subsequent representation of herself as a servant playing the woman's part 'trimmed in Madam Julia's gown' (4.4.153), and thus crucially with the exchange about the nature of spectatorship that we are told takes place at that performance. Sebastian tells Silvia of 'Julia's' bitter tears at 'his' 'lively' performance of 'the lamentable part' – Ariadne 'passioning for Theseus's perjury and unjust flight' (158–60). This complex imaginative engagement of player and spectator, together with the player's own response to it ('would I might be dead If I in thought felt not her very sorrow' [163–4]) suggests that, while a 'part' may well be identified by a single descriptor such as 'lamentable', neither its performance nor the experience of it by player or spectator should be seen as a nameable entity, but as an exchange between parties which creates a counterpart within the duty circle of theatre to the mesh of male/female third party interests operating in cases like *Levett v Hawes*. The action described by the interchangeably male/female position occupied by Sebastian/Julia 'concerns' Silvia (in the sense of the term used in 'Eliz 22': 'the daughter should have the action...for more specially it concerns her') as Sebastian's spectator, as well as the hypothetical 'Julia', the spectator of the hypothetical 'Sebastian'. In fact, Silvia responds in exactly the same way as 'Julia' – 'I weep myself to think upon thy words' – but significantly she rewards him/her in far more material terms: 'There is my purse. I give thee this... because thou lov'st her' (168–9). At this point, where Silvia's payment for the satisfaction she has received from this bond places it identifiably within the economic paradigm of professional performance, we realise why it is important that Julia should be 'dispossessed': she has become the embodiment of the '*poor* player' who provides the metaphor for the conception of 'life' his spectator brings to the theatre to test the truth of its feigning.[27]

The ontological status of this exchange is marked by its affective range: paradoxically, the marker of its 'liveliness' as a performance is the wish, by the performer, to be dead: 'I so lively acted with my tears That my poor mistress, moved withal Wept bitterly; and would I might be dead If in thought I felt not her very sorrow' (4.4.163–6). This range underpins the conception of value that validates the exchange as worthy of payment. Looking back at the cold-hearted Crab from this position in the action, it might now appear that the point of the animal's carefully staged presence in three scenes, the last of which immediately precedes this, is precisely to set the criteria for a valorisation of professional performance by embedding within the action a non-responsive body that parodies its exemplary affectivity. The problem about poor old Crab is that we have all too little sense in his apparently inert presence of the things of pleasure so magnificently on display in *The Taming of the Shrew* – except, of course, that, unlike Merriman, Clowder, Silver, Belman and Echo, this dog really can act.

I hold the world but as the world

Antonio: I hold the world but as the world, Graziano –
A stage where every man must play a part
And mine a sad one.

The Merchant of Venice 1.1.77–9

Shylock: What should I say to you? Should I not say
'Hath a dog money? Is it possible
A cur can lend three thousand ducats?' Or
Shall I bend low, and in a bondsman's key,
With bated breath and whisp'ring humbleness
Say this: 'Fair sir, you spat on me on Wednesday last;
You spurned such a day; another time
You called me dog; and for these courtesies
I'll lend you thus much moneys'?

1.3.115–24

The Two Gentlemen of Verona's juxtaposition of a cold-hearted dog and a lively player's performance of the lamentable part makes a surprisingly good starting point for my discussion of The Merchant of Venice.[28] Six or seven years later, the idea of theatre presented in this play draws on elements of formal construction already in place in Shakespeare's earliest work. But it also demonstrates the institutional enhancement of the relationship between player and spectator that followed the formation of the Lord Chamberlain's Men and their establishment at the Theatre in 1594.

At the very start of the play, Shakespeare plays Antonio's assertion that his demeanour is simply that of a theatrical part and therefore needs no further explanation against his fellow characters' insistence that it demands an explanation as behaviour in a 'world' they mutually inhabit. One of the reasons the confrontation between Antonio and Shylock is so compelling is that it sustains this stand-off between fictional and theatrical concepts of world until 4.1, the court scene, where the nature of the bond between player and spectator, and its conditions for satisfaction, severely challenge Two Gentlemen's now obviously rather innocent equation of reciprocal tears. Refusing to explain his behaviour, Shylock remains an impenetrable cur, his insistence on his pound of flesh a grotesque parody of the principle of beneficial satisfaction I discussed at the end of Chapter 4. Antonio's insistence on Bassanio's presence to witness it is, in its turn, the condition for satisfaction of bonds that are simultaneously bonds both of debt and of spectatorship: 'Debts are clear'd between you and I, if I might but see you at my death (3.2.317); 'pray God Bassanio come To see me pay his debt, and then I care not' (3.3.35–6). As the stark contrast between an idea of performance rewarded with a simple purse and one conceived as a temporally limited debt makes clear, the play takes Two Gentlemen's reading of the exchange between a dispossessed player and his rewarding spectator to a level of complexity that elicits another kind of explanatory dilemma: given the consolidation of his status that followed the developments of 1594, why, in 1596–7, should Shakespeare's imagination of theatre be so dark and destructive?

A relatively easy answer might be that the play responds to the kind of general anxieties about socio-economic conditions in late sixteenth-century English society we noted in Sir Edmund Anderson's discussion of Nebuchadnezzar's tree in Chapter 2. Up to this point, I have pursued the idea that changes to the laws of property in this period should be seen as an 'openness' to socially widening circles of rights and obligations, and that this openness finds a particularly cogent expression in the development of the custom-built theatre as a property and of the property rights that underpin the stabilisation of the Lord Chamberlain's Men as they moved into the Theatre in 1594. But *The Merchant of Venice* tests the optimism of this reading severely. Where *Two Gentlemen* arrives at the idea of 'a world counted as stranger' at the beginning of Act V, but immediately converts it to a renewed law of friendship, *The Merchant* starts from a circle that is already defined by the interests of its strangers. Both Belmont and Venice operate under the rubric of this obligation from the outset, and both pursue it to the point of catastrophe. If Valentine's notion of a tenantless mansion growing ruinous in its owner's absence provides the basis for an idea of performance based on a correlation between embodiment and the ownership of space, Antonio appears to be intent both on materialising that image on stage and on forcing its audience to witness its ruin.

The play is also intent on exposing the questions of temporality that structure this ownership. At the beginning of the play, its three strands of action have widely differentiated projected durations, but what follows creates a counterpoint that leads inexorably to the dissonant climax of 4.1. In 1.1, we hear of the supposed long-term security of Antonio's finances and of Bassanio's immediate need for money. At the end of 1.2, in Belmont, we learn that the Prince of Morocco comes 'tonight'; in 1.3, Antonio agrees to be bound for three months. In 2.1 the Prince arrives and we hear that he will take the hazard of the caskets that same night after dinner. In 2.2, Bassanio announces the feast attended by Shylock, during which Jessica (and *her* casket) are to be 'taken' from her father's house by Lorenzo in 2.5 and 2.6. At the end of 2.6 we hear that the feast has been cancelled and that Bassanio will sail that night. In 2.7, the Prince of Morocco takes the hazard. In 2.8 we learn that Shylock tried to have Bassanio's ship searched for his daughter before it sailed, hear early news of the first of Antonio's shipwrecks, and see Bassanio and Antonio parting. Thus, by implication, everything up to this point has taken place on the same day. In 2.9 we learn of Bassanio's arrival at Belmont; in 3.1 we hear confirmation of Antonio's losses, and Shylock begins his action on the bond. This means that three months have passed. We can just about infer that it does so somewhere between Venice in 2.8 and Belmont in 2.9; but Shylock's reaction to his daughter's flight in 3.1 is intended to create an effect of continuity with the report of it in 2.8. Furthermore, in 3.2, we see Bassanio decide to take the hazard immediately despite Portia's urging to wait, and also hear news of Antonio's danger. In other words, it takes one person one day to get to Belmont and another three months. My point here is not simply that Shakespeare did not observe strict principles of continuity.[29] It is, rather, that these complex spatio-temporal articulations create a continuum of dramatic duration within which Antonio's stipulation of Bassanio's witness of the embodied display of his ruin maps the term of Shylock's 'merry bond' and the conditions for its satisfaction onto the organisation of the text and the audience's experience of the play.

It is hard to avoid the conclusion that this scenario keys to the particular difficulties facing the Chamberlain's Men in the particular circumstances in which Shakespeare was writing this play. The lease on the Theatre had expired in 1595, and by the end of 1596 all attempts at renewal had failed. The company's plan to move into the second Blackfriars was defeated when the Privy Council upheld the petition against them. In 1596–7, they toured extensively, and in late 1597 began what would be a two-year stint at the Curtain, leaving the Theatre empty. When James Burbage died in 1597, Robert Miles continued litigation against Cuthbert and Richard in an effort to force them to 'to take Downe such buyldinges as by the covenaunte aforesaid were to be taken downe and to allow this complainant the moytye of the tymber and other thinges or the value of the moytye therof ...[30] Even though Miles' efforts came to nothing, the period was one in which a number of still unanswered questions hung over the physical integrity of the Theatre. Two years later, when it was finally dismantled and reassembled as the Globe, Giles Allen deposed that it was the Burbages who refused to renew, not him; that he had allowed them to stay on mainly in the interests of the inhabitants of the tenements; that the tenements were in desperate need of repair because of Burbage's neglect; and that Burbage 'never in truth meant to take the lease as he pretended but only sought to take occasion when he might privily and for his best advantage pull down the said Theatre'.[31]

The process of neglect described here – and the accusation implicit within Allen's deposition – is that of waste. Waste was subject to a common law prohibition that forbad tenants of land from doing permanent damage to property to the prejudice of its future owners. The courts of equity made it possible to extend this prohibition to types of tenant overlooked by the common law, typically those who come under the category of acts of commission (people who have been granted permission to commit waste) rather than omission (people who commit waste maliciously).[32] The idea of waste, and the tension between permission and malice within it, is central to this play. Everyone in Venice is guilty of it, and what is probably more pertinent to the play's ambiguous evaluation of Shylock than the mere question of his Jewishness is the fact that where the Christians are collectively guilty of permissive waste, Shylock's isolated attack on the tenantless mansion of Antonio's uninhabited breast takes the action into the domain of malice. The play's preoccupation with the idea of waste could be said to constitute the basis of the difference between this play as a comedy and predecessors like *The Taming of Shrew* and *The Two Gentlemen of Verona*. In contrast to Petruchio, who has 'bettered rather than decreased' his father's lands and goods (2.1.116), Bassanio is a waster: we hear from his own lips 'How much I have disabled mine estate By something showing a more swelling port Than my faint means would grant continuance' (1.1.123–5). Antonio's ruin is directly the result of the same act of commission. Indeed, he invites it: 'you do me now more wrong In making question of my uttermost Than if you had made waste of all I had' (155–7); 'Try what my credit can in Venice do, – That shall be rack'd even to the uttermost To furnish thee to Belmont to fair Portia' (180–2). Where Petruchio comes to his own wedding poorly dressed (which he justifies by anticipating the potentially disabling effects of marriage on his estate [3.2.111–13]) Bassanio ruins Antonio in order to put on a lavish appearance in what is probably the only imaginable situation of courtship in which it makes no difference whatsoever whether he is 'furnished' or not. The term emerges at important points in the action, particularly in Shylock's attacks on the 'unthrifty' Christians. Discussions of Shylock as a usurer may be less to the point than (or at least meaningless without also drawing attention to) the fact that he consistently and accurately identifies habits of waste which we are unquestionably invited to disapprove. While Antonio tells us that his estates are not endangered, from Shylock that we learn the evident truth that he has too many ventures 'squand'red abroad' (1.3.18); and Shylock is happy to see Launcelot leave his service for Bassanio because he is 'huge feeder' and will 'help to waste [Bassanio's] borrowed purse' (2.5.45).

Even Portia is given an insight into the ruinous relationship between Antonio and Bassanio as companions 'that do converse and waste the time together' (3.4.12). Her role in the management of such behaviour is a clear point of comparison with Silvia, enjoined by Valentine to 'repair' him with her presence. Waste was one of the range of equitable actions available to support a woman's third party interest, even within coverture, and hence an action that strongly reinforces our sense of the third party as a form of theatrical agency in its own right. In 1583 *Halghe v Howson* argued the case of Nicholas Halghe who, in 1558, assigned a term of years to trustees upon consideration that if he 'should fortune to waste or consume his inheritance, as in truth he did, that yet the same lease shold be to them in trust for the relief of his wife and children'.[33] Portia's role as the woman's part is thus to 'repair the ruin': first of Bassanio's fortunes, then of Antonio on behalf of Bassanio, but most of all of her own interests in both. At the very outset, she has already begun to pursue those interests in the action her father has put in place for her transfer from the role of daughter to that of wife. At first, she affirms her apparent non-agency: 'I may neither choose who I would nor refuse who I dislike; so is the will of a living daughter curbed by the will of a dead father' (1.2 19–22). But faced with the truly encyclopaedic range of excesses embodied in each of her prospective husbands, we find that there are ways she can begin to act on her own behalf. In response to 'the young German's' drunkenness, she imagines the subterfuge of setting 'a deep glass of Rhenish wine on the contrary casket... I will do anything, Nerissa, ere I will be married to a sponge' (1.3.83).

It is not necessary to fall into the trap of wondering what covert signals are embedded in the scene in which the profligate Bassanio, furnished in Antonio's wealth, chooses the right casket on the manifestly fraudulent grounds that 'so may outward shows be least themselves' (3.2.73). The point is not so much *his* eventual choice as the fact that Portia anticipates it. She characterises herself as in a relation of property to him even before he has made the choice, and that relation as one of spectatorship:

> Beshrew your eyes,
> They have o'erlooked me and divided me.
> One half of me is yours, the other half yours –
> Mine own, I would say, but if mine, then yours
> And so all yours. O, these naughty times
> Puts bars between the owners and their rights:
> And so, though yours, not yours.
>
> (3.2.14–20)

If what Portia says appears to anticipate her assimilation into coverture, her almost excessive rhetorical play on first and second persons insists on maintaining her separation. After Bassanio's success, she restates this assimilation – 'This house, these servants, and this same myself Are yours, my lord's. I give them with this ring ...' (3.2.171) – but expresses the conversion in terms of Bassanio's obligation to maintain the property he has acquired in the process, to the failure of which she retains the right of action: '...which when you part from, lose, or give away, Let it presage the ruin of your love, And be my vantage to exclaim on you' (72–3).

Thus, if Antonio's body, bared for Shylock's knife, materialises Valentine's image of a ruinous tenantless mansion within this play, for Portia, the scene might appropriately be seen as, above all, an opportunity to *ensure* that Bassanio gives her ring away, thus returning to her the interest she has formally conceded by marrying him, enabling her to act on it (in a court of law) and restoring to her the rights of ownership that act as a guarantee to the fragility of this theatrical duty circle. What Portia has achieved by the end of this play is exactly what Valentine invites Sylvia to do: she has repaired its world with her presence. I suggested above that Bassanio's witness of Antonio's ruin maps the duration of the bond, and its conditions for its satisfaction, onto the rewarding experience of spectatorship offered by the play itself as a similar guarantor against ruin in the difficult world of professional theatre. For Shakespeare and his fellows, looking into the uncertain future of 1566–7, the stakes were that high.

Owner of the house

> O benefit of ill! Now I find true
> That better is by evil still made better
> And ruined love when it is built anew
> Grows fairer than at first, more strong, far greater,
>   So I return rebuked to my content
>   And gain by ills thrice more than I have spent.
>
> Sonnet 119

The institution of the Globe in 1599, and the plays written for it in its first few years, present an exemplary instance of the 'benefit of ill' which could be derived from rebuilding a ruin. The supreme formal ease of *As You Like It* keys to this hopeful, winning time. Its 'building anew' of the material of comedy developed over the preceding years – in particular the woman's part – is best seen not from the retrospective position of a concept of genre largely derived from the naturalisation of a Shakespearean *oeuvre* into the vocabulary of literary criticism, but in its contemporary role in the play-by-play renegotiation of the bond between the Shakespeare company and what the plays themselves quite clearly see as an increasingly identifiable audience. Rosalind and Celia form a partnership that is unlike all previous women's part pairings. Julia and Lucetta act briefly as a pair in the early scenes in Verona; as a servant Lucetta is asked to function as an agent for her mistress, but we do not see her thereafter; Nerissa accompanies her mistress to Venice and also disguises, but remains a servant in the household of which both women are already a part when the play begins, and to which they return. More so than either Julia or Portia, Rosalind's and Celia's disguise arises from dispossession; but it is a dispossession that is reconfigured as exemplary performance not merely within an imagined moment of affective exchange between player and spectator, but as a form of institutional agency sustainable beyond the limits of the single play. This sustainability is realised in the fact that in *As You Like It* the woman's part is contextualised within a transformation of the property base from which it acts within the world of the play. Unlike either Julia or Portia, Rosalind and Celia do not retain a place in the home they leave, nor do they return to it; unlike Julia, but like Jessica, they take their wealth with them when they go; unlike Jessica they use it thriftily to buy a house. Unlike all of them, their roles are defined not by service or marriage within a pre-established household, but by the voluntary assumption of the rights and responsibilities of ownership.

Appropriately for a play written for the Globe, reconstructed from the dismantled Theatre, these rights and responsibilities begin where *The Merchant of Venice* ends: with an act of repair. In desperate need of hospitality when they arrive at Arden, they learn from Corin that the local household, Silvius's 'cot, his flocks, and pasture Are now on sale, and at our sheepcote now By reason of his absence there is nothing That you will feed on' (2.4.78–81). Rosalind proposes its purchase – 'And thou shalt have to pay for it of us' (88) – and Celia adds, 'and we will mend thy wages' (89). Their combined action saves the farm from tenantless neglect, but also establishes our sense of the forest as a place of both habitation and work. Celia follows the offer to mend Corin's wages with two important statements: 'I like this place and willingly could waste my time here' (89–90). Corin's response ('if you like upon report The soil, the profit and this kind of life, I will your very faithful feeder be' (92–4) – puts in place the precise relation between ownership and the industry it takes to sustain it. It is worth noting in passing that here, in contrast to Launcelot in *The Merchant of Venice*, a 'feeder' is someone who responsibly feeds others in a relation of trust, not someone who feeds himself excessively at others' expense. In this context, Celia's use of the word 'waste' picks up the resonance of the idea of neglect, but here – again in contrast to the use of the phrase in *The Merchant* – its conjunction with the word 'time' alerts us to the fact that, with their purchase of their own house, Rosalind and Celia become owners, not wasters, of time. With its sustained discussion of contrasting modes of duration ('time travels in divers paces with divers persons' [3.2.236]) and coordination of these 'divers paces' to the time required to bring its formidable range of interlocking courtships to a single coordinated conclusion, the play creates a 'working-day world' in which the woman's part, like the unnamed daughter of '*22 Eliz.*' licensed to transport herrings to Spain, becomes the play's agent for the creation of property, not merely the medium for its transmission from one man to another.

The scene that precipitates this conclusion is the one in which Celia meets Oliver (4.5). Oliver asks Rosalind and Celia for directions to their own house, and Celia replies, 'At this hour the house doth keep itself. There's none within' (80–1). The link between this imagined off-stage space and the onstage action is probably one of the most innovative aspects of this play in Shakespeare's new situation in The Globe.[34] Gay McAuley has suggested that, in scenography, the interplay between the space of the stage and the fictional world presented has been seen as 'constitutive of theatre'. If that is the case, we might do worse than suggest that this, and here, is where it became that. This house that 'keeps itself' while its owners are on stage is on one level an offstage element of the fictional world, but on another the Globe itself: the spatial envelope within which that world is now securely embedded. What follows in this dialogue develops the relation between ownership and performance already underpinning the relationship between Rosalind and Celia. Realising he is looking at the two people he has been sent to find, Oliver asks Celia, 'Are not you The owner of the house I did enquire for?' (87–8). Celia answers in the plural: 'it is no boast, being asked, to say we are' (89). This is true to the earlier representation of the point at which Rosalind and Celia *became* owners together, but Oliver's already obvious focus of attention on Celia also picks up the crucial division of labour (Rosalind offers to buy the house, Celia to mend the wages). That division now becomes important. Noting Celia's plural answer, Oliver responds, 'Orlando doth commend him to you both' (90) and Rosalind maintains the plural in her question about the napkin: 'what must we understand by this?' Oliver's reply begins the play with pronouns noted in Portia's courtship of Bassanio: 'if you will know of me What man I am ... ', beginning his story of 'Orlando's elder brother' in the third person and responding to Celia's exclamation, 'O I have heard him speak of that same brother' (120), with the first person that will reveal itself within ten lines: 'well I know ... 'Twas I but 'tis not I' (123/134).

From this point on, Rosalind's and Celia's attentions are divided. Despite the fact they both begin with the same focusing device, 'was't you...?', Rosalind's questions are about Orlando: 'was't you he rescued?' (132), and Celia's are about Oliver: 'was't you that did so oft contrive to kill him?' (133). The growing responsiveness between Celia and Oliver is a subtle and quite beautiful linguistic presentation of the beginnings of a courtship, later given formal shape in the rhetorical figure of *gradatio* which Rosalind uses to tell the story to Orlando (one of the additional pleasures of which, for the spectator, is the fact that while it was happening, Rosalind herself was obviously not in any fit state to engage in this process of observation):

> For your brother and my sister no sooner met but they looked; no sooner looked but they loved; no sooner loved but they sighed; no sooner sighed but they asked one another the reason; no sooner knew the reason but they sought the remedy; and in these degrees have they made a pair of ladders to marriage, which they will climb in continent, or else be incontinent before marriage. They are in the very wrath of love, and they will together. Clubs cannot part them.
> (5.2.28–36)

I have followed this episode through in detail to show that it is a remarkable account, first, of the separation of the partnership between Rosalind and Celia into individual agencies; second, of the affiliation of these individual agencies with new forms of partnership; and third, of the beginnings of the reassimilation of these new partnerships into a broader reconfiguration of the duty circle of which their purchase of the house has made them a part. In the light of this, it is surprising but appropriate to realise that Celia's last words in the play are spoken to Oliver at the end of 4.3.176 ('good sir, go with us') and that, while Rosalind and Celia as a pair are so unlike previous woman's part pairings, Celia is *like* Silvia, Hermia and Helena in *A Midsummer Night's Dream* and later woman's parts such as *Measure for Measure*'s Isabella in entering her marriage in complete silence. But *As You Like It* makes it clear how strong the agency is in this apparent retreat into the kind of 'pure' third party position I associated with young Elizabeth's non-presence at the end of *Richard III*. If we fail to recognise this in contemporary performances of plays like *Dream* and *Measure for Measure*, it may be because we have not had the benefit of the play-by-play education in the skills of spectatorship which Shakespeare gave his audiences across the 1590s. Celia and

Oliver's courtship precipitates a transition from 'idle talking' (5.2.46) to *doing* which brings together those whose interests Rosalind claims she will 'satisfy' at their wedding (106). It also brings about a complete redistribution of property, as it moves towards a position in which Oliver settles their father's estate on Orlando, Orlando marries Rosalind and thus also becomes heir to the restored Duke Senior's estate, and Oliver stays in the forest, presumably living in his wife's and sister-in-law's cottage and working as a shepherd. From a position in which Celia and Rosalind are presented as joint owners of their own house (and it would be reductive to ask exactly what kind of joint ownership this is) the play works, through Celia, towards a far more complex conception of joint or collaborative action. The point of this co-ownership is precisely the fact that it drives the action towards this radical reconfiguration of a duty circle that is gathered, like a timely harvest, into the final scene.

Sharing the good

> Welcome, young man
> Thou offer'st fairly to thy brothers' wedding:
> To one his lands withheld, and to the other
> A land itself at large, a potent dukedom.
> First in this forest let us do those ends
> That here were well begun, and well begot.
> And after, every of this happy number
> That have endured shrewd days and nights with us
> Shall share the good of our returned fortune
> According to the measure of their states.
>
> (5.4.155-64)

If in *The Merchant of Venice* conflicting durations of indebtedness reflect the ill facing the company in 1566-7 and the uncertainty of its ultimate benefit, then the 'divers paces' of duration coordinated around Rosalind's and Celia's ownership of their own house articulate the extent to which the duty circle created by the Globe indenture turned Shakespeare's early imagination of a special property of theatre into a reality. It is not, however, easy to find the right word to describe it. For Andrew Gurr, the general term 'company' does the job: 'a gathering of like-minded people, a theatre audience or a group of players conjoined to produce a play ... the durability of this word for the ensembles who produce any live play certifies it as the right signifier for a collective working as a team'.[35] But the very scope of Gurr's sense of the difference between *this* ensemble and its competitors suggests that, beyond its obvious relevance as a general frame of reference, it might not be adequate to the task: 'Their management was unique in keeping the sharing co-operative system of the early travellers'; 'in the core of their team they were both tenants and landlords of their own properties';[36] '[they created] the only effective democracy of its time in totalitarian England'.[37] These very strong statements combine notions of joint holding, conjoint agency and rights of association, and as such place Shakespeare in an economic context in which the term 'partnership', an idea that has been circulating rather freely around my discussion up to this point, could be far more useful. At the end of the sixteenth century the notion of partnership served as a collection point for an amalgam of powerful but not always coherent ideas about collective agency. It drew on a confused, and often confusing, synthesis of Roman law (the idea of the *societas*, which combined common holding with rights of association), medieval law merchant (the unit entity concept embodied in the idea of the corporation) and common law principles of joint tenancy. Within a few years, this tradition of economic thought would be further complicated by the assimilation of the work of the courts merchant into the courts of the common law, a development that had significant implications at a time when political ideas of association in general were responding to the pressures of the Jacobean succession.

In this situation, contemporary writers were concerned to define their terms. Writing on 'the custom, or law' of 'the ancient law merchant' in 1622, Gerard Malynes distinguished between mercantile associations 'done by publike authoritie of Princes or States, vpon Grauntes made by Letters Patents, which are properly called Societies' and those 'done by and betweene Merchants of their owne authoritie, ioyning themselues together for to deale and trade either for yeares or voyages ...'

> and this is properly called Partnership, where one man doth aduenture a thousand pounds, another fiue hundreth pounds, another three hundreth pounds, and another foure hundreth pounds, more or lesse, as they agree amongst themselues, to make a stocke, euerie man to haue his profit, or to beare losses and aduenture according to their seuerall stockes, in one or many voyages, for one or more yeares; besides the moneyes taken vp at vse to trade withall, proportionably according to the rates of their stocks by parts and portions, to be diuided into so many parts as they agree: wherein the conditions be

diuers, which must be obserued truely, and the accounts accordingly; otherwise all will run into a Laborinth and confusion.[38]

As a description of the financial arrangements of a joint stock company, the application of this account to the Shakespeare company is straightforward, but we should also note ideas of institutional *durée* which resonate strikingly with the questions of temporality I have been discussing in this chapter. In its sense of the interchangeability of time and action ('years *or* voyages'); of the contrasting and unpredictable durations that arise from this ('one or many voyages for one or more years'); of individual contributions as 'parts' whose 'profit' are subject to 'divers conditions'; not to mention the recognition that these conditions 'must be obserued truly... otherwise all will run into a Laborinth and confusion', Malynes' account echoes the complex flow of time in *The Merchant of Venice* and *As You Like It,* and the awareness within these plays that this flow is the medium within which the difficult coordination of differentiated skills must be achieved. We thus arrive at an approach to Shakespearean authorship in which we can distinguish two constitutive elements: Shakespeare's *writing*, as his conjoint act within the partnership; and his *plays*, both as the 'agreement' of 'parts' that is itself partnership and as the partnership's most profitable joint holding. From this perspective Shakespeare's relation to his *own* plays as a form of property – like his relation to other peoples' – can be seen as one of beneficial ownership, in the sense that their value to him comes not from limited questions of possession, but from the range of institutional interests they served, from rehearsal and performance in the playhouse to publication. This being the case, Malynes' distinction between a form of association 'done by publike authoritie of Princes or States' and one 'done by and betweene Merchants of their owne authoritie' provides the context I need to turn my attention to *Hamlet* in its relation to the Elizabethan culture of monopoly and the rise of what Joseph Loewenstein has called 'possessive authorship'.[39]

6
The Only Man: *A Midsummer Night's Dream* and *Hamlet*

Elizabethan grievances against monopoly gathered momentum throughout the 1580s and 1590s, coming to a head in the Parliament of 1600–1, just as Shakespeare was finishing *Hamlet*. Elizabeth's 'Golden Speech' in November 1601 brought an end to the immediate crisis, but monopolies continued to cause problems until Coke's bill of 1621, enacted as the Statute of Monopolies of 1623, which declared all monopolies void, except charters to 'corporations, companies or fellowships of any art, trade occupation or mystery' and those that could be presented as a defence of economic innovation.[1] As these exemptions suggest, particular monopolies might be considered offensive, but monopoly as a principle was recognised as a structural element of the late Elizabethan and Jacobean commonweal. Joseph Loewenstein has argued that the rise of what he has called 'possessive authorship' was poised between the anti-monopolistic stance of the individual writer battling against the institutions of print[2] and the advantages of forms of economic association, like that of the professional theatre company, which worked openly under its rubric:

> Operating in an urban economy in which commerce was frequently shaped by monopoly, the business of theatre was hardly a sphere of competitive freedom. Days and sites of playing were limited, as was the number of companies allowed to perform in London and its environs: this enabled theater owners and company shareholders to monopolize performers, actors and audiences, and focused the competition for those resources. (It also especially sharpened the difference between sharers in theatrical enterprises – Henslowes, Burbages, and Shakespeares – and those who did piece work – Jonsons, Greenes and Chettles.) Monopoly inflated ticket prices: it should have

constrained theatrical wages, and no doubt did so, though the prices paid for plays rose between, say, the beginning of Shakespeare's career and the end of Jonson's. There is manifold evidence for increased appreciation of authors' contributions to the theater: lengthening scripts; a decline in improvisational performances, at least in the venues with highest ticket prices; plenty of theatrical satire focusing on authors.[3]

For the study of Shakespeare, the problem about this is that, while all of it is true, none of it is true *only* of Shakespeare, and it thus leaves us looking elsewhere for an explanation of why, as early as 1592, well before the establishment of most of the professional practices to which Loewenstein refers, Robert Greene saw him not just as a competitor, but as the very embodiment of monopoly: 'in his owne conceit the only Shake-scene in a countrie'. In this situation, the idea of an 'author's theatre', implicit in Loewenstein's analysis and an influential element of recent reappraisals of a 'literary' Shakespeare,[4] will be inadequate for an account of his rising status as a writer, since it elevates something his contemporaries saw as the basis of his difference from themselves to the status of a historical category that effaces that difference.

All the textual readings I have presented so far suggest that Shakespeare's creative energies were monopolistic from the outset. Throughout his career, but particularly from the establishment of the Chamberlain's Men onward, he built into his work a concept of professional excellence – 'the best in this kind'; 'the only men' – that raised the idea of theatre from the level of the everyday, so painstakingly constructed by the Theatre litigation, to the ontological: 'life's ... a poor player', 'all the world's a stage'.[5] Anne Righter has shown that the theatrical metaphor was a well-established literary topos long before the 1590s.[6] Shakespeare's innovation lay in his use of it to shape the the coincidence of his own institutional aspirations with the competitive dynamic that underpinned the rise of monopoly in that decade.

Each man should prefer himself

If an artificer acquires for himself more customers than another of the same art, for instance a Scrivener, or a Schoolmaster who has more pupils than another because he is more erudite, this is damage to the other but not an injury, because each man should prefer himself ...[7]

As *Fyllol v Assheleygh* shows, the sixteenth-century case for the creation of property by industry led, by an inexorable logic, to a defence of the right to be better than everyone else. This was a right Shakespeare ruthlessly exploited. The term 'preferment' is useful because it focuses the question whether the Chamberlain's Men's advancement, and that of their increasingly famous leading writer, came, in Malynes' words, 'by their owne authoritie', or by that of 'Princes or States'. Written around 1595–6, probably for an aristocratic wedding but also undoubtedly performed at the Theatre, *A Midsummer Night's Dream* might appear to argue the case for the latter. Quince and his company have the opportunity to perform only because they are involved in the celebration of Theseus's wedding, and Theseus appears to be the locus within the play of a critical evaluation of the difference between their 'wretchedness' (5.1.85) and the hypothetical exemplarity with which they are generously but unfavourably compared: 'The best in this kind are but shadows, and the worst no worse if imagination mend them' (208–9). Of course, they are 'preferred' notwithstanding (4.2.33). Theseus courteously dismisses Egeus's reservations – for him, their play is 'nothing, nothing in the world' – in favour of their 'simpleness and duty' (78/83). But nobody who has watched the play up to this point would imagine that these players are all that dutiful, or that the source of their preferment really is Theseus. Their motivations range from Snug's hope of general reward – 'if our sport had gone forward, we had all been made men' (4.2.16–17) – Flute's precise calculation of financial gain – 'O sweet bully Bottom! Thus hath he lost sixpence a day during his life' (18–19) – to Bottom's more intellectual concern with critical success – 'I do not doubt but to hear them say it is a sweet comedy' (36–7).

It is relevant that the scene where we learn of their selection is the one in which we are asked to see them as professional performers, and that it *precedes* the point at which Theseus actually makes his choice.[8] This analepsis keys their success to Bottom's confident virtuosity in Acts II–IV rather than to Theseus's courtly condescension, and isolates them from the competitive field of performance outlined in the 'brief' of entertainments at 5.1.42. More significantly, it ensures that the extradiegetic audience makes a distinction between Theseus's obviously limited insight into the action they have just witnessed and what or whoever it is they infer to be the source of the strange and admirable 'constancy' so acutely perceived by yet another remarkable female spectator, Hippolyta. Theseus's most significant contribution to the play of which he is a part may thus be his role in bringing to it a recognition of the agency of his own creation: the authorial imagination that 'bodies forth The forms of things unknown', and the pen that subsequently gives shape to them (5.1.14–17).

Good and beneficial to the subject in general

If Shakespeare's role as a writer is increasingly foregrounded in the plays produced from 1594 on, the result is not, I think, something I would want to describe, with Loewenstein, as 'possessive' authorship; at least not without recontextualising the idea of 'possession' in terms of the debates about property I have been discussing in the preceding chapters.

Loewenstein illustrates his analysis with an account of the 'passionate speech' performed by the Tragedians of the City's leading player in *Hamlet* 2.2.415–500. Most of the play's editors have seen 'Aeneas' Tale to Dido' as an imitation of Marlowe and Nashe's dramatisation of Virgil's *Aeneid* in *Dido Queen of Carthage*, and have therefore glossed it as a form of theatrical rivalry.[9] Loewenstein takes the argument further. In a discussion that aims 'to expose the specifically ethical and psychological threshold to modern intellectual property',[10] he proposes that Shakespeare's 'remembering' of *Dido* constitutes a homage to Marlowe as a playwright from whom one 'could learn ... to privatize by copying', and suggests that the resulting 'affiliation' of Shakespeare's play to a Virgilian genealogy carries an 'autobiographical charge' that underpins the creation of this speech as an 'object of connoisseurship'.[11] In all these readings, the argument that Shakespeare is engaged in the production of himself as a possessive author hangs on the assumption that the speech is Virgilian. But there is another affiliation in this speech, one that suggests a very different reading of the play as a form of literary property. When the players arrive at court Polonius announces them as

> The best actors in the world, either for tragedy, comedy, history, pastoral, pastoral-comical, historical-pastoral, tragical-historical, tragical-comical-historical-pastoral, scene individable or poem unlimited. Seneca cannot be too heavy nor Plautus too light. For the law of writ and the liberty, these are the only men.
>
> (2.2.379–84)

The framing of this speech between two phrases that neatly encapsulate the dynamic of monopoly – Polonius's rhetorical progression from 'the best' through a parodically inclusive repertoire of theatrical kinds to 'the only' – ensures that the name of Seneca is at the forefront of our response to the Tragedians of the City even before they came on stage.

As David Harris Sacks has shown, the Senecan discourse of benefits underpinned the Elizabethan defence of monopoly as a reward for good service.[12] An interest in Seneca spanned the period both of the political debates about monopoly, and of the rise of Elizabethan professional theatre, from the publication of Arthur Golding's translation of *De Beneficiis* in 1578 – 'The work of the excellent philosopher L. A. Seneca concerning benefits, that is to say the doing, receiving and requiting of good turns' – to Thomas Lodge's translations, *The Workes of Lucius Annaeus Seneca, both morrall and naturall* in 1614, and the W*orkes of Lucius Annaeus Seneca newly inlarged and corrected* in 1620. Seneca's conception of a society based on profitable mutuality is figured in his account of the Three Graces:

> Why do the sisters dance hand in hand in a ring that returns upon itself? For the reason that a benefit passing in its course from hand to hand returns nevertheless to the giver; the beauty of the whole is destroyed if the course is anywhere broken, and it has most beauty if it is continuous, and maintains an uninterrupted succession.[13]

This image was influential in contemporary characterisations of the Elizabethan court, notably in Book VI of *The Faerie Queene*, published in 1596, in which Calidore's vision of the Three Graces dancing with a fourth maiden on Mount Acidale consummates his presentation of Gloriana and her circle of knights across the poem as a whole. Elizabeth's Golden Speech, given in response to her confrontation with the Commons over patents in the Parliament of 1600–1, demonstrated the extent to which it informed her own understanding of the interaction between prince and subject, from the use of patents as a reward for good service to the discourse of gratitude she used so brilliantly to respond to grievances against them:

> My heart was never set on any worldly goods. What you bestow on me, I will not hoard it up, but receive it to bestow on you again. Therefore render unto them I beseech you Mr Speaker, such thanks as you imagine my heart yieldeth, but my tongue cannot express.... Since I was Queen, yet did I never put my pen to any grant, but that upon pretext and semblance made unto me, it was both good and beneficial to the subject in general though a private profit to some of my ancient servants, who had deserved well at my hands. But the contrary being found by experience, I am exceedingly beholden to such subjects as would move the same at first.[14]

Mark Archer has provided a useful formulation of the way we might read Elizabeth's understanding of the bond between prince and servant as beneficial exchange back into the literature that was itself part of that exchange. Writing of *The Faerie Queene*, he suggests that 'what the reader finally takes from the poem is what the poem has subliminally taught him to bring to it: the satisfaction of knowing his own mind through the courteous activity of attending to Spenser's'.[15] In a similar way, Shakespeare courteously attends to Seneca's presence in 'Aeneas' Tale to Dido' at precisely the point at which he most conclusively demonstrates his ownership of it. From the outset, the speech raises the question of property:

> We'll e'en to 't like French falc'ners, fly at anything we see.
> We'll have a speech straight.
> Come, give us a taste of your quality.
>
> (2.2.412–14)

Unlike a straying bloodhound, when a tamed bird of prey was let fly at a quarry, not only did the bird remain the property of its owner, its quarry also became his.[16] When Hamlet describes his chosen speech, he does not tell us the name of the play from which it is taken or the name of its writer. But he does tell us about its style, and from there he proceeds to what is effectively an 'occupation' (in the sense of the word we saw in *Fyllol v Assheleygh*) of its unacknowledged sources:

> – let me see, let me see:
> The rugged Pyrrhus, like th'Hyrcanian beast –
> 'tis not so. It begins with Pyrrhus –
>
> (2.2.429–31)

Critics agree that this 'accidental' reference to the Hyrcanian beast is taken from *Dido* ('But thou art sprung from *Scythian Caucasus* And Tygers of *Hircania* gave thee sucke' [5.1.1564–7]),[17] and that the allusion is an indirect reference to Robert Greene's attack on the upstart Crow 'with his Tyger's heart wrapt in a Players hide', itself a parody of York's denunciation of Queen Margaret from *Richard Duke of York (3 Henry VI)* 'O tiger's heart wrapped in a woman's hide!' (1.4.138) – in turn followed by an earlier borrowing from *Dido*, 'But you are more inhuman, more inexorable, O, ten times more than tigers of Hyrcania' (155–6).

There is thus already a remarkable 'passing ... from hand to hand' going on here, though it is not yet clear what its 'benefit' will be. For Loewenstein, Hamlet's 'misremembering' is part of the speech's autobiographical charge.[18] But the idea of autobiography does not do full justice to the institutionalising energy that is being unleashed in this complex system of exchange. *Dido* was published in 1594 with a title-page that informs us that it was acted by the Chapel Children (the children's company that became so fashionable in London at the turn of the century) and which Hamlet, Rosencrantz and Guildenstern discuss earlier in this scene. They were also the company that leased the Blackfriars from the Burbages after the Chamberlain's Men had been refused permission to play there, so there is much at stake when Shakespeare alludes to this source in a speech presented as a demonstration of the 'quality' of a company of adult players professionally dispossessed by their young competitors.

It is not surprising that, as the speech moves towards its climax, its engagement with Marlowe–Nashe gathers a quite ferocious intensity (or that the subject matter that articulates this intensity is hand-to-hand combat). Editors have noted two main points of comparison. First, lines 453–4: 'But with the whiff and wind of his fell sword Th' unnervèd father falls'. According to Harold Jenkins, this is 'seemingly a reminiscence' of Marlowe–Nashe's 'He ... whisk'd his sword about And with the wound thereof the King fell down' (2.1.253–4).[19] But it reverses the order of events. In *Dido*, Priam's confrontation with Pyrrhus is a response to an attack on Hecuba; in *Hamlet*, it is itself the subject of a response by Hecuba, which in its turn is the subject of the Player's response to her, and of Hamlet's response to him – another remarkable passing from hand to hand. The more obvious Shakespeare's reference to Marlowe–Nashe, the more obviously he seems to insist on rewriting them. But then we reach Pyrrhus's notorious 'pause':

> For lo, his sword
> Which was declining on the milky head
> Of reverend Priam, seemed i'th'air to stick.
> So, as a painted tyrant, Pyrrhus stood,
> And like a neutral to his will and matter,
> Did nothing.
>
> (2.2.457–62)

For most commentators, this is yet another Marlowe–Nashe allusion. Jenkins notes that 'Leech supposes this to derive from *Dido*, II.i.263: 'he stood stone still'.[20] Ann Thompson and Neil Taylor agree, describing the derivation as 'possibly a recollection'.[21] If this were correct, it would constitute another significant reversal, and once again it would give emphasis to Hecuba: in *Dido*, Pyrrhus's pause comes *after* Priam's death; in *Hamlet* it comes *before* it. But Jenkins thought the parallel 'dubious', and I agree, though not that it should figure in our response. Rather, the recognition, once again, that *Dido* is *not* what we should be trying to remember, together with the emphasis on Hecuba 'accidentally' generated by the fact that we do, prepares us for the revelation of a source that rewrites the whole process of rewriting: Seneca's *Troades*, translated by Jasper Heywood as *Troas* and published in 1581 in Thomas Newton's collection of 'Englished' Senecas.

Seneca's play is set in the aftermath of the fall of Troy. Anxious to return home after ten years of siege, the Greeks are becalmed on the Trojan coast. To appease the ghost of Achilles, they agree to sacrifice Polyxena, once his betrothed, and one of Hecuba's only two surviving children. As she is led out to death at the hands of Achilles' son Pyrrhus, a crowd gathers to witness the event:

> Astonied much the people were, and all, they her commende.
> And nowe much more then euer earst, they praysde her, at
>   her ende.
> Some with her beauty moued were, some with her tender
>   yeares:
> Some to behold the turnes of chaunce, and how eche thyng
>   thus weares.
> But most them mones her valiant mynd, and lofty stomake hye,
> So strong, so stout, so ready of heart, and well prepaide to dye.
> Thus passe they furth, and bolde, before kyng Pyrrhus gothe
>   the mayde,
> They pittie her, they meruell her, theyr heartes wer all afrayde.
> As soone as then, the hard hyll top (where dye she should)
>   they trode.
> And hye vppon his fathers tombe, the youthfull Pyrrhus stode.
> The manly mayde she neuer shronke, one foote, nor backwarde
>   drewe
> But boldely turnes to meete the stroke, with stoute
>   vnchanged hew
> Her corage moues eche one, and loe a strange thing
>   monstrouse lyke.
> That Pyrrhus euen himself stoode styll, for dreade, and durst
>   not stryke.[22]

'So as a painted tyrant, Pyrrhus stood And like a neutral to his will and matter Did nothing' (2.2.460–2). It is, I suggest, a direct parallel and it completely changes not only the way we understand this speech, but also the way it informs our understanding of Shakespearean authorship. At an immediate level, the 'manly mayde' Polyxena's 'entry' into the action provides a paradigm for the paradoxically positive agency of Ophelia's suicide, described by her gravediggers in 5.1, and in so doing affiliates her with the comic 'daughters who have the action' discussed in Chapter 5.[23] But it also demonstrates Shakespeare's proprietary relation to the authorial field of which his work is now so dominant a part. In *Hamlet*, he reveals himself, triumphantly, as a literary *cestuy que use*. His virtuosic exploitation of his sources; his equally virtuosic display both of the Senecan discourse of benefits as its justification and of Seneca himself as its authorising antecedent; all this comes together in a distinctive Shakespearean concept of beneficial literary ownership.

The institutional aspirations of this beneficial ownership extend its bond, and the conditions for its satisfaction, beyond the spatial framework of theatre spectatorship. 'Aeneas' Tale' gives us proof, if any were needed, that Shakespeare saw literary readership as a structural element, not so much of theatre in general, as of theatre at its best.[24] Hamlet tells us that the play from which the speech is taken was

> never acted, or if it was, not above once; for the play, I remember, pleased not the million. 'Twas caviare to the general.
>
> (416–18)

He also tells us that he once heard the First Player speak it, but obviously knows it primarily as a reader looking at a page: he refers to scenes, lines and phrases. (Shakespeare has already used the word 'phrase' to make us 'see' Polonius close-read Hamlet's letter to Ophelia earlier in the scene [2.2.111]). In strong contrast to Theseus, the skills he brings to the selection of this speech for performance, particularly in his emphasis on style, are those of a reader, not a prince or courtier. As he hands it over to the First Player for performance ('begin at this line' [428]) his reader's memory merges with the memorial skills of the professional player, and the speech becomes a complex act of convergence, a multi-media event that brings together Hamlet's imagined page and its performance, *Hamlet's* page and its imagined performance, *Hamlet's* performance and its imagined page.[25]

Interestingly enough, the same act of convergence is to be found in another text dating from 1601, which just about gives its author time to have had some kind of contact with Shakespeare's play or page. We encountered Sir William Cornwallis in Chapter 4, where I suggested that his *Encomium of Richard III* was part of a Yorkist tradition of historiography which finds its way into *Richard III*. I noted there that the *Encomium* was possibly circulated among the Earl of Essex's supporters at the end of the 1590s and that one version of the manuscript bears a possible dedication to members of Essex's circle. Cornwallis may have been caught up in Essex's rebellion in February 1601, a possibility that makes the dedication of his *Discourses Upon Seneca the Tragedian* to Sir John Popham – who undertook the interrogatories in the subsequent investigations – particularly evocative. The *Discourses* use Seneca's moral philosophy to present close readings of his plays as commentaries on princely power.[26] The work is organised around eleven 'heads' (short quotations from the plays). Four are taken from *Troades*, and the longest from the opening speech in which Hecuba presents herself as the object of public gaze in the tragedy of human mutability:

> *Quicunque regno fidit,* & magna potens
> Dominatur aula, nec leues metuit Deos,
> Animumque rebus credulum laetis dedit
> *Me videat,* & te Troia, non vnquam tulit
> Documenta sors maiora, quam fragili loco
> Starent superbi.[27]

Like 'Aeneas' Tale to Dido', Cornwallis's text is at once a translation and a critical reading of Seneca's play:

> Are kingdomes then such holdes, as their possession shall make vs proclayme warres against God and man? or is power so confidently to bee trusted, as leaning vpon that pillar, the warres of the world cannot stirre vs? Who beleeueth so, let him behold Troy, let him behold *Priam,* let him behold *Hector,* Cities too weake to resist ruine; Principalitie, not able to shunne the miserable parte of calamitie; Valure made the footestoole of the Conquerour. Which examples if either by age thought weake, or by passing through the handes of a Poet, a fiction: let it serue to stirre vp our memories, which can produce examples of these kindes more fresh, and to our knowledge more sure.

Of course, it is not necessary to read his very Senecan observation about the passing of examples 'through the handes of a Poet' directly back to

Shakespeare – Hecuba and the fall of Troy were popular literary topoi towards the end of Elizabeth's reign[28] – but since the main reason to avoid doing so is contemporary academic preference for context and discourse over personal interaction rather than the intrinsic unlikelihood of such an exchange, the argument is worth making. There is a particularly striking consonance between Seneca's '*Quicunque regno fidit ... Me videat, & te Troia*', Cornwallis's translation, 'Who beleeueth so, let him behold Troy' and the point in 'Aeneas' Tale' where the Player responds to Hamlet's injunction to 'come to Hecuba':

> But who, Oh who had seen the mobbled queen –
> ...
> Who this had seen ...
> ...
> But if the gods themselves did see her then
> When she saw Pyrrhus ...
> ...
> The instant burst of clamour that she made –
> ...
> Would have made milch the burning eyes of heaven ...
>
> (492–507)

Before Pyrrhus's pause, the speech's omniscient narration had not drawn our attention to its place in a dramatic structure of spectatorship. Now, Hecuba's presence triggers a startling mesh of intersecting perspectives embedded in a chain of spectatorships connecting Hamlet to Player, the audience to *Hamlet*, the 'world' to the Globe. Thinking back to Thomas More and to his scepticism about theatre's capacity to advance the interests of 'the people', and then forward to the Essex rebellion as what might now appear to be a very powerful example of the dangers of 'stepping up', how do we understand the exchange that takes place between the disparate positions of interest mapped out by this collective public gaze?

I am Richard II, know ye not that?

Elizabeth herself may provide the answer. In August 1601, she had a conversation about the Essex rebellion with the antiquarian William Lambarde, now an old man retiring from service as archivist in the Tower of London. As Leeds Barroll observed in 1988, this episode had become 'something of a cliché in [then] current historical discussions'. Certainly, it was central to all attempts to see early modern theatre in general, and Shakespeare in particular, as 'subversive'. In readings by Stephen Greenblatt and the cultural materialists Jonathan Dollimore and Alan Sinfield, Elizabeth's famous dictum 'I am Richard II, know ye not that?' emerged as an accusation not only against Essex's attempted insurrection, but against all those involved in the performance of a play about Richard II that preceded it, including the Chamberlain's Men.[29] John Popham interrogated members of the company (though not, as far as we know, Shakespeare himself) and Augustus Phillips' argument in their defence has become almost as famous as Elizabeth's accusation, as a desperate disavowal of their involvement in what was now potentially a treasonable offence:

> On Thursday or Friday sevennight, Sir Chas. Percy, Sir Josceline Percy, Lord Monteagle, and several others spoke to some of the players to play the deposing and killing of King Richard II, and promised to give them 40s. more than their ordinary, to do so. Examinate and his fellows had determined to play some other play, holding that of King Richard as being so old and so long out of use that they should have a small company at it, but at this request they were content to play it.[30]

I have indicated above that I consider the identification of the play in question as Shakespeare's to be sound and do not intend to rehearse the whole of this controversy here.[31] My concern is primarily with the extent to which discussions of Elizabeth's conversation with Lambarde have been manipulated to give weight to the 'political Shakespeare' argument, against the far more compelling evidence it gives to the contrary. In these accounts, Elizabeth emerges as a monologic figure, as passive within the political process of her own time as in the critical process of ours. Thus, according to Greenblatt in 1982, ' "I am Richard II. Know ye not that?" *exclaimed* Queen Elizabeth'. For Dollimore and Sinfield in 1985, 'Queen Elizabeth afterwards *anxiously acknowledged* the implied identification between her and Richard II'. And, in 1997, Katherine Eisaman Maus continued the tradition in her introductory notes to the play in the *Norton Shakespeare*: ' "I am Richard II" *snapped* the *furious* queen. "Know ye not that?" '[32] The snowball effect here is so striking that it is almost impossible not to conclude that what these writers were reading was each other, not the document in which Elizabeth's words are actually recorded (see Figure 6.1).[33]

As Lambarde's 'Memoir' makes clear, what Elizabeth has to tell us about Shakespearean theatre is something quite different from the anxious, querulous queen of New Historicism. As in the Golden Speech, this exchange is above all a gracious yielding of thanks to an ancient servant who has deserved well at her hand. Elizabeth is intelligent, relaxed and communicative; Lambarde open and responsive. Both are familiar and easy with the frame of reference they share in the central part of the conversation: the theatre. Certainly, Elizabeth's statement can be been as an identification of herself with the role of Richard II, but such an inference is preceded by a more basic recognition of the shared skills of spectatorship that are its precondition. It is the question of mutual knowledge that is important here, knowledge that ranges from the performance of and attendance at a play to more complex questions of critical interpretation. Of course, Lambarde's reply – 'Such a wicked imagination' – refers to Essex, but it is just as important that neither of them needs to say it. Elizabeth's response to Lambarde is far more illuminating than any subsequent commentary on it: 'He that will forget God, will also forget his benefactors; this tragedy was played forty times in open streets and houses.' In contrast to accounts like Stephen Orgel's, for whom her words grotesquely articulated 'a fantasy whereby the whole city became a stage for a continual performance in which, in the person of her ancestor, she was mimed and deposed',[34] we might say, more simply, that Elizabeth articulates the iterative nature of a habit of spectatorship now naturalised as a general form of social competence.

If that is the case, what this conversation tells us about Shakespearean theatre may be that its status was such that, by 1601, it was above political accountability. In Chapter 4, I referred to Douglas Bruster's proposal of a 'nascent public sphere' grounded in the public theatre of the 1590s and in the developing market for printed plays.[35] Ultimately, it is the extent to which the Elizabeth we meet in this dialogue has more in common with Hippolyta or Titania, or even Manningham's Citizen, than with New Historicism's peevish queen which makes it clear that the model of the public sphere simply does not fit. What I have been examining in this chapter demonstrates not so much a Habermasian ideal of public association reflexively monitored by public opinion, the rise of authorship and literary property, as the establishment of a generic institution of theatre grounded in the Elizabethan culture of monopoly

APPENDIX.

Nº. VII.

"That which paffed from the Excellent Majeftie of Queen ELIZABETH, in her Privie Chamber at Eaft Greenwich, 4º Augufti 1601, 43º reg. fui, towards WILLIAM LAMBARDE.

He prefented her Majeftie with his Pandecta of all her rolls, bundells, membranes, and parcells, that be repofed in her Majefties Tower at London; whereof fhe had given to him the charge 21ft Jan. laft paft.

Her Majeftie chearfullie received the fame into her hands, faying, "You intended to prefent this book unto me by the Counteffe of Warwicke; but I will none of that; for if any fubject of mine do me a fervice, I will thankfully accept it from his own hands:" then opening the book, faid, "You fhall fee that I can read;" and fo, with an audible voice, read over the epiftle, and the title, fo readily, and diftinctly pointed, that it might perfectly appear, that fhe well underftood, and conceived the fame. Then fhe defcended from the beginning of King John, till the end of Richard III. that is 64 pages, ferving 11 kings, containing 286 years: in the 1ft page fhe demanded the meaning of *oblata, cartæ, literæ clauſæ, et literæ patentes*.

W. L. He feverally expounded the right meaning, and laid out the true differences of every of them; her Majeftie feeming well fatisfied, and faid, "that fhe would be a fcholar in her age, and thought it no fcorn to learn during her life, being of the mind of that philofopher, who in his laft years began with the Greek alphabet." Then fhe proceeded to further pages, and afked, where fhe found caufe of ftay, as what *ordinationes, parliamenta, rotulus cambii, redifeifines*.

W. L. He likewife expounded thefe all according to their original diverfities; which fhe took in gracious and full fatisfaction; fo her Majeftie fell upon the reign of King Richard II. faying, "I am Richard II. know ye not that?"

W. L. "Such a wicked imagination was determined and attempted by a moft unkind gent. the moft adorned creature that ever your Majeftie made."

Her Majeftie. "He that will forget God, will alfo forget his benefactors; this tragedy was played 40ᵗⁱᵉ times in open ftreets and houfes."

Her Majeftie demanded, "what was *præſtita*?"

W. L. He expounded it to be "monies lent by her progenitors to her fubjects for their good; but with affurance of good bond for repayment."

Her Majeftie. "So did my good grandfather King Henry VII. fparing to diffipate his treafure or lands." Then returning to Richard II. fhe demanded, "Whether I had feen any true picture, or lively reprefentation of his countenance and perfon?"

W. L. "None but fuch as be in common hands."

Figure 6.1 'I am Richard II, know ye not that?'

Her Majeſtie. ". The Lord Lumley, a lover of antiquities, diſcovered it faſtened on the backſide of a door of a baſe room ; which he preſented unto me, praying, with my good leave, that I might put it in order with the anceſtors and ſucceſſors ; I will command Tho. Kneavet, keeper of my houſe and gallery at Weſtminſter, to ſhew it unto thee."

Then ſhe proceeded to the Rolls,

Ròmæ; Vaſcon: Aquitaniæ, Franciæ, Scotiæ, Walliæ, et Hiberniæ.

W. L. He expounded theſe to be records of eſtate, and negotiations with foreign princes or counteries.

Her Majeſtie demanded again, " if *rediſeiſnes* were unlawful and forcible throwing of men out of their lawful poſſeſſions ?"

W. L. " Yea; and therefore theſe be the rolls of fines aſſeſſed and levied upon ſuch wrong doers, as well for the great and wilful contempt of the crown and royal dignity, as diſturbance of common juſtice."

Her Majeſtie. " In thoſe days force and arms did prevail ; but now the wit of the fox is every where on foot, ſo as hardly a faithful and vertuouſe man may be found." Then came ſhe to the whole total of all the membranes and parcels aforeſaid, amounting to . . . . . ; commending the work; " not only for the pains therein taken, but alſo for that ſhe had not received ſince her firſt coming to the crown any one thing that brought therewith ſo great delectation unto her ;" and ſo being called away to prayer, ſhe put the book in her boſom, having forbidden me from the firſt to the laſt to fall upon my knee before her ; concluding, " Farewell, good and honeſt Lambarde !"

Figure 6.1 (Continued)

and in the distinctively Shakespearean mode of beneficial authorship that was probably its most triumphant production.[36] The question for my next two chapters is whether this production could survive Elizabeth's death and the accession of James I.

7
A Stranger to My Heart: *King Lear*

The Lord Chamberlain's accounts for the Royal Household on 15 March 1604 record a grant of four and half yards of cloth to Shakespeare and his fellows for their liveries as King's Men in James's coronation entertainments. Their entry is the 63rd item in the list for the 'The Chamber'. It comes after 'falconers' and before 'officers', a category that includes the butler and cook of Star Chamber, and the keepers of Whitehall, St James, Hampton Court and Richmond House. Thomas Dekker and Ben Jonson both record the celebrations; Dekker tells us that Edward Alleyn, one of Prince Henry's players, gave a speech.[1] We do not know whether Shakespeare took part. Scholars have debated what shade of red the cloth he received was, and whether it was cheap or expensive.[2]

The elevation of the Chamberlain's Men to the position of King's Men was obviously some kind of climax in their history, but what kind? What, if any, were its implications for their status as an institution? Shakespeare's brilliant exploitation of an aesthetic of monopoly; the company's pre-eminence in their profession and in a culture of spectatorship that aspired to the condition of a general social competence; the patent issued at James's accession: all this seems to confirm the suggestion made at the end of Chapter 6, that by the end of Elizabeth's reign Shakespearean theatre had achieved generic institutional status in the London theatrical scene. However, I have already had cause to note significant changes in the balance of agencies within the company. In Chapter 5 I discussed the question of partnership; in Chapter 6 I noted the increasing reflexivity within the role of the writer with the consolidation of their position as the Chamberlain's Men and resulting changes in the bond of spectatorship created by the individual play, particularly its opening up of a duty circle of theatre to writer and reader as well as player and spectator. As we saw, a bond of this kind could be seen as structural to the mutuality of the Elizabethan commonwealth. However, its role in the culture of praise and profligacy that attended the rise of Jacobean absolutism may call for a radical reassessment.[3] My aim in this chapter is to consider *King Lear*, one of the first plays Shakespeare wrote after becoming a King's Man, with such questions in mind. Ostensibly a rewriting of the old play *The True Chronicle History of King Leir and His Three Daughters*, *King Lear* was based on a story that was told and retold in a variety of forms throughout Elizabeth's reign. It is this ideological drift – the place this narrative holds, not in one particular text or another, but in an underlying dynamic of social transformation – to which I attend in this discussion.

So much as you have, so much are you worth

Entered for publication in 1594, *The True Chronicle History of King Leir and His Three Daughters* was preceded by *The Mirrour for Magistrates* (published in every decade of Elizabeth's reign by various authors, most latterly by George Whetstone in 1584), the second edition of Raphael Holinshed's *First and Second Volumes of Chronicles* (1587) and Edmund Spenser's Second Book of the *Faerie Queene* in 1590. All tell the story of a king who plans to divide the kingdom among his three daughters, but instead gives it to the elder two when the youngest, his favourite, fails his test of love. What is interesting about these variant narratives is the degree of inconsistency in the way they approach the precise questions of property raised by Lear's decision. In Holinshed, when Cordeilla fails to provide a convincing account of her love for him, Leir marries Gonorilla and Regan to Cornwell and Albany, 'wills' the division of his lands after his death and 'assigns' half his land to them immediately. When the prince of Gallia seeks to marry Cordeilla, he is told that all Leir's land is 'assured' to her sisters. Leir continues as king until he is 'reft ... the governaunce' by Albany and Cornwell, who are not prepared to wait until he dies, but he is allowed a 'portion', which is then systematically reduced in 'going from the one to the other'. When Cordeilla helps reinstate him, 'it was accorded .that [she] should ... take possession of the land, the which he promised to leave unto hir, as the rightful inheritour after his decesse, notwithstanding any former grant made to hir sister'.[4] In *The True Chronicle History* Leir decides to 'resign' the crown 'in equall dowry to my daughters three', though he also refers to the divided estates as 'jointures'. When Cordella is discounted as an 'heir', the kingdom is shared by Gonorilla and Regan. When she restores him to his crown, he 'wills' it to her, and after his death she reigns peaceably 'for a long time'.[5]

If these discussions of property are marked by the kind of descriptive fluidity we noted in the Theatre litigation in Chapter 3, or indeed in the legal material I considered in relation to Shakespeare's comedies in Chapter 6, they also raise similar questions. Who exactly owns what? If, in Holinshed, Leir's allocation of lands to Gonorilla and Regan is an assign, the legal transfer of a property or a right, then they would have both title and possession; if it is an assurance they would have the expectation of title, but not necessarily yet the possession. The wording suggests that there is an assign of half the lands with immediate effect and an assurance of the other half after his death. Is the assign made directly to the daughters and the assurance to the sons as their husbands? If so, does Leir somehow retain a title as king over the lands assigned to his daughters, to which he no longer has title or possession, or merely title and possession until his death of estates assured to Albany and Cornwall? Are Gonorilla and Regan queens, or wives of kings, or merely owners of private estates? If the latter, do they own them in their own name or that of their husbands? If the latter, why is it an assign rather than an assurance? Are Cornwall's and Albany's actions to 'reave' Leir of his 'governaunce' taken on their wives' behalf, or in their own right as owners of the lands assured to them? If Leir then gives possession of all his former estates to Cordeilla, does this mean that he has been restored to the title, including the title of those lands already assigned to her sisters? How does either Cordeilla's possession or her prospect as title-holder after his death affect the fact that he has made 'grants' to the others? In *The True Chronicle History*, if Leir 'resigns' the crown 'in equal dowry to my daughters three', does this mean that he is giving title and possession of his lands to his daughters' husbands on their marriages? Or if the settlement is a 'jointure', that the lands are to be either joint estates for husband and wife, or life estates for the wives after their husbands' deaths? Either way, are the daughters queens, or the husbands kings? When Leir subsequently 'wills' the crown to Cordella, she reigns 'peacably for a long time', so she obviously is a queen; but what is the status of her husband? And so on.

Clearly, one of the compelling things about the three daughters story was the fact that it could and did precipitate, endlessly, questions like these: Anthony Mildmay would probably have found it fascinating. If we doubt whether such questions would have occurred to readers or spectators of these texts, we have only to look at Spenser, because his treatment of the story works to close down this kind of litigiousness, replacing a register of conveyance with one of royal succession. The crux of these variant readings is, of course, the Cordelia character's speech to her father. Exactly what kind of speech act is it? What part does it play in the division of the kingdom? In Holinshed, there are no speeches from either Gonorilla or Regan, so there is no question of her comparing unfavourably. Instead, her speech is presented as a forthright statement of a quantitative relation between love and property that would have been comprehensible, and probably entertaining, to spectators of *The Taming of the Shrew*, and which draws on a similar open-endedness about what the quantity in question is: 'so much as you haue, so much are you worth, and so much I loue you, and no more'. In *Leir*, the older daughters explicitly state their intention to 'flatter' the king 'as he was never so flattered in his life'. When they do, Cordella refuses to reciprocate – 'But looke what loue the child doth owe the father, The same to you I beare, my gracious Lord' – and is scorned by her sisters for 'plain dealing'. Spenser merely describes Cordeilla's statement that she loves her father 'as behoou'd' as 'simple'.[6]

Shakespeare's Cordelia alone introduces the idea of silence. Given the fact that all these earlier versions suggest that she is dispossessed by her father because of what she does say rather than what she doesn't, why? Because Cordelia's silence is heavily invested in the theoretical discourse of contemporary Shakespearean feminism, it has been too easy not to ask this question.[7] For literary historians, the obvious answer is that Shakespeare assimilates his character to conduct book discourses of female virtue. But this creates more problems than it solves because there is nothing in any of the three daughters stories currently recognised as sources for Shakespeare's play to suggest that this is a conduct book 'world'. But there is another Elizabethan three daughters story – *not* identified as the story of Lear – which *is* centrally placed in the conduct book tradition and in which the favourite youngest daughter is presented as an embodiment of the virtue of silence. Since it is a work by Robert Greene, I want to suggest that it offered the Upstart Crow, now a King's Man, an opportunity not just to put its author firmly in his place, but to look back at the personal and professional metamorphosis that had taken place over the years since Greene's envious announcement of his appearance on the London scene in 1592.[8]

The clothworker's art

First published in 1587, but reprinted in 1601, *Penelope's Web* takes the same narrative point of departure as 'Aeneas' Tale to Dido'. It begins at the point 'when as the stately Citty of Troy was sackt by the Grecians, & al the Princely brood of *Priamus* either vtterly extinguished by the sword...'[9] But where 'Aeneas' Tale' follows the Trojan story to Hecuba, *Penelope's Web* follows the Greek strand of the narrative to the woman who, as the very type of marital chastity, might have been a more obvious exemplum for a son preoccupied with a mother he sees as a faithless wife. It presents the well-known story of Penelope, in the prolonged absence of her husband Ulysses, presiding over a court besieged by suitors trying to force her into marriage. Her strategy of deferral is well known: promising to choose a suitor when she finishes the cloth she weaves by day, she spends her nights unravelling the fabric. As she does, she and her maids, Eubola, Vygenia and Ismena, discourse on the 'three speciall vertues, necessary to be incident in euery vertuous woman ... namely obedience, chastity, and sylence'. The third of the illustrative 'comicall histories' that follow tells the story of Ariamenes of Delphos, a prince who decides to set a test in order to decide which of his three sons will succeed him. I provide two quite long extracts of what is probably an unfamiliar text:

> *Ariamenes* blest thus euery way with earthly fauours, seeing his gray hayres were summons vnto death, and that olde age the true limiter of time, presented vnto him the figure of his mortality, that he was come from the cradle to the Crouch, and from the Crouch had one legge in the graue: knowing that the kingdome of *Delphos* was not a Monarchy that fell by inheritaunce, but that bee might as well appoint his youngest sonne successor as his eldest, being affected to them all alike: was perplexed with contrary passions, to which of the three hee should bequeath such a Royall Leagacy, sith by such an equall proportion Fortune had inriched them with fauours. Nature, who is little partiall in such peculiar iudgements, was by the seuerall thoughts that troubled *Ariamenes* head, almost set at an *non plus;* insomuch that the olde King driuen into a Dylemma, fell into this consideration.

> That all his sonnes were married to women descended from honourable parents, and that sith his Sonnes were so equal in their vertues, he was to measure his affection by the conditions of their wiues: for he knew that kings in their gouernment proued oft such Iusticiaries as y[e] good or il disposition of their wiues did afford: for the greatest Monarches haue bene subiect to the plausible perswasions of women, and Princes thoughts are oft tied to the wings of beautie. ... These things considered, *Ariamenes* was thus resolued for himselfe, to bestowe y[e] kingdome on that sonne whose wife was found to be most vertuous.

In the test that follows, the two older wives – referred to as sisters – vie with each other to outdo their claims to virtue. At this,

> The yongest Sister hearing how vnreuerently they brabled before the King, began to blush: which *Ariamenes* espying, noting in her face the very purtraiture of vertue, demanded of her why hearing her sisters so hard by the eares for a Crowne shee said nothing? her answere was thus briefe and pithy. He that gaineth a Crowne getteth care, is it not folly then to hunt after losse? The King looking for a longer discourse, and seeing contrary to his expectation that she was onely short and sweete, prosecuted still in questioning, and demaunded what vertues she had that might deserue so royall a benefit? This quoth she, that when others talke, yet being a woman I can hold my peace. *Ariamenes* and all the Nobility of *Delphos* wondred at the modestie of the young Lady, that contrary to her naturall disposition could so well bridle her affections. Therfore debating the matter betwixt them which of the three were most vertuous: although they found by proofe that the other Ladies were both obedient and chast: yet for that they wanted silence, which (sayd *Ariamenes*) comprehended in it all other vertues, they mist of the cushion, and the King created his youngest Sonne heire apparant to the Kingdome.

This narrative has an instantly clarifying effect on the way we understand the 'analogic' relation between the King Lear story and Norton and Sackville's *Gorbuduc*. Greg Walker has argued that a performance of the play presented at Elizabeth's court over Christmas 1561–2 during the festivities that attended Swedish ambassador Nicholas Guildenstern's pursuit of a royal match with the Swedish king Eric, was designed to advance the argument for Elizabeth's marriage to Robert Dudley.[10] In 1587, the year he was succeeded by Essex as Master of the Horse, Dudley's ascendancy was all but over, and Greene's text helps us trace the way the story re-presented the succession crisis in the face of the realisation that Elizabeth would now neither marry nor give birth. First published the same year as the republication of Holinshed's *First and Second Volumes of Chronicle*, it reorganises the Lear story's three sisters as wives of three sons, and presents the story of a contest for succession as an act of wisdom rather than folly. If, as Walker argues, *Gorbuduc* is to be seen as a direct commentary on the Elizabethan marriage crisis at the point when it was still possible for Elizabeth to consolidate an English line of succession, *Penelope's Web* updates the situation by presenting her position as that of a strong queen ruling in a single state now mythologised as the indefinitely deferred absence of an idealised husband.

However, if this background illuminates Shakespeare's decision to rewrite the Lear story in the aftermath of Elizabeth's death, it also suggests that we may now need to return to Loewenstein's notion of the 'autobiographical charge' to understand its role in Shakespeare's response to his new position in James' court. In a topical development of the conventional analogy between writing and weaving, *Penelope's Web* aligns its claim for authorial status with a scathing allusion to the 'Cloath workers arte':

> But some may obiect that Homers pen deawd forth such sugred eloquence, as beseemed the discourse of Vlisses trauailes: whereas my harsh style and method makes the Web that of it selfe was as soft as the Seres wool, be as rough as Goates haire. I confesse my fault, and therefore by custome claime pardone of course: yet thus farre dare I answere for my selfe, that although Demosthenes had a Plaudite for his Oratio~ because it was curious: yet Nemius got the sentence for the trueth of his plaine tale. Penelope her self was more chast then eloquent. Virgill was seene to haue Ennius in his hand. The Romain Ladies spurned at the sweet verses of Ouid, when they read ouer the Satyres of Inuenall· And I hope your Ladiships will vouchsafe of Penelopes Web, at least for the vertue of the woman that first wrought it, though the Cloath workers arte haue giuen it so bad a glosse.

Since the 1560s, the Clothworkers and the Merchant Adventurers had been engaged in what was probably the longest-running political confrontations of Elizabeth's reign. Their 'relentless feud' concerned the Clothworkers' insistence, rejected by the Merchant Adventurers, that English cloth sold for export should be finished by English workers. The artificers had scored a success in the 1566 when it was enacted that for 'every nine cloths shipped undressed one must go fully dressed ... al cloths made in Kent and Suffolk must go fully dressed', but the Merchants found a way round this by packing cloths up 'privily' and sending them out without inspection.[11] With high levels of unemployment among artisan clothworkers, Elizabeth's grants of licences to ship undressed cloth to favoured courtiers like Francis Walsingham severely exacerbated the problem, and the stand-off continued throughout the 1590s when the cloth industry's troubles took more parliamentary time than any other interest group.[12] In 1601, Elizabeth granted a licence to ship undressed cloth to the Earl of Cumberland, husband of Greene's dedicatee, Margaret. This was a decisive point in the confrontation: Cumberland came to an uneasy alliance with the Merchant Adventurers, and 'the artisan clothworkers were left to nurse their resentment'.[13] With its celebration of Greene's 'harsh style and method' contrasting favourably with 'the Clothworkers art', the republication of *Penelope's Web* could well have had something to do with Cumberland's new monopoly and as such it presents a particular reading of the relation between authorship and patronage; a reading that contrasts strongly with the underlying argument about authorship and style in 'Aeneas' Tale' in *Hamlet*.

This may have been a red rag to a bull. In 1601, also the year of his father's death, Shakespeare would have retained the painful memory that his family, though not clothworkers as such, had suffered directly from restrictive practices in the cloth industries. In the early 1570s, John Shakespeare faced prosecutions in the Exchequer on charges of illegal trading in wool. James Langrake brought information that Shakespeare, whose work as a glover involved the handling of wool taken from the animals used to produce hides, had bought 200 and 100 tods of wool in violation of a statute of 1552 which restricted the purchase of wool to Merchants of the Staple. These quantities make it clear, as Thomas and Evans have suggested, that 'John Shakespeare was a wool dealer on a considerable scale', a fact that 'makes his fall from public position all the more surprising':

> Having attained the highest elective office that Stratford had to offer, John Shakespeare withdrew from borough life after 1576; he ceased attending meetings of the council and was ultimately removed from his position as alderman. At the same time he got into debt and sold land. His decline was dramatic but is as yet unexplained.[14]

Cathy Shrank has suggested that Stratford's civic culture provided a 'vibrant background' for 'Shakespeare as a playwright':

> From 1556 to 1576, Shakespeare's father, John, was deeply involved with this corporation, holding a series of civic offices of increasing responsibility ... The young William would consequently have been exposed to civic values of duty and participation in local affairs even before he started at the town's free grammar school.[15]

But she does not consider the possibly negative consequences for young William's idea of civic values of whatever it was that happened in 1576.[16]

Since the figure of the clothier was one of a contemporary repertoire of 'upstarts' who 'doeth most harme of all other degres in this land by purchasing lande or leses or by meyteyning his son in the Ynes of Cort like a gentleman or by byeng offices for him',[17] we might observe that Shakespeare should have been able to expect but did not enjoy similar advantages from his father's early success. As we know, he took steps to restore his father's position with the purchase of the title of gentleman in 1596, an act glanced at in the heraldic imagery of 'Aeneas' Tale'. But it is *King Lear* that demonstrates fully the significance of this memory for Shakespeare's imagination of his theatre's future under the patronage of James I.

If only to go warm were gorgeous

In the reading of *King Lear* that follows, I return to Christopher St German's account of the use in *Second Dialogue* of *Doctor and Student* first discussed in Chapter 2.[18] I will argue that, when Shakespeare began to work on *Lear* shortly after James' accession, this passage was on his mind too, for reasons that will become obvious. As we saw earlier, the *Second Dialogue* offered an account of the use that set the terms for the popularisation of forms of beneficial ownership in private conveyancing across the sixteenth century:

> He that hath lande and intendeth to gyue onely the possessyon and freeholde thereof to another and to kepe the profytes to hym selfe ought in reason and conscyence to haue the profytes seynge there ys no lawe made to prohybyt but that in conscyence suche reseruacyon may be made.[19]

As the discussion unfolds, St German records the argument that, since the *cestuy que use* had no title in law, the conveyance would be *nudum pactum* (a naked promise) without some kind of valuable consideration. But he also argues that, even without consideration, such promises should hold good in conscience:

> Yf a man seased of land make a gyfte thereof by a nude promyse without any lyuerey of season or recompense to hym made: & graunt that he shall be seased to his vse: that though that promyse be voyd in the law: that yet neuertheles yt must holde and stande good in conscyence & by the law of reason.[20]

Referring to a class of promise called an avow – a promise made 'upon a deliberate mind entending to perform it ... though it be only made in the heart without pronouncing of words' – the Doctor asserts that

> in all such promises it must be understand that he that made the promise intended to be bound by his promise for else commonly after all doctors he is not bounde unless he were bound to it before his promise. As if a man promise to give his father a gown that hath nede of it to kepe him from cold and yet thinketh not to give him, nevertheless he is bound to give it for he was bound thereto before.[21]

I want to argue that St German's discussion, in particular this striking illustration of the naked promise as a son's obligation to provide his father with a gown to keep him warm, provided Shakespeare with an imaginative template for the literal and metaphorical journey Lear makes from the beginning of the play to his confrontation with the naked Edgar and subsequent self-exposure, and for the autobiographical position from which he approached it. I am not suggesting that the text invites us to see Lear's division of the kingdom as in any technical sense a 'use'. Indeed, the words Lear uses to vest his divided kingdom in Goneril and Regan are those traditionally associated with the granting of a fee simple: 'to thine and Albany's issues be this perpetual' (1.1.64–5):[22] 'To thee and thine hereditary ever ...' (77–8). But the fundamental principle of the use, described by St German as 'giving the possession' and 'keeping the profit', and the trust-based principles on which it is based, unquestionably underpins Lear's negotiations with his daughters.[23] In this situation, his request for a quantitative statement of his daughters' love ('which of you shall we say doth love us most' [48]), and Goneril and Regan's provision of it, can be seen as a rhetorical form of consideration; as we saw in Chapter 5, the 'recompense' without which such promises could not be held to be binding in law. It is noticeable that legal terms from St German's discussion emerge onto the surface of Shakespeare's language, very much in the same way that the term 'assure' straddles legal and everyday senses in *The Taming of The Shrew* – notably the term 'reservation' ('the action or fact of reserving or retaining for oneself some right or interest in property which is being conveyed to another; an instance of this; a right or interest so retained; the clause or part of a deed by which something is thus reserved'),[24] which Lear uses to refer to his group of knights ('Ourselves by monthly course With reservation of an hundred knights By you to be sustained' [132–4]), and the term 'consideration' itself, ironically used by Kent to urge Lear 'in thy best consideration check This hideous rashness' (148–9).

Despite the fact that they have provided the requisite quantities of love and affection, Goneril and Regan do not consider their undertaking to their father to be binding, and this 'reservation' becomes the focus of their cancellation of their 'deed of love' (2.2.69). The speech that responds to this breach of trust at 2.2.430 is a brilliant adaptation of St German's metaphor of the needy father as the figure of the naked promise. It is also the dramatic starting point for the process by which Lear comes to embody this figure in the scenes that follow:

> O, reason not the need! Our basest beggars
> Are in the poorest thing superfluous.
> Allow not nature more than nature needs,
> Man's life is cheap as beast's. Thou art a lady;
> If only to go warm were gorgeous,
> Why, nature needs not what thou, gorgeous, wearest,
> Which scarcely keeps thee warm. But, for true need –
> You heavens, give me that patience, patience I need.
>
> 2.2.430

It is in the scenes on the heath that we become aware that questions of clothing have acquired the force of theatrical reflexivity and of the autobiographical charge; and that these hitherto opposing institutional energies are becoming one. Edgar's sympathetic tears – 'my tears begin to take his part so much They mar my counterfeiting' (3.6.17–18) – invite comparison with the plays I have discussed in Chapter 5 as episodes where such an exchange signalled a mutual recognition by player and spectator of the shared value of performance. Here, the exchange is between a king precipitated by his experience of a performance into a mental state in which he no longer knows that he is a spectator or the player a player, and a player knowingly engaged in a performance that is intended to render its spectator incapable of making these distinctions. When Lear, faced with the spectacle of the naked Edgar, identifies him as 'the thing itself', there is a startlingly modern effect of phenomenological reduction that brings St German's needy father face to face with John Shakespeare and the clothworker's art: 'Is man no more than this? Consider him well. Thou owest the worm no silk, the beast no hide, the sheep no wool, the cat no perfume' (3.4.92–7).[25]

I would like to be able to propose that what we are witnessing in these scenes is a stern challenge to the emerging aesthetics of Jonsonian masque, with its idealisation of a passive royal spectatorship and assimilation of performance into the spectacle of Jacobean absolutism: Jonson's first masques, *The Coronation Triumph, The Entertainment of the Queen and Prince Henry at Althorp, The Masque of Blackness*, had begun to be presented in early 1604–5. But *Lear*'s variant readings complicate such an idea.[26] Q1 suggests that Lear has some insight into the Shakespearean values he is confronting at this point, and aligns our understanding with his: 'Come on, be true' (11.92). But F shows him engaged only in the physical act of disrobing, and in doing so distances our response to him by making us aware that we are watching him: 'come, unbutton here' (3.4.97–8). In other words, at a climactic point in an argument about the very nature of theatre, the play's textual variants appear to take opposing sides. How do we approach the institutional implications of such a thing?

The contrast between the ways Q1 and F handle the question of consideration in 1.1 may help answer the question. Where Q1 states simply that Lear intends to 'shake all cares and business *off our state*' (1.37), F emphasises his age: 'shake all cares and business *from our age ... while we Unburdened crawl toward death*' (1.1.37–9). It also tells us, as Q does not, that in this situation he has decided 'to publish Our daughter's several dowers, that future strife May be prevented later' (42–4). (This increased detail about precise mechanisms of conveyance might almost suggest that Shakespeare went back to his sources between Q1 and F or even perhaps read some of them for the first time when he was thinking about rewriting it.) Thus, by the time F's Lear turns to his daughters with the all-important question 'which of you shall we say doth love us most?' (49) we can (just about) understand his action as the result of a considered, even responsible, decision. At this point, F's insertion of an additional two lines between the two parts of that question – 'Tell me my daughters '*Since now we will divest us both of rule, Interest of territory, cares of state* – Which of you shall we say doth love us most?' (47–8) – tells us exactly what that decision is: that he intends to retain beneficial ownership of his property. He will divest himself of rule, interest and cares, but *not* title. We *infer* from Q1 that the underlying paradigm of property is that of beneficial ownership, but F states it, and in doing so provides justification for Lear's request for, and Goneril and Regan's subsequent offers of, a rhetorical form of consideration. On the other hand, Q1 provides more insight into the questions of conscience raised by it. When Cordelia replies to her father, both Q1 and F tell us that she loves him 'according to my bond, no more, nor less'. But their treatment of the preceding asides give this bond very different weight. Q1 has 'What shall Cordelia do? Love and be silent' (1.54), followed by 'Then poor

Cordelia – And yet not so since I am sure my love's More richer than my tongue' (69–70). Here, the idea of silence is presented as a positive form of agency explicitly contrasted with her sisters' quantitative statements of love. As such, it echoes St German's identification of a promise made 'upon a deliberate mind entending to perform it ... though it be only made in the heart *without pronouncing of words*'. In other words, Q1 gives us a Cordelia who is silent, not because she does not intend to be bound, but because her love constitutes an undertaking *that was binding even before it was made*. Having created a situation in which the audience could understand why Lear might ask for 'recompense', F suggests that the only reason Cordelia fails to provide it is that her language is inadequate to the task of calculation: 'What shall Cordelia speak? Love and be silent' (1.1.59); 'Then poor Cordelia – And yet not so since I am sure my love's More ponderous than my tongue' (74–6).[27]

Since Shakespeare did not *have* to bring Greene's idea of silence into this story, and the idea of silence is ultimately what makes most sense of the play's engagement with St German, should we not decide that the text that most clearly demonstrates the rationale for its inclusion should be described, as Stanley Wells and Gary Taylor describe it, as 'the play as Shakespeare first conceived it, probably before it was performed'?[28] In Q1, we arrive at the crux of Shakespeare's *use* of Greene. Q1 presents Cordelia's 'silence' as an inward act of conscience rather than public performance, thus encouraging us to align her defence of the nakedness of her promise – 'so young, my lord, and true' (1.1.105) – with Lear's later revelation of his own nakedness on the heath. With its affiliation to the principles that underpin the worlds of his Elizabethan comedies, in particular their systematic development of the father–daughter relationship as a template for the innovative creation of theatrical property, this perception carries the weight of the older Shakespeare's obligation to his own younger imagination of theatre; an obligation given further weight by a son's obligation to the father with which that imagination is so intimately bound.

If that is the case, we have to acknowledge the full implications of F's Lear-like expulsion of the Cordelia-like Q1. In both versions, Cordelia has been made a stranger by the end of the first Act. Lear describes her as such, twice: 'a stranger to my heart and me' (1.105; 1.1.113); 'strangered with our oath' (1.191; 1.1.201). F's effective endorsement of the principle of consideration against Q1's trust in the naked promise aligns the action with Lear's analysis of this estrangement. In the dialogue that precedes Q1/F's joint statement, 'so young, my lord, and true' (1.97; 1.1.105), Q1 asserts, 'Sure, I shall never marry like my sisters / To love my father all', but then asks, 'But goes this with thy heart?'(1.92–4).

F asserts, 'Sure, I shall never marry like my sisters', but asks 'But goes thy heart with this?' (1.1.101–2). *Both* echo St German's notion of the 'deliberate mind entending to perform ... *though it be only made in the heart* without pronouncing of words', but where Q1 retains the implicit distinction between an intending mind and the heart, F amalgamates the two, preparing us for the play's sustained attention to Lear's heart as where, and indeed *what*, we experience throughout the play that follows. I suggested that these textual variants make it hard to generalise about the relation between Shakespeare's vision of theatre in *Lear* and Jonsonian masque. We know that *King Lear* was the first play performed at court at the beginning of the Christmas season acted before James at court 1606–7, and that Q1 was entered into the Stationers' Register after this in 1607. Grace Ioppolo has proposed that the revisions from Q1 to F were 'almost certainly made during the same period in the course of preparing the original play for later performances'.[29] If this is the case, can we surmise that the effect of those changes, the shift from Q1's conscientious resistance to the reduction of Cordelia's love to contract, to F's redemption of contract by Lear's passion, is also associated with the play's performance at court? I think so. From an institutional perspective, we might then see *King Lear* as a protracted period of writing (but not, *pace* Ioppolo, open-ended)[30] radically divided between the conditions of its own past and those of its future; between the principles of beneficial ownership associated with the Elizabethan world of Shakespearean comedy, and the rise of the Jacobean contractualism.

It is tempting to assume that, for Shakespeare, the first of these was 'good' and the second 'bad', but his extraordinary capacity to keep reinventing the institutional conditions for Shakespearean theatre suggests otherwise. F affiliates it to a modernity that might now, cautiously, be seen as the basis of something like a public sphere. I noted above that F's 'come, unbutton here' distances us from Lear by isolating our critical response to him within the physical process of observation, of 'seeing feelingly' (4.5.141). The play consistently exploits effects of 'close up', both in narration and in direct action, that serve paradoxically to make spectators aware how far away they are, even in a custom-built theatre, and how difficult it is to understand, most notably in the all-but-unimaginable visual chaos of the final scene, which culminates in Lear's business with the looking glass, the feather, and his final words, only in F, 'Do you see this? Look on her. Look, her lips Look there, look there' (5.3.285–6). I suggested at the end of Chapter 6 that the mesh of intersecting perspectives in 'Aeneas' Tale' creates a collective public gaze embodied in Hamlet's single position of spectatorship. *Lear*'s techniques of visualisation create a spectator who is private within the auditorium, an effect that is enhanced by its distinctive approach to dramatic duration. Just as *The Merchant of Venice* and *As You Like It* negotiate the 'terms' of their occupation of theatrical space in highly characteristic spatio-temporal articulations, so *Lear* balances a continuum of shared history against intensely focused moments of private experience: references to 'time' (1.1.14; 1.2.175); 'this (sad) time' (5.3.323); 'the time' (3.2.93; 4.6.183; 5.1.54; 5.3.31, 233); 'my ... ', 'his ...' and 'our time(s)' (*passim*) are counterpoised against urgent, often desperate, calls to act 'in time' or 'in good time' (2.4.253; 4.7.92; 5.1.54; 5.3.247).

This brings the play to a conclusion that presents itself as a mapping of the duration of the play onto the space within which the audience 'feels' its 'weight': 'The weight of this sad time we must obey, Speak what we feel, not what we ought to say' (5.3.298–9). It is in this idea of a theatre that is both private and passionate that the status of Shakespearean theatre as public (in the sense implied by the concept of the public sphere)[31] can most convincingly be argued, since it is here that Shakespearean theatre engages in debates about the nature of obligation that look *beyond* institutional interests towards theories of association that would change the direction of seventeenth-century political thought. Victoria Kahn has identified 'a new discourse of the passions', which 'performed a crucial role in helping construct a subject who consents to be bound, who consents to bind himself'.[32] Her concern there was with the work of William Gouge, John Milton and Thomas Hobbes, but the 'trajectory' she identified – a transformation within the history of contract from 'the derivation of passion from obligation to the derivation of obligation from passion' that she was prepared to read back to 1604 and Thomas Wright's *The Passion of the Minde in General*[33] – is evident in case law across the same period. If *Levett v Hawes* suggested that, in 1599, questions of natural love could still take priority over contract, *Dutton v Poole* (1680) marks the final triumph of the doctrine of consideration over third party interest. This case is particularly illuminating for the study of *Lear*, though it might more appropriately be said that *Lear* is illuminating for the study of *Dutton v Poole*. Before her marriage to Sir Ralph Dutton, Grizil Poole's father decided to fell a stand of oak trees to raise her dowry. As the heir of the estate, her brother asked him not to do so, and in consideration promised that he would pay his sister £1000 after her marriage. After the marriage, the father died, the money was not paid and Grizil and her husband brought assumpsit for non-payment. The defence maintained that, since the promise had been made not to her but to her father, Grizil was neither privy nor interested in the consideration.

Notwithstanding, the King's Bench decided that she could maintain an action on a promise made to her father for her benefit. This decision was made, not because she had a third party interest, or even because natural love could be held to make the promise binding in conscience, but because her father's love was held to constitute a valuable consideration in which she could claim to have a direct interest.[34]

According to Vernon Palmer, 'the great difference between this case and any previous gift case of the 17th century was the assumption that the beneficiary's action must satisfy the consideration test or it would not lie'.[35] If so, its importance lies in the fact that it was not until duty of care was brought within the domain of the enforceable promise that such an assumption could be made. As a scenario that assimilates the priority Q1 gives to filial obligation into F's emergent framework of contract, *Dutton v Poole* might almost be seen as a conflation of these two texts. Ioppolo has described the 'type of editorial treatment' that produces a conflated text, somewhat provocatively, as 'fraudulent'.[36] One might open her description to a wider historical reading by suggesting that there is perhaps something within an agency of writing that keeps a play open to structural transformation in the way I have described in this chapter that might itself be described as fraudulent, albeit in that very creative sense of the word associated with the Elizabethan law of fraudulent conveyance: the transfer of one's property to another owner in order to avoid its loss to contractual obligations such as the payment of debt (and we saw in Chapter 2 that there were occasions when the Burbages were able to retain ownership of the Theatre only by such creative means).

If we return to the idea I put forward at the end of Chapter 5, that we can see Shakespeare's writing as a conjoint agency within a partnership in which the 'play' is a joint holding, then *Lear* might best be approached as a process of writing in which Shakespeare sought ways of preserving the value of the play to his company by moving it from one text to another, in a situation in which that value was subject to the incalculable fluctuations associated with the accession of James. It is in the reading *across* these texts, rather than in one or the other, and in their place, not simply in the history of an institution of theatre, but in the wider social history of which an institution of theatre is a part, that *Lear* explores the implications for Shakespearean theatre of what Roy Kreitner has described as 'a conception of contracting individuals as knowing and willful, as taking on obligations in measured, calculable increments, exchanging their obligations for precise values'.[37] The question that remains for my final chapter is how long such an exploration would remain satisfying for Shakespeare himself.

8
'Tis Time: *The Alchemist* and *The Tempest*

In 1608, the King's Men took possession of the Blackfriars theatre. After ten years of its occupation by the Chapel Children, the indoor theatre originally built by James Burbage as a relacement for the Theatre reverted to the ownership of the consortium that had been running the Globe: Richard and Cuthbert Burbage, who had inherited the lease from their father, John Hemminges, Henry Condell and William Shakespeare. Within a year, the King's Men had instituted a year-round schedule of performance, playing at the Globe in the summer and Blackfriars in the winter. Andrew Gurr describes the decision to play in two theatres as the realisation of James Burbage's 'vision' of 1594:

> The most conspicuous feature of the company's new grandeur was its display of absolute pre-eminence, a company with seasonal playhouses that could afford to keep one of them shut for half of each year at a time when other companies were seriously short of places to perform at.... The deal of 1608 made the company unique. Deciding to run two playhouses was the most hegemonic act of all its forty-eight years.[1]

However, it also radically altered the institutional ethos that characterised the company up to this point. The outdoor Globe played to popular audiences, the indoors Blackfriars to what Gurr refers to as 'high society':[2] from now on, the company would have to cater for both. To do so, they began to use writers who had previously written for the boys at the Blackfriars, notably Beaumont and Fletcher and Ben Jonson. The plays produced by these new writers imagined a theatre which was fundamentally different from the open duty circle of Shakespearean theatre, a theatre knowingly presented as an elite exploitation of vulgar gullibility.

It was also a theatre that was changing in its relation to the institutions of publication. If, at the end of Elizabeth's reign, Shakespeare dominated the market for printed plays, by the second decade of the seventeenth century that market was beginning to display a more nuanced mode of demand. As Zachary Lesser has shown, publishers began to pursue the profit potential of an elite readership. In 1613, Walter Burre published *The Knight of the Burning Pestle*, which had played unsuccessfully at the Blackfriars in 1607, presenting it as a play that was 'privy' not to the 'vulgar braine' but to 'good wits'. Burre specialised in plays, including Jonson's *The Alchemist*, written for the King's Men and first performed in autumn 1610, which were organised around a spectator-figure who is himself a 'wit' and whose activities are themselves seen as an exploitation of gullible spectators.[3] Gurr has argued that Lovewit, the owner of the house in Blackfriars in which the action of *The Alchemist* takes place, was intended to represent Shakespeare, now a 'housekeeper' at the Blackfriars but no longer a full-time presence with the company in London.[4] Jonson's rising status in the wake of Shakespeare's partial withdrawal may be seen in the fact that, with *Epicoene* in 1609, he made what Richard Dutton has described as 'a deliberate and calculated switch to recognisably Jacobean London settings'.[5] In the Prologue to *The Alchemist*, he begins with the familiar call for a discriminating reception (couched paradoxically in the suggestion that 'judging spectators' should stay away in order to avoid being duped), followed immediately by a claim for the pre-eminence of London as the setting for a play 'cause we would make it known No country's mirth is better than our own'. I argued in Chapter 4 that the London setting of *Richard III* can be seen as institutionally performative, a welcome to the 'chamber' of Shakespearean theatre in its pre-duopoly years. At the redefining point in the history of the institution of theatre that arose from Shakespeare's success, Jonson's dramatisation of London for the King's Men may have had a comparable function. If so, Shakespeare's corresponding switch to temporally and spatially distant locations may constitute an equally calculated means of distancing Shakespearean theatre from this new principle of occupation.

The implications of the possibility that the 'hegemony' of 1608 was founded on a clash of incompatible institutional values are considerable.[6] They raise the question how we should understand the King's Men *as* an institution after the establishment of the two-theatre set-up: as a continuation of the process of institutionalisation that had taken place up across the 1590s and into James' reign? As its apotheosis in the establishment of a generic institution of theatre now aspiring to the condition of a public sphere? Or as something completely different? Andrew Gurr has proposed that 'The Blackfriars was the company's ultimate security. It tied them to their royal patrons and courtly interests, and when royalty fell they did so too.'[7] I suggested in Chapter 2 that the Globe lease and indenture gave the Chamberlain's Men a future 'as secure as an Elizabethan future could be'. Do we really see that company as one that within a few years would be 'tied' to courtly interests? If in 1608 they had passed up on the Blackfriars, maintained only the Globe with its traditional audience base and confined their courtly interests to formal appearances, what would their future have been, or that of professional theatre in London over the next few decades? Once again, much virtue in 'if'; but the question does at least allow us to consider the possibility that what evolved over the years between 1603 and 1608 was a *different* institution: different principles of legitimation; different prerogatives, different occupied social space. Since the most significant contrast between the pre- and post-Blackfriars partnership lies in the nature of Shakespeare's agency within it, this could be a useful discrimination. I suggested in Chapter 7 that alterations across the two versions of *Lear* display a 'drift' from the trust-based duty circle of the Elizabethan plays towards a new Jacobean contractualism. I want to suggest in this final chapter that this drift comes to an arrest in the face-off between Jonson and Shakespeare in *The Alchemist* and *The Tempest*, and that this arrest is perhaps the best way to approach both Shakespeare's withdrawal from London around 1609–10 and our understanding of the institution of theatre that survived it.

'Twas time

Andrew Gurr has described the relationship between the two men as a friendship, but his own account suggests that that might not be quite the right word: 'initially...colleagues and rivals', their relationship became a 'more complex interaction' around 1605, when Jonson satirised aspects of *Lear* in *Volpone*, and thereafter, on Jonson's side, openly critical: his scathing derogation of '*Tales, Tempests* and such-like drolleries' in the Induction to *Bartholomew Fair*; his sarcasm about *The Winter's Tale*'s nonexistent Bohemian coastline in the 'Conversations' with Drummond of Hawthornden, and the description in his 'Ode to Himself upon the Censure of his *New Inn*' of *Pericles* as a 'mouldy tale'.[8] Gurr concludes that the links between the two playwrights are so intense and consistent that we cannot doubt a close human link, too. The bond may have been especially potent in 1610, when Shakespeare was beginning to detach himself from daily work with the King's Men, and Jonson had returned to write for the company.[9]

Such a relationship may indeed have been a 'bond', but was it a merry one? The word is useful, since in the very flexibility of its conditions for satisfaction it draws our attention not only to fundamental differences in the way both men articulate their sense of professional obligation, and indeed obligation to their profession, but also to the possibility that they were in some sense bound *to each other*, as Shylock and Antonio were bound to each other, by opposing claims to the same set of interests. In chapters which deal with *The Alchemist* and *The Tempest* separately and make no cross-reference between them, Luke Wilson notes an equivalence in both writers' work between the contracts that underpinned theatrical employment and a conception of dramatic action based on notions of promissory performance.[10] But in any comparison between the two, we repeatedly come up against the implications of the difference between a beneficial ownership in which the interests of all parties remain open and negotiable, and one-to-one contractual obligation.

This contrast manifests itself at every level of their professional lives. Shakespeare was committed to long-term institutional continuities; Jonson to an immediate critical and financial return on the individual play. Where Shakespeare created open-ended formal and thematic continuities between plays across all stages of his career (and would unquestionably have seen those continuities as part of his audience's experience of individual productions), Jonson gave priority to a neoclassical conception of the individual play based on self-contained principles of formal and stylistic unity. Shakespeare worked with one company of players, with a remarkably consistent membership, for almost the whole of his career. Jonson seems to have had no consistent ties within the theatre profession even after 1608: following the disaster of *Catiline* in 1611, he took his next play, *Bartholomew Fair*, to the newly formed Lady Elizabeth's Men playing at the new Hope theatre in an effort, according to Luke Wilson, 'to distinguish his own work from the kind of material the King's Men had been putting on, particularly, as the Induction [to *Bartholomew Fair*] hints, plays like *The Winter's Tale* and *The Tempest'*.[11] Of course, he had no obligation to loyalty, but he also seems to have had little inclination to it, and it is not surprising to find a clash between

Shakespearean and Jonsonian values given embodiment in these two plays.

It is also not surprising to find that in *The Alchemist*, the brunt of Jonson's satire against the theatre in general and the King's Men in particular lay in accusing *them* of grasping contractualism. Gurr describes Lovewit as an 'application' of Shakespeare,[12] but if aspects of the play suggests that the application may be more general than that, it is certainly a satirical representation of the King's Men at the Blackfriars, written in terms that purport to expose their relation to their audiences as one of exploitation. This representation is explicit in the 'Argument' provided in Walter Burre's edition, published after *Catiline* in 1612, which describes how

> The sickness hot, a master quit, for fear,
> His house in town, and left one servant there.
> Ease him corrupted, and gave means to know
> A cheater and his punk...
> ...only wanting some
> House to set up, with him they there contract,
> Each for a share, and all begin to act.[13]

If in performance at the Blackfriars the audience lacked this paratextual direction, they only had to wait 45 lines, at which point Face (played by Richard Burbage) points out to Subtle, presumably with an appropriate physical gesture to the theatre itself, that he has 'lent you beside A house to practise in', and Subtle scathingly replies 'Your master's house... Yes, in your master's house. You and the rats kept possession' (1.1.47; 49–50).

Despite Gurr's confidence in identifying this 'master' as Shakespeare, subsequent dialogue suggests that the roles of sharer are spread loosely across the four main parts. There are hints of an association between Subtle and Shakespeare, and of the Subtle-Face relationship as something like Manningham's account of personal and professional one-upmanship between Shakespeare and Burbage. Subtle tells Face that he has 'raised thee from brooms and dust and watering pots' (do we catch here a faint echo of the famous episode with the broomhandle in the Theatre yard?)[14] 'put thee in words and fashion? Made thee fit For more than ordinary fellowships... Made thee a second in mine own great art?' (67; 72–3; 77). Jonson refers not simply to the allocation of professional responsibilities within the company, but also to the relationship between those responsibilities and broader questions of political association raised by the notion of partnership. Doll refers to Face and Subtle as Sovereign and General, and to herself as their 'republic' (110) and she tries to reconcile them by reminding them of their mutual obligations: 'As if... the work Were not begun out of equality? The venture tripartite? All things in common? Without priority?' (133–6). In reply, Face blames Subtle: ''Tis his fault. He ever murmurs and objects his pains, And says the weight of all lies upon him'. When Subtle confirms this opinion, Doll insists, in terms that anticipate Gerard Malynes, 'Do not we Sustain our parts?'

> *Subtle*: Yes, but they are not equal.
> *Doll*: Why if your part exceed today, I hope
> Ours may tomorrow match it.
>
> 144–7

However we allocate the parts in this partnership, the play drives a public wedge between them and follows it home in its representation of the bond they offer their customers. Luke Wilson present an excellent account of the play as 'a series of bargains and agreements, of mutual promises to do or refrain from doing' and suggests that 'the close correspondence' between Lovewit's house and the Blackfriars playhouse helps produce 'a palimpsestic relation between the contractual exchanges performed on stage and the contractual exchanges by which the play itself, and its performance, have come into being'.[15] But he does not discuss Lovewit at all, and therefore brackets off the fact that the play clearly proposes that ownership of the house is the precondition for this kind of behaviour. He thus subordinates an account of the *particular* institutional situation engaged by this play to the proposal that its 'contractual nexus' reflects the *general* condition under which 'dramatic and theatrical labor was conducted in early modern London'.[16] In the process, he excludes from consideration an 'autobiographical charge' of almost Frankensteinian proportions:

> As we have seen, contract in *The Achemist* is closely tied to the aggressive impulses evident throughout much of Jonson's work... This sort of violent scatological aggression has been explained as a symptom of Jonson's personality; I propose here instead that in the contract-permeated theatrical business, aggression is systemic, a result of the competition for scarce resources.[17]

The problem with this is not only that it does not apply to this particular context of production – as Gurr suggests, the King's Men were not strapped for cash – but that *The Alchemist* itself, a play written *because* the company now owned two theatres, is evidence of this. Unless we attend to the details of this specific institutional interaction we cannot account for the way Jonsonian authorship emerges through this play, not just as part of a general historical trend towards possessive authorship, but as a highly particular response to Shakespeare and the King's Men at a highly particular point in their history, or indeed for its effect on the institution they had created. This is not, of course, to suggest that this was the only occasion on which Jonson articulated a distaste for the theatre and preference for publication; only that the force of that articulation was, so to speak, structurally personal. Zachary Lesser points out that the Latin epigram appended to Burre's publication of *The Alchemist* 'makes explicit Jonson's hope of finding a better audience in print than in the theatre: "*Neque, me vt miretur turba, labore*: *Contentus paucis lectoribus.*"' ("Nor do I work so that the crowd might admire me: I am satisfied with a few readers.")'.[18] But Jonson's aim was not a simple act of textual remediation. What he had in mind was nothing less than a structural transformation: from an institution of theatre to the institution of literature.

Ultimately, this is what binds and divides these two men: the unique but incompatible institutionalising energies of their creative ambitions. Gurr suggests that the play's 'application' to Shakespeare and the King's Men may not have been recognised by its audiences,[19] but such a statement may constitute more an implicit acknowledgement of the Jonsonian disavowal of Shakespearean theatre than a fact about its spectators, who, as we have seen, were perfectly capable of associating their response to individual plays with entertaining stories about its leading men sleeping with the customers. At the very least we can assume that the application would have been recognised by Shakespeare and his fellows, and that their response to it in *The Tempest* would in its turn have been recognised by Jonson. The curious circularity of this relationship – that sense again of opposing claims to the same set of interests – informs the way these two plays rewrite, or better, *un*-write, each other. Where Subtle tells Face that he has 'put thee in words and fashion...made thee fit For more than ordinary fellowships', Prospero reminds Caliban he 'took pains to make thee speak...endowed thy purposes With words that made them known' (1.2.357; 360–1); Doll's idea of herself as a republic under the sway of a sovereign and a general opens up into Gonzalo's Utopian musings about king and commonwealth. Point by point, Shakespeare's apparent aim, and achievement, in *The Tempest* was not simply to answer *The Alchemist*; it was to turn the mirror of Shakespearean theatre on the social and political framework by which the play's contempt for popular theatre legitimated itself. If, within 45 lines, Jonson's spectators knew that what they were looking at and thinking about were the Blackfriars and the King's Men, by the end of 1.2 Shakespeare's spectators could have been in no doubt that the object of their gaze was the very image of Jonsonian monarchy. *The Alchemist* begins with a parodic account of theatrical labour undertaken in absence of the owner of the house; *The Tempest* responds with a spectacular contrast between sovereignty and collective labour which proceeds to a comprehensive vindication of that labour. Prospero's injunction to Ariel, 'the time twixt now and six Must by us both be spent most preciously' may lay down the terms for what David Lindley describes as an 'exceptional observance of temporal unity',[20] but those terms are dishonest, and Ariel confronts them as such. In reply to Prospero's subsumption of his labour into the specious profligacy of 'precious spending', he demands, 'is there more toil?' and proceeds to remind Prospero of the reciprocality of their mutual obligation: 'Let me remember thee what thou hast promised Which is not yet performed me' (1.2.241–4).

Prospero and Ariel's initial confrontation opens up into a thoroughgoing exposure of the ethical values that underpin the Jonsonian principle of unity: the isolation of its contributory elements into a series of alienated one-to-one contractual exchanges. Once Face, Subtle and Doll have lured their dupes to the Blackfriars house, the success of their scheme depends on being able to keep each strand of the action separate. There is no privity between the parties seeking to enter into agreements with these fraudsters, and the play's 'comedy' derives from the ruses by which their isolation from each other is maintained – emblematically, Dapper's distasteful sequestration in the privy – and from the sequence of temporal crises that threatens to collapse it. The play is punctuated by temporal markers that constantly alert us to the coordination of activities under the pressure of the play's running time, figured as a process of alchemical 'casting'.[21] Pretending to talk Subtle into accepting Dapper's *assumpsit*, Face urges, 'he may make us both happy in an hour' (1.2.119). They only just have time to usher him out before Drugger comes in: 'Conduct him forth, by the back way. Sir, against one c'clock, prepare yourself' (164–5). They then only just succeed in getting Drugger offstage in time for Mammon's arrival, 'coming along, at far end of the lane (1.4.7). The Mammon plot, occupying most of 2.1–2.3, is then ushered offstage with an injunction to return 'within two hours' (2.3.298), again only just in time for Ananias and then Tribulation: 'O are you come? 'Twas time' (3.2.1). This hectic momentum almost gives way in the lead-up to Mammon's return at the beginning of 4.1: "'Yonder's your knight, Sir Mammon" "God's lid, we never thought of him, till now. Where is he?" "Here, hard by, at the door"' (3.5.51) – a crisis that leads up to the 'explosion' at 4.5.64. They appear to be getting away with it all until Lovewit's unforeseen return and entry at the beginning of 5.1, but if Lovewit's conference with his neighbours leads directly to his triumph, it produces no exposure, because he covers up for them and steps in to take the profit.

The hour's now come

Where *The Alchemist* presents this crisis-based temporal sequencing of multiple strands of action as the intensification of promissory performance, *The Tempest* identifies it as radically split between Prospero's intention and Ariel's agency, and it is in this split that the play's presentation of the unity of time reveals itself as exposure rather than observance. Prospero describes Ariel's 'disposition' of the royal party into 'troops...dispersed 'bout the isle' (1.2.220) as an 'exact' performance of his command, and repeatedly asks him if he is continuing to perform exactly. Equally repeatedly, Ariel makes it clear that the exactness of his performance both anticipates and exceeds Prospero's demands. The most spectacular example of this is, of course, the masque and its dissolution at 4.1. Once again, Prospero subsumes Ariel's agency into his need for exorbitant display ('I must Bestow...Some vanity of mine art' [4.1.39–41]), and identifies it as *his* obligation to Ferdinand and Miranda ('It is my promise And they expect it from me' [41–2]). Ariel, who has been 'given power' over the rabble who will perform, collapses the promissory interval, thus demonstrating the fact that his agency in this display precedes the command to perform it 'presently: 'Before you can say come and go...Each one tripping on his toe Will be here...' (43–6).

Thus, in reply to the Jonsonian insinuation that the Shakespearean owner-master who gives the use of his house to his servants but keeps the possession is the precondition for the fraudulent activities that take place within it, Shakespeare presents a Jonsonian sovereign-master whose expensive 'art' may be 'power', but is demonstrably not agency. For this, he relies on servants whose skill is self-evidently the precondition of his capacity to command. To confirm this, the play's temporal unity – reflexively presented in the masque of Iris, Ceres and Juno – is disrupted by Prospero's 'forgetting' of 'the foul conspiracy' of Caliban and his confederates. Of course, when he calls Ariel, we learn that Ariel had the situation under control all the time: 'At last I left them I' th' filthy-mantled pool beyond your cell, There dancing up to th' chins' (81–3). This is worth emphasising, because the famous 'our revels now are ended' speech, with its vision of the ephemerality of theatre, is actually made in the 'twink' (Prospero's word at 43) between Ariel's exit at the end of the masque (if we assume his participation as Ceres) at l.143 and his re-entry at l.163. That is to say, it articulates Prospero's position as master-provider of the masque, but *not* that of Ariel and his fellows as the servant-labour that turns its hand supremely to whatever 'toil' the maintenance of this vision requires – strictly on the understanding that what they will eventually receive as satisfaction for their bond will be 'freedom'.

Prospero's 'forgetting' is not, as in *The Alchemist*'s point of danger prior to Mammon's return, simply a crisis within the control of 'his' plot. It alerts us to the idea that shapes this Shakespearean reflection on Jonsonian drama. What brings unity of time in *The Tempest* to the point of collapse is not the conspicuous Jonsonian investment in a display of formal virtuousity; it is the fact that, as in the Elizabethan comedies, 'time travels in divers paces for divers persons' (*As You Like It* 3.2.236), and that a single point within it, whether that of a single play within a career of writing, or a moment of action within the single play, is part of a theatrical *longue durée* intersected by multiple narratives, each with its own distinct organisation of time. Each member of the group that makes up the complex temporal nexus of *The Tempest* has a past and a future in a way that is unknown in Jonson. Just as the two opening scenes together establish the play's defining contrast between power and agency, so they also counterpoise the extreme presentness of the sea storm ('we split, we split...we split, we split, we split!' [1.2.55–6]) with Prospero's equally extreme act of recall, initiated by the signals "tis time...the hour's now come' (1.2.23; 36), in his narrative to Miranda. Throughout this account of his past, which his daughter tells us he has begun many times before but many times delayed until now, his narrative is similarly marked by constant prompts to the present ('Dost thou attend me?...thou attendst not!...Dost thou hear? [78; 87; 106]). A similar balance between moment and *durée* structures his relationship with Ariel, where it makes us aware of the precise nature of the personal and professional values that lie in the balance between the two: 'what ist thou can demand? My liberty. Before the time be out?' (246–8). Throughout the play, Jonsonian unity is subjected to the violent pressure of the 'dark backward and abyss of time' (50), with its multiple points of retrospect (Miranda's women; Dido; Sycorax; the man in the moon) and the pressure of *Jetzheit*, now-ness, wrenching the present from the past and forcing it into the future. And where *The Alchemist* simply closes its unity around Lovewit, its owner figure, *The Tempest* brings its multiple strands together, like *As You Like It*, into a single coordinated collective co-presence, ending with a recapitulation of the 'dark backward' of the play's beginning in Alonso's 'longing to hear the story of your life' and the *mise-en-abyme* of Prospero's undertaking to 'deliver all' (5.1.3–3.7).

This institutional reunification of time is our key to Miranda. As David Lindley points out, Miranda challenges both contemporary perspectives on the play – he cites Ann Thompson's rather bleak assertion that there is no available pleasure in her for contemporary women – and any attempt to find continuities with earlier Shakespearean creations such as Rosalind or Viola.[22] To a certain extent, reading the play as a response to Jonson solves this problem, since it suggests that this discontinuity might be the point: Miranda is a Jonsonian 'ripe daughter', a sacrificial offering to the principle of royal husbandry whose sole purpose is to secure the Jacobean succession, and with it the presiding power of Jonsonian authorship.[23] But her institutional role in what Giddens refers to as the 'tie between the *durée* of the passing moment, and the *longue durée* of deeply sedimented time-space relations' is the key to understanding this Shakespearean recuperation of *The Alchemist's* Dame Pliant.[24] The focus of Shakespeare's un-writing of Jonson is neither, singly, Miranda nor Prospero. It is, rather, the father–daughter *relation*, recapitulated in this play both as the heart of its own action and as the generative principle of Shakespearean theatre throughout Shakespeare's career. Miranda is an instantiation of the third party agency I discussed in Chapter 5. Indeed, in some ways she is a return to the kind of 'pure' third party position I noted in non-present characters like young Elizabeth in *Richard the Third* and in characters like Celia, who go silently into their marriages at the end of their plays. The father–daughter relationship, with the apparently irresistible imaginative impetus we noted in *Levett v Hawes* and in the 'phantasticall conceit' Sir Anthony Mildmay took all the way through the courts in an effort to secure his daughter's inheritance,[25] puts at the centre of this play what Shakespeare has asserted throughout his career as the underlying principle in his creation of a special property in theatre – and of course, in so doing, comprehensively answers the accusation levelled at theatrical ownership embodied in the figure of Lovewit. Prospero tells us that twelve years have passed since Miranda was a baby in Milan; *The Winter's Tale* has a temporal break of sixteen years between Perdita's abandonment at the end of Act III and reappearance as a young woman in Act IV. This disjunction – the time it takes a daughter to leave a father and become a wife – takes the plot back to the beginning of its action, but it also plots Shakespeare's career back to the point at which the present of this play was still the future he worked to create and sustain, and from which, writing this last solo performance at home in Stratford,[26] he now began to take his well-earned leave.[27]

After times

> Poor Poet-Ape, that would be thought our chief,
> Whose works are e'en the frippery of wit,
> From brocage is become so bold a thief,
> As we, the robbed, leave rage, and pity it.
> At first he made low shifts, would pick and glean,
> Buy the reversion of old plays; now grown
> To a little wealth, and credit in the scene,
> He takes up all, makes each man's wit his own,
> And told of this, he slights it. Tut, such crimes
> The sluggish, gaping auditor devours;
> He marks not whose 'twas first, and after times
> May judge it to be his, as well as ours.
> Fool! as if half-eyes will not know a fleece
> From locks of wool, or shreds from the whole piece![28]

In this poem, part of the collection 'Epigrams' published in the Folio *Works* in the year of Shakespeare's death, Jonson executes the use of a Shakespearean beneficial literary ownership. A reversion is a procedure by which the interest in a property or estate, transferred by an instrument such as a use, deed of trust or mortgage, reverts to its titleholder after that interest is exhausted; the sale of reversions was yet another way of exploiting the separation of possession and use.

Although 'Poet-Ape' has been popularly held to be what Loewenstein has described as 'one of [Jonson's] several famous swipes at Shakespeare',[29] most Jonsonians prefer to read it in a more general relation to the conceptual categories that would emerge from an institution of literature. Timothy Murray locates the poet-ape in Jonson's anti-theatrical bias, and reads his 'retreat from the public theater' into a wider concern with the 'degradation' of poetry and authors;[30] Marjorie Swann sees the poem as an attack on plagiarism.[31] To a certain extent approaches like this could be said to reproduce Jonson's un-writing of Shakespeare by submitting what is obviously and distinctively a Shakespearean approach to dramatic authorship to the adjudication of a concept of literary value that purports to precede the practice of writing to which it is in fact a response. Jonson's account of the act of 'taking up all' which 'makes each man's wit his own' invests the authors of the 'old plays' with a 'title' to their work that has priority over its transfer to another owner. It gives 'the old play' a retrospective moment of self-possession – 'he marks not whose 'twas first' – which is mirrored in the *mistaken* judgement by 'after times', who 'may judge it to be his...'. The curious little afterthought that follows this – '*as well as ours*' – gives the game away, since it is clearly designed to disguise the poem's possessive energies as a principled concern for a public domain. Jonson's animus against a writer whom he accuses of thinking of himself as 'the best in this kind' articulates itself *against* the poet-ape's creation of a special property in theatre as a literary authorship that is not so much possessive as *re*possessive, an action of recovery. Is there in these last lines – 'Fool! as if half-eyes will not know a fleece From locks of wool' – a mocking allusion to John Shakespeare and the clothworker's art? The buried reference here to the story of the golden fleece reinforces the notion that the old text had a value that is lost when exploited by its new owner; paradoxical, of course, because, as John Shakespeare's son knew very well, it is only in its *use* as wool that a fleece has value.

We may have to face the fact that the categories that underpin the modern institution of literature are grounded in a paradigm of authorship that is at some fundamental level *anti*-Shakespearean. This idea of a right of possession poised between retrospect to a lost original and the prospect of its future misrecognition, reveals the underlying temporality of a concept of literary property that seeks to combine a literary *longue durée* with the limited term of copyright. It is a temporality that Jonson used Shakespeare to legitimate in the commendatory verse he supplied seven years later for the first Folio edition of *Mr.William Shakespeare's Comedies, Histories & Tragedies*: 'To the memory of my beloved, The Author Mr WILLIAM SHAKESPEARE: AND *what he hath left us*'. We note again the bad faith, not just of 'my beloved', but of a first-person plural afterthought, here with its hint both of a 'will', a legacy, and of a public domain. In contrast to 'Poet-Ape"s metaphor of property, this poem uses a notion of immortality – 'not of an age but for all time' – based on aristocratic ideals of nature and lineage. In other words, where 'Poet-Ape' placed the Shakespeare-figure's industry *outside* the public good, 'To the memory of my beloved', evidently captivated by the prospect that its writer is about to profit privately from his loss, places the public idea(l) of the dead poet at its heart.

However, Shakespeare's afterlife – the remarkable capacity his work has to create an apparently open-ended series of historical and cultural contexts for its continued production and reception – owes more to its extraordinary institutional creativity than to that of the institutions of literature into which it has been assimilated. Trite as it may be to conclude on such a note, it is impossible to imagine what status the institution of literature would have if not a word of Shakespeare's work had survived the burning of the Globe. Happily, this counterfactual is given meaning by the fact that here at least we can identify a single act intentionally directed towards the preservation of this work: as Andrew Gurr explains,

> the Globe's fire during a performance meant that enough bright sparks were on hand to save the company's vital assets. Such a rescue act must have been what saved for posterity the half of Shakespeare's plays that were not yet in print.[32]

One of the unintended consequences of this act is the existence of modern traditions of production and reception that are largely responsible for the attention we continue to give, not only Shakespeare, but to contemporaries, like Ben Jonson, whose work would arguably be relatively insignificant without his.

To some extent, the phenomenon of the Shakespearean afterlife has been one of the reasons why I have sought to reconsider the question of might be involved in an institutional approach to his work. The fact that its *durée* is qualitatively different from that of any other writer suggests that it is a structural rather than accidental feature of his practice of writing, and that unless we approach it on those terms we risk mistaking structural features of our own practices of writing, as members of institutions of research, performance, or production, for his. I began this discussion with an argument that New Historicist applications of institutional analysis disabled the approach by subsuming the model of the institution into that of the market. Writing in the *Guardian* in November 2006, Anthony Giddens sent out a call for a 'return' to his own discipline, sociology, as a response to the market-based philosophies that have dominated the humanities and social sciences since the early 1980s. According to him, 'market fundamentalism' – 'the belief that the realm of the market should be extended as far as possible, since markets are the most rational and efficient means of allocating resources' –

reduces the scope of social thought.[33] Writing at a time when the extreme instability of the global market suggests that such a reduction may hold more than intellectual dangers, the benefits of returning to an approach that encourages attention to the potential creativity of the basic mechanisms of institutionalisation seem to me self-evident. If in the 1980s Shakespeare could stand as guarantor for the dream of a global market, he can certainly help us think the process of social reconstruction that must follow its replacement by something more genuinely open and creative. Of course, I do not pretend that this study goes all, or even much, of the way towards this. My aim has been to bring together the basic shape of a descriptive model, a comprehensive series of contexts for its elaboration, and perhaps above all an open range of connections between them. I have asked more questions than I have myself been able to answer. Perhaps there will be afterthinkers who will do that for me.

Notes

Chapter 1

1. See, for instance, P. Bűrger (1979), trans. L. Kruger (1992) 'The Institution of Art as a Category of the Sociology of Literature', in P. Bűrger and C. Bűrger (1992) *The Institutions of Art* (Lincoln, NB and London: University of Nebraska Press); R. Williams (1981) *Culture* (London: Fontana); J. Wolff (1981) *The Social Production of Art* (London: Macmillan) and (1983) *Aesthetics and the Sociology of Art* (London: Allen & Unwin).
2. See, for instance, C. Metz (1971) *Psychoanalysis and the Cinema* (London: Macmillan); J. Ellis (1975) 'Made in Ealing', *Screen* 16.1; and (1976) 'The Institution of Cinema', *Edinburgh '76*; S. Neale (1981) 'Art Cinema as Institution', *Screen* 22.1; S. Heath (1981) *Questions of Cinema* (Bloomington, IN: Indiana University Press). For an exemplary combination of theoretical and empirical description, see also G. Born (1995) *IRCAM, Boulez and the Institutionalization of the Musical Avant-Garde* (Berkeley and Los Angeles, CA: University of California Press).
3. S. Greenblatt (1990) 'Psychoanalysis and Renaissance Culture', in *Learning to Curse: Essays in Early Modern Culture* (New York: Routledge, Chapman and Hall). Greenblatt's essay took its point of departure from N. Z. Davis (1983) *The Return of Martin Guerre* (Cambridge, MA: Harvard University Press).
4. Greenblatt (1990) p. 137.
5. Ibid.
6. Ibid., p. 141.
7. Ibid., p. 142.
8. Ibid., p. 143.
9. See S. Greenblatt (1980) *Renaissance Self-Fashioning: From More to Shakespeare* (Chicago: Chicago University Press).
10. Greenblatt 'Towards a Poetics of Culture' in (1990), p. 147.
11. This question became notorious during the McCarthy HUAC (House UnAmerican Activities Committee) hearings of the late 1940s and early 1950s. For contrasting treatments, see E. Rolfe, 'Are You Now or Have You Ever Been', in C. Nelson and J. Hendricks (eds.) (1993) *Collected Poems* (Urbana, IL: Illinois); and Eric Bentley's documentary drama (1972) of the same title.
12. For discussions of the New Historicist anecdote, see J. Fineman (1989) 'The History of the Anecdote', in H. A.Veeser (ed.) *The New Historicism* (New York: Routledge), pp. 49–77; C. Porter (1990) 'After the New Historicism', *New Literary History* 21.2, pp. 253–72.
13. C. Prendergast (1999) 'Circulating Representations: New Historicism and the Poetics of Culture', *SubStance* 28.1, Issue 88, p. 98.
14. Greenblatt (1990) p. 154.
15. S. Greenblatt (1988) *Shakespearean Negotiations: The Circulation of Social Energy in Renaissance England* (Berkeley and Los Angeles, CA: University of California Press) p. 14.

16. C. Pye (1994) 'The Theater, the Market and the Subject of History', *ELH* 61.3, p. 502. On the function of the economic metaphor in New Historicist discourse, see also H. A. Veeser's introduction to Veeser (ed.) (1989), pp. xiv–xv.
17. For the concept of the media-scape, see A. Appadurai (1996) *Modernity at Large: Cultural Dimensions of Globalization* (Minneapolis, MN: University of Minnesota Press), p. 35. For 'synergy' ('the enhanced profit potential brought about by the cross-marketing of a commodity or related commodities in multiple media') see S. Neale and M. Smith (eds.) (1998) *Contemporary Hollywood Cinema* (London and New York: Routledge), p. xvi.
18. See, for instance, L. Hutcheon (1988) *The Poetics of Postmodernism* (London and New York: Routledge); and (1989) *The Politics of Postmodernism* (London and New York: Routledge); F. Jameson (1991) *Postmodernism, or, The Cultural Logic of Late Capitalism* (Durham, NC: Duke University Press). D. Lanier (2002) 'Shakescorp Noir', *Shakespeare Quarterly* 53.2, pp. 164–5, has pointed out that this period also saw the beginning of the 'Screen Shakespeare' boom 'initiated in 1989 with Branagh's *Henry 5* and Zeffirelli's *Hamlet*'. He correctly identifies the context for this boom as 'the unprecedented consolidation and vertical integration of global multimedia conglomerates ... and with it the consolidation of a cultural dominant founded on the mass-market screen image'. The compression of past and present is one of the features of New Historicism most consistently identified by its critics: see, for instance, A. Liu (1989) 'The Power of Formalism: The New Historicism', *ELH* 56.4, p. 749: 'the membrane of history between the Renaissance and postmodernity sometimes stretches so thin that there is virtually no separation at all'.
19. J. C. Agnew (1986) *Worlds Apart: The Market and the Theater in Anglo-American Thought 1550–1750* (Cambridge: Cambridge University Press).
20. Ibid., p. 56.
21. Ibid., p. 131. For applications of Bakhtinian theory to Renaissance theatre, see also M. D. Bristol (1983) 'Carnival and the Institutions of Theater in Elizabethan England', *ELH*, 50.4; and (1985) *Carnival and Theatre: Plebian Culture and the Structure of Authority in Renaissance England* (New York: Methuen).
22. D. Bruster (1992) *Drama and the Market in the Age of Shakespeare* (Cambridge: Cambridge University Press).
23. Ibid., pp. 1, 3, 4, 10.
24. Ibid., p. 37.
25. In the context of his own interest in the institutional relations between theatre and law, Luke Wilson has drawn attention to the 'almost obligatory' chiasmic formulations of 'reciprocal influence' in studies of the 1980s. See L. Wilson (2000) *Theaters of Intention: Drama and the Law in Early Modern England* (Stanford, CA: Stanford University Press), pp. 3–4.
26. For an account of the unstable dichotomies of Cold War thinking, see S. J. Whitfield (1991) *The Culture of the Cold War* (Baltimore, MD: Johns Hopkins University Press).
27. L. Barroll (1991) *Politics, Plague, and Shakespeare's Theater: The Stuart Years* (Ithaca, NY and London: Cornell University Press).
28. Ibid., p. 3.
29. Ibid., p. 4.
30. Ibid., p. 7.

31. Ibid., p. 8.
32. Ibid., p. 15.
33. Such as Patrick Cheney's account of a Shakespeare for whom the closure of the theatres offered the opportunity to write poems and thus 'capitalize' on a 'leadership role' in the emergence of the national poet-playwright, thereby 'chang[ing] the institution of authorship forever'. See P. Cheney (2004) *Shakespeare, National Poet-Playwright* (Cambridge: Cambridge University Press), pp. 4, 28 and 64. Cheney discusses and rejects 'plague theory' on pp. 62–4.
34. For *Schenck v United States* see *Cornell University Law School Legal Information Institute Supreme Court Collection* <http://supct.law.cornell.edu.supct/htm/historics/USSC_CR_0249_0047_20.html>. Accessed 1 August 2008.
35. *Clear and Present Danger* (Philip Noyce, 1994).
36. Barroll (1991) p. 13.
37. P. Yachnin and A. B. Dawson (2001) *The Culture of Playgoing in Shakespeare's England: A Collaborative Debate* (Cambridge: Cambridge University Press).
38. Ibid., p. 5
39. Ibid.
40. Ibid., p. 6.
41. Ibid., p. 29.
42. Ibid., p. 50.
43. Ibid., p. 28.
44. To be fair, they make it quite clear in their 'Afterword' that 'their disagreement goes too deep to be capable of easy resolution' and that 'we do not ourselves regard it as desirable to synthesize our positions into a univocal view' (pp. 209; 208). But my point is that the level of their disagreement might have made it appropriate to make basic questions of description the starting point of their inquiry. As it is, the differences between their positions may be an effect of indefinition rather than debate.
45. P. Yachnin (2005) '"The Perfection of Ten": Populuxe Art and Artisanal Value in *Troilus and Cressida*', *Shakespeare Quarterly* 56.3, p. 308. Yachnin records Dawson's comment, in his edition of *Troilus and Cressida*, that '"the play as a whole ... suggests the possibility of a more moderate interpretation: that value is located in the field of communal work and systems of belief rather than in the marketplace, where value can rise and fall in a moment" (Dawson, ed., 39)' (p. 311).
46. Ibid.
47. Ibid., p. 327.
48. A. Patterson (2002) '"Ideas Seldom Exist Apart from Practice": Turning Over Millennial New Leaves', *The Journal of British Studies* 41.3. For an example of 'the cultural turn' and its implication for a rereading of New Historicism, see D. Bruster (2003) *Shakespeare and the Question of Culture: Early Modern Literature and the Cultural Turn* (New York and Basingstoke: Palgrave/St. Martin's Press). Bruster responds to the characteristic elisions of New Historicism with the idea of a literary deep focus ('thin description') that aims 'to keep multiple planes of a culture in view without the abrupt editorial cuts between part and whole, anecdote and culture, that remain so characteristic of thick description' (pp. xvi–xvii).

49. *Making Publics 1500–1700: Media, Markets and Association in Early Modern Europe Project Summary*. <http://makingpublics.mcgill.ca/summary.php>. Accessed 30 August 2008.
50. Ibid., *Detailed Project Description: Year 5: Networks and Publics from Early Modernity to the Twenty-first Century* <http://makingpublics.mcgill.ca/details.php#year 5>. Accessed 30 August 2008.
51. Prendergast (1999), p. 110; M. D. Bristol (1990) *Shakespeare's America, America's Shakespeare* (London and New York: Routledge), *passim*.
52. Witness the brief, puzzling reference at the end of 'Towards a Poetics of Culture' (pp. 158–9) footnoted only to an earlier publication of the essay in *The Aims of Representation: Subject/Text/History* (New York: Columbia University Press 1987). More extended discussions include Wilson (2000), pp. 28–30; 272–4.
53. A. Giddens (1979) *Central Problems in Social Theory: Action, Structure and Contradiction in Social Analysis* (London: Macmillan), p. 2.
54. J. B. Thompson (1989) 'The Theory of Structuration', in D. Held and J. B. Thompson (eds.) *Social Theory of Modern Societies: Anthony Giddens and his Critics* (Cambridge: Cambridge University Press), p. 61.
55. A. Giddens (1981) *A Contemporary Critique of Historical Materialism* Vol. 1 (London: Macmillan), p. 42.
56. J. B. Thompson (1990) *Ideology and Modern Culture: Critical Social Theory in the Era of Mass Communication* (Cambridge: Polity Press) p. 149. For an application of this theoretical model to the analysis of early cinema, see J. Kember (2001) *Intimacy at a Distance: Towards an Institutional Account of Early British Film, 1896–1910* (PhD, University of Sheffield), and (2009) *Marketing Modernity: Victorian Popular Shows and Early Cinema* (Exeter: Exeter University Press).
57. Ibid., p. 4.
58. Ibid., p. 5.
59. Thompson, in Held and Thompson (eds.) (1989), p. 72.
60. Giddens (1979), p. 43.
61. Ibid., pp. 43, 42.
62. For the decline of literary patronage in the 1590s, see A. Fox (1995) 'The Complaint of Poetry for the Death of Liberality: The Decline of Literary Patronage in the 1590s', in J. Guy (ed.) *The Reign of Elizabeth I: Court and Culture in the Last Decade* (Cambridge: Cambridge University Press) pp. 229–57; and D. Bruster (2000) 'The Structural Transformation of Print in Late Elizabethan England', in A. F. Marotti and M. D. Bristol (eds) *Print, Manuscript and Performance: The Changing Relations of the Media in Early Modern England* (Columbus, OH: Ohio State University Press), p. 76.
63. For the idea of the duopoly, see A. Gurr (1996) *The Shakespearian Playing Companies* (Oxford: Clarendon Press); and (2004) *The Shakespeare Company 1594–1642* (Cambridge: Cambridge University Press). For a challenge to it, see D. Kathman (2005) 'The Shakespeare Company, 1594–1642 (review)', *Shakespeare Quarterly* 56.3, pp. 360–2.
64. See, for instance, R. Weimann (1978) *Shakespeare and the Popular Tradition in the Theatre: Studies in the Social Dimension of Dramatic Form and Function*, ed. R. Schwarz (Baltimore, MD: Johns Hopkins University

Press); M. D. Bristol (1985); and (2000) 'Shamelessness in Arden: Early Modern Theater and the Obsolesence of Popular Theatricality', in Marotti and Bristol, pp. 279–306. For 'popular culture', see P. Burke (1978) *Popular Culture in Early Modern Europe* (New York: New York University Press); and (1985) 'Popular Culture in Seventeenth-century London', in B. Reay (ed.) *Popular Culture in Seventeenth-Century England* (New York: St. Martin's Press), pp. 36–9; T. Harris (1989) 'The Problem of "Popular Political Culture" in Seventeenth-Century London', *History of European Ideas* 10, pp. 43–58.

65. See, for instance, Bristol (2000), p. 280: 'Early modern public theaters are institutions created within a rapidly expanding culture of the printed book that fundamentally transformed the aims of social authority as well as the mechanisms of social discipline and control'; and on the idea of a 'nascent' public sphere of the 1590s, Ibid., p. 65: 'The public sphere that works of the 1590s began to establish was ... highly theatrical in nature. ... During the 1590s, publishers found that readers were eager to buy the plays they had seen and heard in London's theatres.' For an account of playbook publication that challenges aspects of this analysis, see A. B. Farmer and Z. Lesser (2000) 'Vile Arts: The Marketing of English Printed Drama, 1512–1660', *Research Opportunities in Renaissance Drama* 39, pp. 77–165; and (2005) 'The Popularity of Playbooks Revisited', *Shakespeare Quarterly* 56.1, pp. 1–32.

66. Thompson (1989), in Held and Thompson p. 70.

67. For an exemplary account of this aspect of the early modern institution, see Joseph Loewenstein's study of the printer and publisher John Wolfe, in (2002) *The Author's Due: Printing and the Prehistory of Copyright* (Chicago and London: University of Chicago Press) pp. 27–51. In an earlier publication of the essay (1988) 'For a History of Intellectual Property: John Wolfe's Reformation', *English Literary Renaissance* 18, pp. 389–412, Loewenstein appended a judicious note on the need to question aspects of the prevailing Foucauldianism of early modern institutional analysis.

68. It has been argued, most recently by Blair Worden (2003), 'Which Play Was Performed at the Globe Theatre on 7 February 1601?', *The London Review of Books*, 25.13, p. 22, that the play in question was not *Richard II*. I see no reason to agree. The arguments why we should decide that the play commissioned from the Chamberlain's Men on 5 February – a play the company could perform at two days' notice and that Essex and his supporters considered compelling enough to influence not just its audience but, by their example, the whole population of London – should be by the playwright Farmer and Lesser (2005) p. 11, have described as 'England's first best-selling playwright', rather than an 'adaptation' of John Hayward's *The Life and Raigne of King Henrie the Fourth*, for the existence of which there is no other evidence whatsoever, seem to me compelling. For earlier stages of this long-running debate, see E. M. Albright (1927) *PMLA* vol. XLII, pp. 686–720; R. Heffner (1930) *PMLA* vol. XLV, pp. 754–80; E. M. Albright (1931) *PMLA* vol. XLVI, pp. 694–719; R. Heffner and E. M. Albright (1932) *PMLA* vol. XLVII, pp. 898–901.

69. Thompson (1989), in Held and Thompson p. 61.

Chapter 2

1. For a discussion of these topics, see J. H. Baker (1990) *An Introduction to English Legal History* (London: Butterworth), particularly Chapter 14, 'Real Property: Feudalism and Uses' and Chapter 17, 'Other Interests in Land'.
2. J. A. Guy (1985) *St German on Chancery and Statute* (London: Selden Society) p. 75.
3. For the 'path to privity', see V. V. Palmer (1992) *The Paths to Privity: The History of Third Party Beneficiary Contracts at English Law* (San Francisco: Austin and Winfield). According to Palmer, the period from the mid-sixteenth to mid-seventeenth centuries was one of remarkable openness to third party actions: 'the common law courts were more flexible about permitting a beneficiary action than at any subsequent time. ... [T]he sheer number of actions and the liberal results were impressive. Relief was given frequently to the beneficiary, indicating that a strict privity rule did not exist before 1670' (p. 28). See also N. Jones (1997) 'Uses, Trusts, and a Path to Privity', *Cambridge Law Journal*, pp. 175–200 for further commentary on what Palmer refers to as the 'interest theory' approach to beneficiary actions.
4. Baker (1990) p. 282. An excellent example of the ambiguities of this exploitation is provided by Shakespeare in Sonnet 94, 'They that have power to hurt' ('They are the lords and owners of their faces,/Others but stewards of their excellence'), where the poem's application of a metaphor of property to the experience of sexual desire is underpinned by an ironic distinction between beneficial owner and feudal trustee.
5. Ibid., p. 287.
6. C. St German (1530–1) 'Second Dialogue', in T. F. T. Plucknett and J. L. Barton (eds.) (1974) *Doctor and Student* (London: Selden Society 1974), p. 222.
7. T. Audley, in J. H. Baker (ed.) (1977) *The Reports of Sir John Spelman* (London: Selden Society), Vol. 2, p. 198.
8. J. H. Baker and S. F. C. Milsom (1986) *Sources of English Legal History: Private Law to 1750* (London: Butterworth), p. 112.
9. 1 Co.Rep.77; 2 And.134; Moore KB 601. References to the English Reports throughout are taken from *Justis: The Law Online* <http://www.justis.com/data-coverage/english-reports.aspx>.
10. W. Burton (1622) *The Description of Leicester Shire*, in Baker and Milsom (1986), p. 162.
11. 2 And. 143.
12. 2 And. 143.
13. *Dillon v Freine* (1594), in Baker and Milsom (1986), p. 155.
14. W. H. Bryson (2001) *Cases Concerning Equity and the Courts of Equity 1550–1660* (London: Selden Society), vol. 1, p. 304, from CUL MS Gg 2.31, fo. 464v, dated 1598–1602.
15. Ibid.
16. Ibid., p. 319, from Herts RO MS Verulam XII A.50, fo. 59. Uncertainty about dating makes it hard to determine which 'Burbage' is referred to here.
17. Ibid., p. 376, taken from a collection of extracts of decrees in BL MS Add. 48097, ff. 61v–66 [Eng]. 'Judgements at the common law examined in the High Court of Chancery'.
18. Ibid., pp. xxiv–xxv.

19. C. W. Wallace (1913) 'The First London Theatre: Materials for a History', *Nebraska University Studies* 13, p. 115. As the only available published collection of these documents, I refer to Wallace throughout. Explanatory terms or expanded abbreviations in square brackets are provided by Wallace; in square brackets in italics by me.
20. More extended discussions of the Theatre litigation are provided by W. Ingram (1992) *The Business of Playing: The Beginnings of the Adult Professional Theater in Elizabethan London* (Ithaca, NY: Cornell University Press) and T. B. Leinwand (1999) *Theatre, Finance and Society in Early Modern England* (Cambridge: Cambridge University Press).
21. Wallace (1913), p. 40.
22. Ibid., p. 139.
23. Ibid., pp. 141–2.
24. Ibid., p. 139.
25. Ibid., p. 137.
26. Ibid., pp. 40; 47.
27. Ibid., p. 140.
28. Ibid., p. 151.
29. Ibid., p. 152.
30. ibid., p. 53.
31. ibid., p. 55.
32. Ibid., p. 137.
33. John Popham, in *Dillon v Freine* (1594): 'Moreover these kinds of assurances and conveyances of future uses impair all natural love which God by the rules of nature has engrafted between kinsmen of one blood, name and progeny' (Baker and Milsom [1986], p. 157).
34. Ibid., p. 135.
35. Ibid., p. 193.
36. The eponymous heroes of *The Producers* (Brooks 1968; Stroman 2005) overfinance a musical they are sure will flop ('Springtime for Hitler') by selling 100% rights in the production to multiple investors. The scheme backfires when the show is runaway success.
37. Ibid., p. 87.
38. Ibid., pp. 100, 105 and 121.
39. Ibid., pp. 114–15.
40. Ibid., p. 101.
41. Ibid., p. 127.
42. Ibid., p. 56.
43. Ibid., p. 192.
44. Ibid., p. 201.
45. Ibid., pp. 40–1.
46. C. C. Rutter (ed.) (1984) 'Introduction', *Documents of the Rose Playhouse* (Manchester: Manchester University Press), p. 8.
47. Wallace (1913), pp. 286, 285.
48. Ibid., p. 286.
49. See, for instance, G. Wickham, H. Berry and W. Ingram (eds.) (2000) *English Professional Theatre 1530–1660, a Documentary History* (Cambridge: Cambridge University Press).
50. Ingram (1992), p. 118.

51. Leinwand (1999), p. 65; S. C. Shershow (2000) *Renaissance Quarterly* 53.3, pp. 931–3.
52. Rutter (1984), p. 8.
53. A. Gurr (2004) *The Shakespeare Company 1594–1642* (Cambridge: Cambridge University Press), pp. 4, 8, 30.
54. Ibid., p. 5.
55. E. Buscombe (1977) 'Sound and Color', *Jump Cut* 17, pp 23–5. The phrase 'Great Man theory' refers to Thomas Carlyle's dictum 'The history of the world is but the biography of great men', in 'The Hero as Divinity'. See T. Carlyle (1901) *Complete Works of Thomas Carlyle: Sartor Resartus and Heroes and Hero-Worship* (New York: P. F. Collier), p. 262.
56. Baker (1990) p. 286 n. 7. 'Use' derives not from the English verb, but from the Latin phrase *ad opus* through the Old French *al oes* or *al ues* meaning 'on behalf of' or 'to the benefit of'.
57. Wallace (1913), p. 69.
58. Ibid., p. 50.
59. Ibid.
60. Ibid., p. 51.
61. Jones (1997), p. 176.
62. Wallace (1913), p. 62.
63. Ibid., p. 69.
64. Ibid., p. 103.
65. Ibid., p. 128.
66. ibid., p. 145.
67. A fraudulent conveyance is a transfer of a property to another party, with the intention to avoid a claim on that property, for instance by a creditor seeking to recover his or her dues. See C. Ross (2003) *Elizabethan Literature and the Law of Fraudulent Conveyance: Sidney, Spenser, and Shakespeare* (Aldershot: Ashgate) for an extended discussion of the highly creative adaptation of this legal device to sixteenth-century literature.
68. *OED Online*, <http://dictionary.oed.com/cgi/entry/50273876>entry la, although at least one of the contemporary quotations supplied, from Jonson's *Cynthia's Revels* V. I, is arguably an instance of the legal sense, a confusion that makes my point for me.
69. Wallace (1913), p. 250.
70. Ibid., p. 258.
71. Ibid., p. 278.
72. Ibid., p. 139.
73. Ibid., p. 140.
74. Ibid., p. 142.
75. On this basis, *pace* Barroll, it can be seen *not* as evidence that its occupants assumed that a theatre would always be open, but as an attempt to establish the institutional basis on which it should or could be.
76. *Twelfth Night*, 5.1, pp. 394–5.
77. Bryson (2001) vol. 1, pp. 80, 83, 86. As noted above, the Theatre was built on dissolved ecclesiastical land, as were the first and second Blackfriars, the Swan and the Whitefriars.
78. Wallace (1913), p. 43.
79. Baker (1990), pp. 120–1.

80. Wallace (1913), p. 192.
81. Ibid., p. 201.
82. Ibid., p. 242.
83. For accounts of early modern theatre as 'subversive', see J. Dollimore (1984) *Radical Tragedy: Religion, Ideology and Power in the Drama of Shakespeare and his Contemporaries* (Brighton: Harvester Press); J. Dollimore and A. Sinfield (eds.) (1985) *Political Shakespeare: New Essays in Cultural Materialism* (Manchester: University of Manchester Press), especially S. Greenblatt, 'Invisible Bullets: Renaissance Authority and its Subversion, *Henry IV* and *Henry V*', pp 18–47.
84. See L. Wilson (2004) 'Renaissance Tool Abuse and the Legal History of the Sudden', in E. Sheen and L. Hutson (eds.) *Literature, Politics and Law in Renaissance England* (London: Palgrave Macmillan), pp. 121–45, for a discussion of tool abuse, or 'use against design'.
85. Baker (1990), p. 136.
86. For an account of Thomas Egerton, see L. A. Knafla (1977) *Law and Politics in Jacobean England: The Tracts of Lord Chancellor Ellesmere* (Cambridge and New York: Cambridge University Press).
87. For a discussion of this episode and complete transcription of Elizabeth and Lambarde's conversation see Chapter 6.
88. For 'natural love', see Popham in n. 33 above.
89. For the text of the royal patent, see *Malone Society Collections* (1909) I.3, p. 264.
90. Thus *Vaughan v. Twisden* (1554) in Bryson (2001), vol. 1, p. 76: 'in tender consideration whereof it may please your good lordship ... to permit the said Elizabeth one of your said orators peaceably and quietly to occupy the premises *without any let or trouble* ...'.

Chapter 3

1. References to Shakespeare's plays throughout are taken from S. Greenblatt, W. Cohen, J. E. Howard and K. E. Maus (eds.) (1997) *The Norton Shakespeare* (New York: W. W. Norton) unless indicated otherwise.
2. B. Morris (ed.) (1981) *The Arden Shakespeare The Taming of the Shrew* (London and New York: Methuen), pp. 50; 65 argued that *The Shrew* 'might be [Shakespeare's] first play' and proposed a date of 1589. MacDonald P. Jackson (2002), 'Pause Patterns in Shakespeare's Verse: Canon and Chronology', *Literary and Linguistic Computing* 17.1 suggests 1593.
3. The term 'special' is 'used with a large number of legal terms to denote particular or distinctive instances or cases of the thing, action, or person in question' (*OED Online* <http:oed.com/cgi/entry/s0232614> entry 7 (Law)).
4. *Fyllol v Assheleygh* (1520) Trin.12 8 fo. 4 pl 3 in J. H. Baker (ed.) (2002) *Year Books of Henry VIII: 12–14 Henry VIII 1520–23* (London: Selden Society), pp. 14–20. Quotations are supplied in Baker's translations from law French and Latin. See E. Sheen (2004) 'Shakespeare's Animations', in E. Fudge (ed.) *Of Animals, Humans, and Other Wonderful Creatures* (Urbana and Chicago, IL: University of Illinois Press) for an early attempt to think about this material; and B. Boehrer (2005) 'Renaissance Beasts: *Of Animals, Humans, and Other Wonderful Creatures* (review)', *Renaissance Quarterly* 58.1, pp. 286–8 for an unilluminating response to it.

152 Notes

5. Baker (2002), p. xvii.
6. J. H. Baker (ed.) (1977) *The Reports of Sir John Spelman* (London: Selden Society), Vol. 2, p. 212, points out that, in the early sixteenth century, '[inns of court] readers who chose to lecture on theft were particularly fond of the finer points relating to the ownership of beasts and fish.'
7. Thomas More, *Utopia*, ed. D.H. Sacks (1999) (Boston: Bedford/ St. Martin's Press), pp. 199–200.
8. Baker (2002), p. 14.
9. Ibid., pp. 14; 17.
10. Ibid., p. 18.
11. Ibid., p. 19.
12. References to the Manners family household records are taken from *The Manuscripts of His Grace the Duke of Rutland*, Royal Commission on Historical Manuscripts, 24 (London: HMSO, 1888–1905), vol. 4, pp. 260ff. Thanks to Alan Bryson, who drew my attention to this material.
13. Baker (2002), p. 20.
14. Ibid., p. 16.
15. For paratext as threshold, see W. Sherman (2007) 'On the Threshold: Architecture, Paratext, and Early Print Culture', in S. A. Baron, E. Lindquist and E. Shevlin (eds.) *Agent of Change: Print Culture Studies after Elizabeth L. Eisenstein* (Amherst, MA: University of Massachusetts Press), pp. 67–81. In his discussion of 'Consideration, Contract and the End of *The Comedy of Errors*', Andrew Zurcher, (2007) *Law and Humanities* 2, pp. 145–6, welcomes a 'properly historical return to the recognition of Shakespeare's preoccupations with legal ideas and practices', but suggests 'we still lack a discussion of the significance of this legal engagement'. 'What, if anything', he asks, 'Could it all be for?' The institutional approach I develop here, in which I try to think about legal ideas and practices as part of an inclusive range of historical and textual perspectives rather than yet another chiasmic formulation – 'law and literature' – is my answer to this question.
16. Sir Thomas Cokayne (London, 1591) *A short treatise of hunting: compyled for the delight of noble men and gentlemen*. British Library, <http:/gateway.19proquest.com/openurl?ctx_ver = 39.88-2003&res_id = xri.eebo:citation.99852060.> Accessed from *Early English Books Online*, 4 April 2007.
17. *Twelfth Night* 5.1.394–5.
18. The phrase 'show of apparel' is from the Proclamation of 1574, which seeks to redress 'the wasting and undoing of a great number of young gentlemen, otherwise serviceable, and others seeking by show of apparel to be esteemed as gentlemen, who, allured by the vain show of those things, do not only consume themselves, their goods, and lands which their parents left unto them, but also run into such debts and shifts as they cannot live out of danger of laws without attempting unlawful acts, whereby they are not any ways serviceable to their country as otherwise they might be' (*Book of Proclamations* fo.154 *seq.*).
19. Walter Benjamin developed the idea of the dialectical image in *Das Passagenwerk* (Gesammelte Schriften, vol. V [1982]. Frankfurt/M: Suhrkamp). According to Susan Buck-Morss (1991) *The Dialectics of Seeing: Walter Benjamin and the Arcades Project* (Cambridge, MA and London: MIT Press), p. 71, 'such images were the concrete "small, particular moments" in which the "total

historical event" was to be discovered, the "perceptible ur-phenomenon (*Urphänomen*) in which the origins of the present could be found'.
20. *OED Online* <http://dictionary.oed.com/cgi/entry/50013581>entry4(Law)>.
21. Commentators have differed on whether he is generous or mean and on whether the arrangement is jointure or dower: see B. J. Sokol and M. Sokol (2003) *Shakespeare, Law and Marriage* (Cambridge: Cambridge University Press), pp. 179–84 for a survey of these positions, and what they present as a corrective account of Petruchio's 'actual words'. The point, however, is not whether Petruchio's law is accurate: rather, it is the difference between the objective value of his offer, and the rhetorical inflation that follows in the negotiations for Bianca.
22. *OED Online* <http://dictionary.oed.com/cgi/entry/50013587>entry7trans.>

Chapter 4

1. F. Bacon, *History of King Henry VII* in *Works of Francis Bacon Baron of Verulam Viscount St Albans Lord High Chancellor of England* (London: 1819), Vol. 5, p. 6.
2. For the 'fisc', see G. L. Harriss (1975) *King, Parliament and Public Finance in Medieval England to 1369* (Oxford: Clarendon Press).
3. B. P. Wolffe (1956) 'The Management of English Royal Estates under the Yorkist Kings', *The English Historical Review*, 71.278, p. 3.
4. Ibid., p. 16.
5. In (1953) *The Tudor Revolution in Government: Administrative Changes in the Reign of Henry VIII* (Cambridge: Cambridge University Press) and (1955) *England under the Tudors* (London: Methuen) Elton argued that the Tudor monarchy instigated the replacement of the medieval household by a planned modern government. A member of the British Intelligence Corps in the Second World War and subsequently an outspoken opponent of Marxist approaches to history, his work was as responsive to the rhythms of contemporary politics as Stephen Greenblatt's, if at an earlier stage in the Cold War.
6. K. Eden (2001) *Friends Hold All Things in Common: Tradition, Intellectual Property and the Adages of Erasmus* (New Haven, CT: Yale University Press), esp. Chapters 4 and 5.
7. E. S. Donno (1982) 'Thomas More and *Richard III*', *Renaissance Quarterly* 35.3 provides an account of these traditions in the afterlife of More's *History of Richard III*.
8. In putting forward this argument I am not overlooking the position put forward by J. Jowett (2000) *The New Oxford Shakespeare Richard III* (Oxford: Oxford University Press), p. 7, that 'the Quarto text itself indicates that a play initially written as if for Strange's Men is given finishing touches towards its close that make it suitable for the new Pembroke company; then later, like Shakespeare's other pre-1594 plays (or at least those that are extant) it appears in the hands of the Chamberlain's Men'.
9. For speculation on Shakespeare's religion, see E. A. J. Honigmann (1999) *Shakespeare: The Lost Years* (Manchester: Manchester University Press); R. Wilson (2004) *Secret Shakespeare: Studies in Theatre, Religion and Resistance* (Manchester: Manchester University Press); S. Greenblatt (2004) *Will in the World: How Shakespeare Became Shakespeare* (New York: W. W. Norton).

10. There is general agreement that Shakespeare 'read More not in the collected edition of the *Works* published by Rastell in 1557, but in Hall's Chronicle'. A. Hammond (1981) *The Arden Shakespeare King Richard III* (London and New York: Methuen), p. 79.
11. Historians have debated the precise focus of this critique. Some have seen it as a specific reflection on the occupation of Tournai; others see *The History* and *Utopia* more generally as oblique critiques of Henry's 'war-making and propensity to tyrannical behaviour'. T. F. Mayer (1991) 'Tournai and Tyranny: Imperial Kingship and Critical Humanism', *The Historical Journal*, 34.2, pp. 258; 259; S. L. Davies (1998) 'Tournai and the English Crown, 1513–1519', *The Historical Journal* 41.1, p. 25.
12. See W. G. Zeefeld (1940) 'A Tudor Defense of Richard III', *PMLA* 55.4; A. M. Kincaid (ed.) (1977) *The Encomium of Richard III by William Cornwallis the Younger* (London: Turner and Devereux). The fact that one version of this manuscript bears a dedication by 'Hen W' is evocative. Michelle O'Callaghan has suggested that 'Hen. W' could be 'possibly either Henry Wotton, secretary to Essex, or Essex's close associate Henry Wriothesly, earl of Southampton', thus drawing the Yorkist narrative within easy reach of Shakespeare's social and professional sphere. M. O'Callaghan (1998) '"Talking Politics": Tyranny, Parliament and Christopher Brooke's *The Ghost of Richard III* (1614)', *The Historical Journal* 41.1, p. 112.
13. References to Cotton MS Tiberius E. x, ff. 121ff from M. Eccles (1933), 'Sir George Buc, Master of the Revels', in Charles J. Sisson (ed.) *Thomas Lodge and Other Elizabethans* (Cambridge, MA.: Harvard University Press), pp. 415–16.
14. *Sir Thomas More: Passages attributed to Shakespeare*, Add. III, 5–14 in *The Norton Shakespeare*, pp. 2018–19.
15. W. H. Dunham Jr. and C. T. Wood (1976) 'The Right to Rule in England: Depositions and the Kingdom's Authority, 1327–1485', *The American Historical Review* 81.4, p. 761.
16. Ibid., p. 738.
17. Ibid., p. 758.
18. For constitutionalist thinking in the later fifteenth century, see A. Cromartie (2004) 'Common Law, Counsel and Consent in Fortescue's Political Theory', in L. Clark and C. Carpenter (eds.) *The Fifteenth Century IV: Political Culture in Late Medieval Britain* (Oxford: Oxbow Press), pp. 45–67.
19. Donno (1982), p. 420.
20. Sir Thomas More, *The History of King Richard the Third*, Renascence Editions <scholarsbank.uoregon.edu/xmluibitstream/handle/1794/801/Kingrichard.pdf.>. Accessed 4 November 2006. Page numbers are provided in parenthesis at the end of each citation.
21. See, for instance, A. N. Kincaid (1972) 'The Dramatic Structure of Sir Thomas More's History of King Richard III', *Studies in English Literature, 1500–1900* 12.2, pp. 223–42.
22. S. Greenblatt (1980) *Renaissance Self-Fashioning: From More to Shakespeare* (Chicago: University of Chicago Press), pp. 13–14.
23. Hammond (1981), p. 78.
24. OED.
25. *The Magnificent Ambersons* (Orson Welles, 1942). I give this example of a long take rather than the more famous opening shot of *Touch of Evil* (Orson Welles,

1958) because the earlier film is more obviously associated with innovations in the relation between sound and camera movement.
26. T. H. Howard-Hill (ed.) (1989) *Shakespeare and Sir Thomas More: Essays on the Play and its Shakespearean Interest* (Cambridge: Cambridge University Press); G. H. Metz (1989) *Sources of Four Plays Ascribed to Shakespeare: The Reign of King Edward III, Sir Thomas More, The History of Cardenio, The Two Noble Kinsmen* (Columbia: University of Missouri Press); S. McMillin (1987) *The Elizabethan Theatre and The Book of Sir Thomas More* (Ithaca, NY: Cornell University Press).
27. S. McMillin (1972) 'Casting for Pembroke's Men: The *Henry VI* Quartos and *The Taming of A Shrew*', *Shakespeare Quarterly* 23.2, p. 159.
28. G. Melchiori, in Howard-Hill (1989), p. 96.
29. *Sir Thomas More* features in strongly contrasting accounts of authorship. Grace Ioppolo (1991) in *Revising Shakespeare* (Cambridge, MA: Harvard University Press), p. 11, cites the play as evidence of Shakespeare's 'later revision practices'; affirming a traditional commitment to the ideology of single authorship, John Jones (1995) *Shakespeare at Work* (Oxford: Clarendon Press), p. 9, is pleased to 'catch' Shakespeare in 'the untidy act of composition', but asserts that 'there is no clear sign that he had even read the rest of the play'.
30. Robert Greene (1592) *Greenes Groats-worth of Wit, bought with a Million of Repentaunce* in A. B. Grosart (ed.) (1881–3) *The Life and Complete Works in Prose and Verse of Robert Greene* (London: the Huth Library), vol. 12, p. 144. See Bruster (2000), pp 67–8 for an account of Greene's insult that reads it into a 'nascent public sphere', and my discussion of this position at n. 37 below.
31. H. Chettle (London, 1593) *Kind-harts dreame Conteining fiue apparitions, vvith their inuectiues against abuses raigning*. Harvard University Library. <http://gateway.proquest.com/openurl?ctx_ver=Z39.88-2003&res_id=xri.eebo&rft_id=xri.eebo.citation.99852060>. Accessed from *Early English Books Online* 4 November 2006.
32. All references to *Sir Thomas More* are taken from the *Project Gutenberg* edition of Harleian MS 7368 at http://www.gutenberg.org. Act/scene references only are provided.
33. See, for instance, McMillin (1987).
34. *A Midsummer Night's Dream* 3.2.346.
35. For an account of Gilles Deleuze and Felix Guattari's distinction between potential and possibility in *Capitalism and Schizophrenia*, see B. Massumi (1996) *A User's Guide to Capitalism and Schizophrenia: Deviations from Deleuze and Guattari* (Cambridge, MA: MIT Press), pp. 35–41.
36. J. Manningham, in R. Sorlien (ed.) (1976) *The Diary of John Manningham of the Middle Temple 1602–1603* (Hanover NH: University Press of New England), Folios 29b–30, p. 75. 'Mr. Touse' is William Towse, bencher of the Inner Temple and Manningham's source for this piece of gossip.
37. My argument here has points of contact with Douglas Bruster's discussion of the relationship between Manningham's anecdote and *Richard III*, but I have reservations about his account of the role of *Richard III* in a 'nascent public sphere': 'the printed play texts that began to appear in great numbers in the 1590s would have offered readers a record of lines they might connect with real bodies on the platform stage ... those who purchased *Richard III*, for instance, would possess a version (however varied in nature) of what they had heard specific actors speak in London's playhouses: these the lines of

Richard Burbage, those the lines of William Kemp...' (Bruster [2000], pp. 66–7). In 1593–4, *Richard III* seems to me to engage its spectator in the memorial skills of professional performance, not print consciousness. In comparison with Bruster's suggestion that 'beginning in 1593-4, texts of public-theater plays began to make up an increasing percentage of literary publications' (p. 65), Farmer and Lesser (2005) agree that there was a 'boomlet' in 1594, but consider it 'a brief anomaly in a period of low production, a one-year surge that did not result in an increased market for printed professional drama' (p. 7).

38. See Hammond (1981), p. 103 for an example of the critical tendency to conflate these two readings: '[Richard's] Vice-like, anti-Christ qualities are linked with those of another familiar medieval horror: the Scourge of God'.
39. A. Leggatt (2002), 'The Audience as Patron: the Knight of the Burning Pestle', in P. W. White and S. R. Westfall (eds.) *Shakespeare and Theatrical Patronage in Early Modern England* (Cambridge: Cambridge University Press), p. 295, demonstrates the way the Vice characters in *Mankind* delay the appearance of the popular devil-character Titivillus by demanding money. He describes this as an articulation of the 'tacit contract between actors and audience: if you want to see the show, you have to give us money'.
40. P. Happé (1966) in Hammond (1981), p. 100.
41. Ibid., p.109.
42. J. Lull (1999) *The New Cambridge Shakespeare Richard III* (Cambridge: Cambridge University Press).
43. See n. 37 above.
44. For an application of the idea of a 'skills hierarchy' to the institutional differentiation between stardom and acting in cinema, see B. King, 'Stardom as an Occupation', in P. Kerr (1986) *The Hollywood Film Industry* (London: Routledge), pp. 154–84.
45. See, for instance, K. E. Maus (1995) *Inwardness and Theater in the English Renaissance* (Chicago: Chicago University Press); L. Wilson (2000) *Theaters of Intention: Drama and the Law in Early Modern England* (Stanford, CA: Stanford University Press); A. Dawson, in Dawson and Yachnin (2001); L. Hutson (2007) *The Invention of Suspicion: Law and Mimesis in Shakespeare and Renaissance Drama* (Oxford: Oxford University Press).
46. *Henry V*, Prologue, 11–12. According to Anthony Giddens (1990) *The Consequences of Modernity* (Stanford, CA: Stanford University Press), p. 18, the social relations of pre-modern societies are largely confined to local contexts of interaction. Modernity disembeds such interactions by 'fostering relations between "absent" others, locationally distant from any given situation of face-to-face interaction'.
47. Marc Augé (1992) *Non-lieux: Introduction à une anthropologie de la surmodernité* (Paris: Editions Seuil). In (1997) *L'Impossible voyage: Le tourisme et ses images* (Paris: Rivages) pp. 170–1, Augé suggests that filmmakers such as Wim Wenders and Nanni Moretti reinvent 'les espaces informes de la ville' where 'l'image... désigne les espaces à construire ou à réinventer... dessine l'espace de la rencontre... s'attarde sur les terrains vagues, les marges, les déserts provisoires, errante et attentive'.
48. This play's focus on London as the place within which the space of performance is embedded gains intensity from the fact that it was written at

a time when the theatres were closed by plague and the players forced to travel, a fact that suggest the extent to which Shakespeare's 'imagination' of London at this turning point in this career was institutionally performative, not representational.
49. For a comprehensive study of the Shakespeare part, see S. Palfrey and T. Stern (2007) *Shakespeare in Parts* (Oxford: Oxford University Press).
50. *As you Like It* 2.7.138–41.
51. 1.2.22. Dympna Callaghan (2000) *Shakespeare Without Women* (London: Routledge), p. 15, notes, but does not pursue, the 'surprising affinity' between Bottom and Richard.
52. As Lull (1999), p. 205 notes, '*In the True Tragedie of Richard the Third*, Richard says "A horse, a horse, a fresh horse", perhaps an echo of Shakespeare, perhaps a precursor.'
53. YB Mich 2 Ric 3 fo 22v pl 52.
54. For an example of this sense of the word 'diversity' not recorded in OED, see St German, *Second Dialogue*, in T. F. T. Plucknett and J. L. Barton (eds.) (1974) *Doctor and Student* (London: Selden Society 1974), p. 221. The Doctor cites two similar cases and asks why the question of intent is not taken into account in the same way in both: 'I pray thee let me know thy mind what dyversity thou puttest between them'. For a discussion of the 'infinite flexibility' of the conditional bond, see A. W. B. Simpson (1987) *A History of the Common Law of Contract* (Oxford: Oxford University Press), pp. 112–13.
55. YB Hil 9 Hen 7 fo 20v pl 16.
56. Ibid. See also YB Hil 10 Hen 7 fo 14 pl 11.
57. YB Pas 11 Hen 7 fo 21 pl 6.
58. *Pynnell v Cole* (1602) at Co.Rep. 117.

Chapter 5

1. *Hamlet* 4.3.53–4. For an account of coverture (the legal fiction that 'a wife's legal identity was covered by her husband'), see A. L. Erikson (2005) 'Coverture and Capitalism', *History Workshop Journal* 59, pp. 1–16.
2. A. W. B Simpson (1971) *History of the Common Law of Contract: the Rise of Assumpsit* (Oxford: Clarendon Press), pp. 316; 326.
3. For the historical background to the principle of consideration in general and Slade's Case in particular, see ibid.; D. Ibbetson (1999) *A Historical Introduction to the Law of Obligations* (Oxford: Oxford University Press); J. H. Baker (1986) 'Origins of the "Doctrine" of Consideration' and 'New Light on the Slade Case', in *The Legal Profession and the Common Law* (London: Hambledon), pp. 361–91 and 393–432.
4. V. Kahn and L. Hutson (2001) (eds.) *Rhetoric and Law in Early Modern Europe* (New Haven: Yale University Press) p. 6.
5. L. Wilson, 'Ben Jonson and the Law of Contract', in ibid., p. 143, citing D. E. Wayne (1982) 'Drama and Society in the Age of Jonson: An Alternative View', *Renaissance Drama* 13, p.104.
6. D. H. Sacks, in Kahn and Hutson (2001), p. 45; Wilson, in ibid., p. 152.
7. See Chapter 2, n. 33 at p. 149.
8. N. G. Jones (1997) 'Uses, Trusts, and a Path to Privity', in *Cambridge Law Journal*, p. 175.

9. Cro. Eliz. 619, pl. 8 (QB).
10. Cro. Eliz. 652, pl. 11.
11. (1688) Moore KB. 550, 'En Bank le Roy le pere de file assume al pere le fits q sil voit donner son consent al le marriage & assure 40l terre a son fits, que il le pere le pere le file voiloit payer 200l al fits en marriage: & le question fuit si le fits mesme ou son pere ava action sur le case sur assumpsit vers le pere le file sil ne pay le 200 l. Popham & Fenner que le fits ava l'action. Clench e contra, absente Gawdy.'
12. 2 Taunt 374.
13. *Hadves against Levit* in Het 176.
14. All references to *The Woman's Prize or the Tamer Tamed* are taken from *Twilight Pictures Internet Beaumont and Fletcher Editions* <http://www.uq.edu.au/emsah/drama/fletcher/ff/prize/prize_firstfolio/prize_fscenes/prize.html>. Accessed 8 August 2007. Act/scene references are provided in parenthesis.
15. The problematic nature of this reference is evidenced in its omission from both Gregory Doran's production of the play for the RSC in 2003 and the production's published performance text, *The Tamer Tamed* (2003) (London: Nick Hern Books). My thanks to Gordon McMullan, textual consultant for this production, who confirmed that it was omitted because it was found to be meaningless in performance.
16. C33/71 ff 472, 563 cited in N. G. Jones (1998) 'Trusts in England after the Statute of Uses: a View from the Sixteenth Century', in R. H. Helmholz and R. Zimmermann (eds.) *Itinera Fiduciae: Trust and Treuhand in Historical Perspective* (Berlin: Duncker and Humbolt), p. 89.
17. *Twelfth Night* (5.1.315).
18. V. V. Palmer (1992) *The Paths to Privity: The History of Third Party Beneficiary Contracts at English Law* (San Francisco: Austin and Winfield), p. 8.
19. For a similar argument about Lear's journey to Dover, see J. Goldberg (1984) 'Dover Cliff and the Conditions of Representation: *King Lear* 4:6 in Perspective', *Poetics Today* 5.3, pp. 537–47.
20. Thus Greenblatt et al. (1997) *The Norton Shakespeare* at p. 100.
21. *OED Online* at http://dictionary.oed.com/cgi/entry/S10188738.
22. For an account of the Deleuzean notion of reterritorialisation, see F. Jameson, 'Marxism and Dualism in Deleuze', in I. Buchanan (1999) *A Deleuzian Century?* (Durham, NC: Duke University Press), pp. 13–36.
23. K. Schlueter (1990) *The New Cambridge Shakespeare The Two Gentlemen of Verona* (Cambridge: Cambridge University Press), p. 133; Greenblatt et al. (1997), p. 127.
24. See, for example, Catherine Belsey's (1985) account of Shakespeare's comic heroines 'dwindling' into marriage: 'Disrupting Sexual Difference: Meaning and Gender in the Comedies', in J. Drakakis, *Alternative Shakespeares* (London: Methuen), pp. 160–90.
25. See, for instance, J. L. Simmons (1993) 'Coming Out in Shakespeare's *The Two Gentlemen of Verona*', in *ELH* 60.4, p. 874.
26. For the woman's separate estate, see A. L. Erikson (1994) *Women and Property in Early Modern England* (London: Routledge).
27. *Macbeth* 5.5. 23–5.
28. Other commentators have observed the connection between Crab and Shylock, but characteristically see it in representational rather performative

terms as evidence of what Gail Kern Paster has described as 'a long association in the history of European anti-Semitism between Jews and dogs'. See G. K. Paster (1999) 'From the Editor', *Shakespeare Quarterly* 50.2, p. iii. Thus, in the article to which Paster refers, Bruce Boehrer proposes that 'Crab's lack of emotion evokes an ethnic association of central importance to *The Merchant of Venice*'. See B. Beohrer (1999) 'Shylock and the Rise of the Household Pet: Thinking Social Exclusion in *The Merchant of Venice*', in ibid., p. 155.
29. My discussion here will inevitably recall the idea of 'double time' in *Othello*. See M. R. Ridley's (1965) introduction to *The Arden Shakespeare Othello* (London and New York: Methuen) for an exposition of this influential theory, and Emrys Jones (1971) *Scenic Form in Shakespeare* (Oxford: Clarendon Press) for an equally influential counterattack on over-naturalistic approaches to Shakespearean time schemes. For recent reappraisals, see S. Sohmer (2002) 'The "Double Time" Crux in *Othello* Solved', *English Literary Renaissance* 32.2, pp. 214–38, and L. Hutson (2007) *The Invention of Suspicion: Law and Mimesis in Shakespeare and Renaissance Drama* (Oxford: Oxford University Press), pp. 118–19.
30. C. W. Wallace (1913) 'The First London Theatre: Materials for a History', *Nebraska University Studies* 13, p. 160.
31. Ibid., p. 197.
32. See W. H. Bryson (2001) *Cases Concerning Equity and the Courts of Equity 1550–1660*, (London: Selden Society) vol. 1, xxviii (2001), p. xxviii. For the relation between waste and 'excess of array', see the discussion of the Acts and Proclamations of Apparel in Chapter 3 above at pp. 45–6 above.
33. *Halghe v. Howson* (1583), in N. G. Jones (1998), in Helmholz and Zimmermann, pp. 184–5.
34. G. McAuley (1999) *Space in Performance: Making Meaning in the Theatre* (Ann Arbor, MI: University of Michigan Press), pp. 126–7.
35. A. Gurr (2004) *The Shakespeare Company 1594–1642* (Cambridge: Cambridge University Press), p. 19.
36. Ibid., p. 87.
37. Ibid., p. xiii.
38. G. Malynes (London, 1622), *Consuetudo, vel lex mercatoria, or The ancient law-merchant*, Ch. XLII: 'Of Associations, Monopolies, Engrossings, and Forestallings'. (Bodleian Library <http://gateway.proquest.com/openurl?ctx_ver=Z39.88-2003&res_id=xri.eebo&rft_id=xri.eebo.citation.99849272>. Accessed from *Early English Books Online*, 15 August 2007. For a discussion of Malynes in relation to *The Merchant of Venice* and *Troilus and Cressida*, see J. G. Harris (2004) *Sick Economies: Drama, Mercantilism, and Disease in Shakespeare's England* (Philadelphia: University of Pennsylvania Press).
39. J. Loewenstein (2002) *Ben Jonson and Possessive Authorship* (Cambridge: Cambridge University Press).

Chapter 6

1. Statute of Monopolies 1623, 21 Jac 1, c.3.
2. Joseph Loewenstein (2002) *Ben Jonson and Possessive Authorship* (Cambridge: Cambridge University Press). Loewenstein characterises the rise of possessive authorship as a 'transformation in the way authors understood

themselves – as producers and (in Mark Rose's nice phrase) as owners', and suggests that this transformation 'conditioned the political struggles that lead to the legal institution of intellectual property' (p. 2).
3. Ibid., pp. 85–6.
4. For discussions of an 'author's theatre', see R. Helgerson (1992) *Forms of Nationhood: The Elizabethan Writing of England* (Chicago: University of Chicago Press); R. Weimann (2000) *Author's Pen and Actor's Voice: Playing and Writing in Shakespeare's Theatre* (Cambridge: Cambridge University Press); J. Knapp (2005) 'What is a Co-Author?' *Representations* 89.1, pp. 1–29.
5. *A Midsummer Night's Dream* 5.1.208; *Hamlet* 2.2.384; *Macbeth* 5.5.23; *As You Like It* 2.7.138.
6. For the history of the theatrical metaphor, see A. Righter (1967) *Shakespeare and the Idea of the Play* (Harmondsworth: Penguin Books).
7. J. H. Baker (ed.) (2002) *Year Books of Henry VIII: 12–14 Henry VIII 1520–23* (London: Selden Society), p. 18.
8. Peter Holland (1994), editor of *The Oxford Shakespeare* edition (Oxford: Oxford University Press) p. 229, argues against the idea that this temporal disjunction has any significance of this kind: 'Though their play is not chosen by Theseus until 5.1.76 the audience has not the slightest doubt that it will be; critics who argue differently have a fine sense of logic and reality and little awareness of how dramatic plots work.' This question has points of contact with the 'double time' debate annotated at p. 159 n. 29 above.
9. See, for instance, the *Arden Shakespeare Hamlet* editors, H. Jenkins (1982), p. 479, and A. Thompson and N. Taylor (2006), p. 267 (citing Loewenstein). For a contrasting reading, see Anthony Dawson, in P. Yachnin and A. B. Dawson (2001) *The Culture of Playgoing in Shakespeare's England: A Collaborative Debate* (Cambridge: Cambridge University Press), pp. 174–9, who approaches the speech as a 'record' of the 'national trauma' experienced 'by English people over the previous seventy years or so, when the struggle raged over what could count as memory, what should be erased, how the nation should be reconfigured in relation to, among others things, an English religion'.
10. Loewenstein (2002), p. 86.
11. Ibid., pp. 87; 89.
12. D. H. Sacks, 'The Countervailing of Benefits: Monopoly, Liberty, and Benevolence in Elizabethan England', in D. Hoak (ed.) (1995) *Tudor Political Culture* (Cambridge: Cambridge University Press), pp. 272–91.
13. L. A. Seneca, trans. J. W. Basor (1928-35) *Moral Essays* (London: The Loeb Classical Library), vol. 3, p. 13.
14. J. Levine (ed.) (1969) *Elizabeth I* (Upper Saddle River, NJ: Prentice Hall), pp. 142–3. For a discussion of Elizabeth's speeches, see L. S. Marcus (2000), 'From Oral Delivery to Print in the Speeches of Elizabeth I', in Marotti and Bristol, pp. 33–48.
15. M. Archer (1987) 'The Meaning of "Grace" and "Courtesy": Book VI of *The Faerie Queene*', *Studies in English Literature, 1500–1900*, 27.1, p. 32.
16. J. H. Baker (ed.) (1977) *The Reports of Sir John Spelman* (London: Selden Society) vol.2 p. 210. We might recall that the family crest for which Shakespeare successfully applied in 1596 consisted of a falcon with wings argent shaking a spear with the motto 'non sanz droict' (not without right). Loewenstein's (2002, p. 86) reading of this crest attends to its representation of 'the writing

and spending hand that had earned and purchased such eminence as the family now had'.
17. C. Marlowe, *The Tragedie of Dido Queene of Carthage*, ed. C. F. Tucker Brooke (1966) *The Works of Christopher Marlowe*, (Oxford: Oxford University Press), 5.1.1564–7.
18. Loewenstein (2002), p. 89.
19. Jenkins (1982), pp. 479–80.
20. Ibid., p. 480. In Tucker Brooke (1966) these lines occur at 2.1.558–9.
21. Thompson and Taylor (2006), p. 269. Loewenstein (2002), p. 89 passes over this crux breezily, as if aware of the challenge it offers to his Oedipal reading: 'though Pyrrhus acts on behalf of his own now-incapable but once-nearly-invincible father, he hesitates when his sense of duty brings him to the brink of unleashing a huge violence against an enfeebled patriarch'.
22. Lucius Annaeus Seneca (London, 1581) *Seneca his tenne tragedies translated into Englysh*. Henry E. Huntington Library and Art Gallery. <http://gateway.proquest.com/openurl?ctx_ver=Z39.88_2003&res_id=xri.eebo&rft_id=xri.eebo.citation.99852323>. Accessed from *Early English Books Online*, 12 December 2007.
23. This affiliation is acknowledged in Gertrude's lament that she 'hoped thou shouldst have been my Hamlet's wife./I thought thy bride-bed to have decked, sweet maid,/And not t' have strewed thy grave' (5.1.228–30). See E. Sheen (2004) 'These are the Only Men: Seneca and Monopoly in *Hamlet*', in C. Martindale and A. B. Taylor (eds.) *Shakespeare and the Classics* (Cambridge: Cambridge University Press), pp. 156–72 for an early attempt to develop this argument.
24. See L. Erne (2003) *Shakespeare as Literary Dramatist* (Cambridge: Cambridge University Press); and P. Cheney (2004) *Shakespeare, National Poet-Playwright* (Cambridge: Cambridge University Press) for compelling accounts of Shakespeare as an author writing for readers as well as players and spectators.
25. My use of the term 'convergence' is informed by its contemporary application to the multi-media platforms associated with conglomerate vertical integration and the rise of a global market discussed in Chapter 1. For a general discussion, see H. Jenkins (2006) *Convergence Culture: Where Old and New Media Collide* (New York: New York University Press).
26. Sir W. Cornwallis (London, 1601) *Discourses vpon Seneca the tragedian*. Henry E. Huntington Library and Art Gallery. <http://gateway.proquest.com/openurl?ctx_ver=Z39.88-2003&res_id=xri:eebo.citation.99844354>. Accessed from *Early English Book Online*, 20 December 2008.
27. Translated by Jasper Heywood, In Seneca (1581) as the first speech of the play:

> Who so in pompe of prowde estate, or kingdome sets delight:
> Or who that ioyes in princes court to beare the sway of might.
> Ne dredes the fates which from aboue the wauering gods
>   downe flinges:
> But fast affiaunce fixed hath, in fraile and fickle thinges:
> Let him in me both see the face, of fortunes flattring ioye:
> And eke respect the ruthfull ende, of the (O rumons [*sic*] Troye)
> For neuer gaue she plainer proofe, then thys ye present se:
> How fraile and brittle is the state of pride and high degre.

28. As Cornwallis (1601) puts it, 'Behold Hecuba, a princess in her youth made happy, with having magnificence and principalitie ... in her age possessed of mortal immortalitie, of all the graces that raigne in man ...'
29. L. Barroll (1988) 'A New History for Shakespeare and His Time', *Shakespeare Quarterly* 39, p. 442. For discussions of the Elizabeth–Lambarde conversation, see S. Greenblatt (1982) *The Power of Forms in the English Renaissance* (Norman, Oklahoma: Pilgrim Books), p. 3; S. Orgel (1982) 'Making Greatness Familiar', in ibid., p. 45; J. Dollimore (1984) *Radical Tragedy: Religion, Ideology and Power in the Drama of Shakespeare and his Contemporaries* (Hassocks: Harvester Press), p. 23; J. Dollimore and A. Sinfield (1985) *Political Shakespeare: New Essays in Cultural Materialism* (Manchester: Manchester University Press), p. 9.
30. S. P. Dom. Eliz. 1598–1601, CCLXXVIII, art. 85.
31. See n. 67 at p. 148 above.
32. Greenblatt (1982), p. 3; Dollimore and Sinfield (1985), p. 9; K. E. Maus, in S. Greenblatt et al. (1997), p. 944, my emphasis.
33. This 'Memoir' is published in J. Nichols (ed.) (1780–90) *Bibliotheca Topographica Brittanica* (London), vol. 1, pp. 493–531.
34. Orgel, in Greenblatt (1982), p. 45.
35. D. Bruster (2000) 'The Structural Transformation of Print in Late Elizabethan England', in A. F. Marotti and M. D. Bristol (eds) *Print, Manuscript and Performance: The Changing Relations of the Media in Early Modern England* (Columbus, OH: Ohio State University Press), p. 65.
36. Farmer and Lesser's demonstration (2005), 'The Popularity of Playbooks, Revisited', *Shakespeare Quarterly*, 56.1, p. 11, that the growth of a market in printed plays at the end of the 1590s was largely driven by the popularity of Shakespeare's plays, lends support to my proposal. Of course, Shakespeare had no formal proprietary rights in these publications, but the property his industry created for a wide range of beneficiaries in institutions of publication and the market confirmed his status within a system of exchange that would lead directly towards the retrospective establishment of a concept of literary property based on the kind of status I am discussing in this chapter. Noting that Shakespeare, Bacon and Milton were 'the perennials of the book trade', whom 'the booksellers had been accustomed to treat as if they were private landed estates', Mark Rose (1988) has shown how Lockean arguments about the origin of property in individual acts of appropriation from the general state of nature were used to advance the idea that writers like Shakespeare were already owners of their own work, and consequently that the transfer of this property to the booksellers gave them a legitimate title ('The Author as Proprietor: *Donaldson v Becket* and the Genealogy of Modern Authorship', *Representations* 23, p. 53). At that point, we might appropriately discuss the centrality of Shakespearean authorship to a Habermasian concept of the public sphere, but not, I think, before. For the public sphere, see J. Habermas (1991) *The Structural Transformation of the Public Sphere: An Inquiry into a Category of Bourgeois Society* (Boston, MA: MIT Press).

Chapter 7

1. Thomas Dekker (Edinburgh, 1604), *The Magnificent Entertainment Given to King James*, British Library, <http://gateway.proquest.com/openurl?ctx_ver=z39.88-2003&res_id=xri.eebo&rft_id=xri.eebo.citation.99850915>. Accessed from *Early English Books Online* 20 November 2007.
2. See S. Schoenbaum, *William Shakespeare: A Documentary Life* (Oxford: Oxford University Press 1977); P. Honan (1998) *Shakespeare: A Life* (1998), p. 303.
3. See C. Perry (1997) *The Making of Jacobean Culture: James I and the Renegotiation of Elizabethan Literary Practice* (Cambridge and New York: Cambridge University Press) for an account of the transition from the mutuality of the Elizabethan commonwealth to Jacobean absolutism.
4. R. Holinshed (London, 1587) *The first and second volumes of Chronicles*. Henry E. Huntington Library and Art Gallery. <http:gateway.proquest.com/openurl?ctx_ver=Z39.88-2008&res_id=xri.eebo&rft_id=xri.eebo.citation.3>. Accessed from *Early English Books Online*, 5 December 2007. Textual references are to this digital file so no further citation are provided.
5. EEBO provides the version of this text attributed to Michael Drayton, published after Shakespeare's play. M. Drayton (London, 1605) *The true chronicle history of King Leir, and his three daughters*, Henry E. Huntington Library and Art Gallery. <http://gateway.proquest.com/openurl?ctx_ver=Z39.88-2003&res_id=xri.eebo.citation.99846511>. Accessed from *Early English Books Online*, 15 November 2007.
6. T. P. Rocher Jr. (ed.) (1978) *Edmund Spensor, The Faerie Queere* (Harmondsworth: Penguin), Book II, Canto X, 28, p. 335
7. See, for instance, D. Callaghan (1989) *Woman and Gender in Renaissance Tragedy: A Study of King Lear, Othello, the Duchess of Malfi and the White Devil* (Atlantic Highlands, NJ: Humanities International Press) for the argument that the silence and absence of women like Cordelia and Desdemona constitutes a 'transgressive' void at the centre of their respective plays.
8. See S. Greenblatt (2004) *Will in the World: How Shakespeare Became Shakespeare* (New York: W. W. Norton) for biographical speculation on Shakespeare's relations with Robert Greene.
9. R. Greene (1601), *Penelopes Web*. Henry E. Huntington Library and Art Gallery. <http://gateway.proquest.com/openurl?ctx_ver=Z39.88-2003&res_id=xri.eebo&rft_id=xri.eebo.citation.99839178>. Accessed from *Early English Books Online*, 15 November 2007.
10. G. Walker (1998) *The Politics of Performance in Early Renaissance Drama* (Cambridge: Cambridge University Press), p. 201.
11. G. D. Ramsay (1977) 'Clothworkers, Merchant Adventurers and Richard Hakluyt', *The English Historical Review* 92.364, pp. 504, 505 and 507.
12. See D. Dean (1996) *Law Making and Society in Late Elizabethan England: the Parliament of England 1584–1601* (Cambridge: Cambridge University Press), p. 133.
13. Ramsay (1977), p. 512.
14. D. L. Thomas and N. E. Evans (1984) 'John Shakespeare in the Exchequer', *Shakespeare Quarterly* 35.3, pp. 317-18. Patrick Collinson (1994) *Elizabethan*

Essays (London: Hambledon Press), p. 246–51, has suggested that John Shakespeare's withdrawal from public life was related to the recusancy with which he was eventually charged in 1592.
15. C. Shrank (2002) 'Civility and the City in *Coriolanus*', *Shakespeare Quarterly* 54.4, pp. 411–12.
16. For a contrasting argument, see D. Armitage, 'Shakespeare's Properties' forthcoming in D. Armitage and A. Fitzmaurice (eds.) *Shakespeare and Political Thought* (Cambridge: Cambridge University Press).
17. Rawlinson MS D vol. 133 f13.
18. See pp. 20–1 above.
19. C. St German, in Plucknett and Barton (eds.) (1974), pp. 222 ff. My emphasis.
20. Ibid., p. 227.
21. Ibid., pp. 229–30. My emphasis.
22. Textual references are to *The Norton Shakespeare*'s Folio *The Tragedy of King Lear* unless indicated otherwise.
23. C. Spinosa (1995) '"The name and all th' addition": King Lear's Opening Scene and the Common Law Use', in L. Barroll (ed.) *Shakespeare Studies*, vol. 23, p. 150, usefully refers to Lear's conveyance of the kingdom to his daughters as a 'proto-use'. However, in the discussion that follows, his concern is with questions of 'identity' rather than property: 'Shakespeare transforms questions about the use, and the affection that the use depends on, into questions about the personal identity of a self (Lear's) constituted as the general unifying style in which common practices and particular actions make sense' (p. 171).
24. *OED Online* at <http:/dictionary.oed.com/cgi/entry/50208901/entry 2(Law).
25. For the phenomenological reduction, see D. Moran (2000) *Introduction to Phenomenology* (London: Routledge), pp. 146–7.
26. References to Q1 and F are taken from *The Norton Shakespeare*'s parallel presentation of both texts.
27. G. Ioppolo (1991), in *Revising Shakespeare* (Cambridge, MA: Harvard University Press), pp. 167–82, presents a well-developed account of the differences between Cordelia in Q1 and F. She suggests that Cordelia is 'powerful and active' in Q1 and 'incidental and subordinate' in F. Even so, she characterises these asides in negative terms: 'In the Quarto she acts badly, and in the Folio she speaks badly ... Where does the difference lie in *doing* love and *speaking* love and why do these texts diverge here in the evolution of Cordelia's character?' Her answer is that 'in each text Cordelia makes a deliberate choice that will govern her dramatic portrayal, form and meaning: in the Quarto she decides to do nothing and in the Folio she decides to say nothing' (p. 169).
28. Noted in *The Norton Shakespeare* at p. 2318
29. G. Ioppolo (1991), p. 182.
30. Ioppolo sees Shakespeare as a 'deliberate, consistent and persistent reviser' whose plays have '[no] "final" form, only a *later* form' (ibid., pp. 5, 186).
31. As this suggests, I consider proposals for the existence of an early modern public sphere in the early seventeenth century more plausible than the 1590s, though *Lear* is earlier than most of the following studies would suggest: D. Norbrook (1994) 'Areopagitica, Censorship, and the Early Modern Public', in R. Burt (ed.) *The Administration of Aesthetics: Censorship, Political Criticism and the Public Sphere* (Minneapolis, MN: Minnesota University Press); S. Achinstein (1994) *Milton and the Revolutionary Reader* (Princeton, NJ: Princeton University Press); A. Halász (1997) *The Marketplace of Print: Pamphlets and*

the Public Sphere in Early Modern England (Cambridge: Cambridge University Press); J. Raymond (1999) (ed.) *News, Newspapers and Society in Early Modern Britain* (London and Portland, OR: Frank Cass); M.O'Callaghan (2000) *The 'Shepheard's Nation': Jacobean Spenserians and Early Stuart Political Culture 1612–1625* (Oxford: Oxford University Press); D. Zaret (2000) *Origins of Democratic Culture: Printing, Petitions and the Public Sphere in Early Modern England* (Princeton, NJ: Princeton University Press); P. Lake and S. Pincus (2007) *The Politics of the Public Sphere in Early Modern England* (Manchester: Manchester University Press).
32. V. Kahn (2001) '"The Duty to Love": Passion and Obligation in Early Modern Political Theory', in V. Kahn and L. Hutson (eds.) *Rhetoric and Law in Early Modern Europe* (New Haven, CT: Yale University Press), p. 260.
33. Ibid., pp. 244, 245.
34. For *Dutton v. Poole*, see V. V. Palmer (1992) *The Paths to Privity: The History of Third Party Beneficiary Contracts at English Law* (San Francisco: Austin and Winfield), pp. 75–8.
35. Palmer (1992) *The Paths to Privity*, p. 76.
36. Ioppolo (1991), p. 185.
37. Roy Kreitner (2001) 'The Gift beyond the Grave: Revisiting the Question of Consideration', *Columbia Law Review* 101.8, p. 1878.

Chapter 8

1. A. Gurr (2004) *The Shakespeare Company 1594–1642* (Cambridge: Cambridge University Press), p. 37, p. 36.
2. Ibid., p. 37.
3. Z. Lesser (1999) 'Walter Burre's *The Knight of the Burning Pestle*', *English Literary Renaissance* 29, p. 22; see also (2004) *Renaissance Drama and the Politics of Publication: Readings in the English Book Trade* (Cambridge: Cambridge University Press).
4. A. Gurr (1999) in R. Cave, E. Schafer and B. Woolland, *Ben Jonson and Theatre: Performance, Practice and Theory* (London: Routledge), pp. 5–19.
5. A. R. Dutton (1974) 'The Significance of Jonson's Revision of *Every Man in his Humour*', *The Modern Language Review* 69.2, p. 242.
6. Andrew Gurr's generous approach to early modern theatre-professional enmities encourages him to read the King's Men's employment of Jonson, Beaumont and Fletcher, after the antagonisms of 'the War of the Theatres', in Shakespearean terms as a 'readiness to forgive' (though he also suggests, more pragmatically, that this 'lack of ill will ... went with the upward mobility that was now able to take on the Blackfriars audiences' [2004], p. 54).
7. Ibid., p. 37.
8. Gurr, in Cave, Schafer and Woolland (1999), p. 6.
9. Ibid., pp. 11–12.
10. L. Wilson (2000) *Theaters of Intention: Drama and the Law in Early Modern England* (Stanford, CA: Stanford University Press). See Chapter 2, 'Ben Jonson and the Law of Contract' and Chapter 4, 'Promissory Performances'.
11. Ibid., p. 107.
12. Gurr, in Cave, Schafer and Woolland (1999), pp. 16–17.
13. All references to *The Alchemist* are taken from G. Campbell (1995) *Ben Jonson: The Alchemist and Other Plays* (Oxford: Oxford University Press).

14. See pp. 29–30 above.
15. L. Wilson (2000), pp. 95; 99.
16. Ibid., p. 99.
17. Ibid.
18. Lesser (1999), p. 29.
19. Gurr (1999) p. 18, describes the allusion as 'at least semi-private in its own time'.
20. D. Lindley (ed.) (2002) *The New Cambridge Shakespeare The Tempest* (Cambridge: Cambridge University Press), p. 111.
21. Wilson (2000) p. 166 discusses the possibility that the verb 'cast' in *The Tempest* ('she that from whom We all were sea-swallow'd, though some cast again' [2.1.245–6]) has theatrical connotations not yet recorded by OED; he does not link it to *The Achemist*.
22. Lindley (2002), pp. 71–3.
23. For the 'ripe daughter', and her role in the mutually consitutive relations between royal husbandry, the Jacobean succession and Jonsonian authorship see 'To Penshurst', written 1611–12, in G. Parfitt (1988) *Ben Jonson The Complete Poems* (London: Penguin) p. 96, l. 54.
24. A. Giddens (1979) *Central Problems in Social Theory: Action, Structure and Contradiction in Social Analysis* (London: Macmillan), p. 110.
25. See pp. 22 above.
26. Of course, he continued to collaborate after this point. See G. McMullan's Introduction to his (2000) *Arden Shakespeare* edition of Shakespeare and Fletcher's play *King Henry VIII or All is True*.
27. I can only glance here at the question of Shakespeare's relationship with his own daughters, particularly Susanna, at the point around the move into the Blackfriars when he began to spend more time in Stratford. His granddaughter, Susanna's daughter Elizabeth, was born in September 1608; Shakespeare's mother died the same year. These personal temporal intersections inform the last plays in the same way that questions about his father inform *King Lear*, but the forms in which they do so were deeply embedded in Shakespearean theatre from its earliest years.
28. Jonson, 'On Poet-Ape', in Parfitt (1988), p. 51.
29. J. Loewenstein (2002) *The Author's Due: Printing and the Prehistory of Copyright* (Chicago and London: University of Chicago Press), p. 108. Parfitt (1988), p.490 describes the attribution of this reference to Shakespeare as a 'groundless tradition'.
30. T. Murray (1983) 'From Foul Sheets to Legitimate Model: Antitheater, Text, Ben Jonson', *New Literary History* 14.3, p. 651.
31. M. Swann (1998) 'Refashioning Society in Ben Jonson's *Epicoene*', *Studies in English Literature 1500–1900* 38.2, p. 305.
32. Gurr (2004), p. 88. Niall Ferguson has controversially proposed that counterfactuals are a valid intellectual exercise if pursued on the basis of what individual historical agents demonstrably considered to be possible alternative courses of action. See N. Ferguson (1999) 'Virtual History: Towards a Chaotic Theory of the Past', in N. Ferguson (ed.) *Virtual History: Alternatives and Counterfactuals* (New York: Basic Books).
33. *The Independent*, 28 June 2007.

Index

'22 Eliz' 76, 83, 92

Acts
  of commission 88
  of permission 87
Admiral's Men 3, 30, 61
Agnew, Jean-Christophe 6, 7, 16
Alleyn, Edward 112
Anderson, Sir Edmund 22, 40, 85
Antiquarian Society 54
Apparel 48–9, 51
  Statute of (7 Hen 8, c. 6) 45–6
Archer, Mark 102
As You Like It 17, 23, 90–6, 126, 137, 138
Assign 113–14
Assurance 21, 27, 28, 49–51, 77, 114
Audley, Thomas 21
Augé, Marc, *non-lieux* 67
Autobiographical charge 100, 103, 118, 133
Avow 121

Bacon, Francis 52, 71
Baker J. H. 20, 34, 37, 38
Bakhtin, Mikhail 6
Barroll, Leeds 7–9, 13, 16
Beaumont, Francis and Fletcher, John
  The Knight of the Burning Pestle 129
Belvoir Castle 46
Beneficial ownership 17, 19–42, 71, 96, 105, 120, 123, 125, 131
  beneficial literary ownership 96, 102, 105, 111, 130
Benefit 26, 36, 40, 75, 90, 93, 94, 101, 102, 105, 117, 127
Benjamin, Walter 4
Bills 23, 24, 37–9, 4
Biography 7
Blackfriars playhouse 13, 18, 24, 31, 33, 39, 128–33
Bloodhounds 44, 46, 102

Body 51, 59, 62, 80–2, 84, 90
  see also embodiment
Bonds 27, 28, 34, 66, 68–71, 72, 77, 79, 83–7, 90, 102, 105, 112, 123, 131, 133, 137
Bowen v Morriss (1810) 75
Brayne, John 26–35
Brayne, Margaret 25–35
Bristol, Michael 11
Bruster, Douglas 6, 7, 9, 16, 109
Bryson W. H. 24, 25, 37
Buc, Sir George
  Daphnis Polystephanos 54
  History of the Life and Reigne of Richard III 54
Burbages, the 13, 17, 24–41, 97
  Cuthbert 26, 29, 30–1, 34–6, 38–9
  James 25–39, 128, 128
  Richard 26, 29, 61, 65, 128
Burre, Walter 129, 132, 134

Camera regis 52, 58, 67, 69
  echo chamber 78
  king's chamber 52, 58, 112
  special chamber 58, 67
  theatrical chamber 67–8, 78–9, 129
Carnival 6, 16
Cestuy que use 20, 21, 35, 105, 120
Chamberlain's Men 13–16, 26, 31, 34, 38, 39, 53, 61, 67, 79, 85–7, 98, 99, 103, 108, 112
Chancery 20, 23, 24, 25, 32, 25, 36, 37
Chapel Children 103, 128
Chettle, Henry 60, 97
Cinema and film 1, 7
Circulation 4, 7
Clancy, Thomas 8
Clear and present danger 7–8
Clifford, George 3rd Earl of Cumberland 118–19
Clifford, Margaret, Countess of 119

Cloth   112, 116, 118, 119
  clothier   120
  clothing   47
  clothworkers   115, 118–20, 122, 140
  gowns   121
  robes   71
Cokayne, Sir Thomas   48
Coke, Sir Edward   54, 71, 97
Cold War   4, 5, 6, 8, 9, 11
Collaboration   17, 54, 60, 61, 66
Company, the idea of the   12–17, 32–42, 61–4, 94–6
Competence, social   109, 112
Condell, Henry   128
Consideration   25, 31, 32, 73–6, 88, 120, 127
Contract   125–7, 130–3, 135
Contractualism   125, 130, 132
Convergence   105
Cope, Sir Walter   30–1, 35–6, 41
Corbett v Corbett (1600)   22–3, 76
Cornwallis, Sir William
  Discourses upon Seneca the Tragedian   106–7
  Essayes of certain paradoxes   53–4
Court, courts   13–16, 20–41, 67, 80, 83, 85, 87, 90, 95, 101
  Chancery   20, 23, 24, 25, 32, 35, 36, 37
  Common Pleas   22, 44
  King's Bench   127
  Requests   38
  Star Chamber   24, 32, 36, 38, 39, 112
Coverture   72, 76, 88, 89
  feme covert   75, 77
Cultural poetics   3, 4,7,11, 33

Daughter, daughters   18, 22, 23, 29, 33, 51, 66, 72, 75–7, 83, 86, 89, 92, 105, 113–27, 137–9
Dawson, Anthony B.   9–10, 16
Debt   79, 85
  indebtedness   94
Dekker, Thomas   60, 112
Deleuze, Gilles   64, 66
  becoming-player   64, 66, 80

reterritorialisation   80
Demurrer   44, 48
Devereux, Robert 2nd. Earl of Essex   15–16, 39, 106–9
Diversity   60, 69–71
Dogs   43, 44–9, 79–80, 84, 85
Dollimore, Jonathan   108
Donno, Elizabeth Story   55
Duopoly   13
Durée   6, 15, 34, 37, 40, 96, 137–8, 140–1
Dutton v Poole (1680)   126
Dutton, Richard   129
Duty circle   20, 37, 40, 78–81, 83, 90, 93–4, 112, 128, 130
Duty of care   127

Eden, Kathy   53
Egerton, Sir Thomas   23–5, 39
Elizabeth I   7, 18, 39, 97, 101, 102, 107–9, 111, 112–18, 124–7
  Golden Speech   97, 101, 109
Elton, G. R.   52
Embodiment   66–9, 76, 78–81, 84, 86–7, 89, 95, 99, 122, 132
Encomium of Richard III   53
English Reports   75
  Croke   74
  Hetley   76
  Taunton   75
Equity   20, 23, 24, 38, 41
  the equitable jurisdictions   66

Fee simple   121
Fletcher, John, *The Woman's Prize, or, The Tamer Tamed*   76–8
Ford Company, the   14–15
Foucault, Michel   1, 3, 5
Fraudulence   21, 36, 89, 127
Fyllol v Ashelleygh (1520)   43–4, 46, 47–9, 78, 99, 102
Fyllol, Sir William   44, 45

Game Act (13 R2, st 1 c. 13)   45
Giddens, Anthony   12–17, 138, 141
Globe playhouse   3, 14, 17, 23–4, 26, 33–4, 37–41, 67–8, 78, 87, 90–2, 94, 128, 130, 141

Gouge, William   126
Great Man theory   33
Greenblatt, Stephen   2–7, 11, 13, 57, 108
Greene, Robert   61, 97–8, 102, 124–5
  Penelope's Web   115–19
Gurr, Andrew   33, 94–5, 128–30, 132, 134, 141
Guy, John   19

Habermas, Jürgen   18, 109
Habit   72, 81, 85
  habitation   91
  inhabit   81
  uninhabited   88
Hamlet   14–17, 41, 64, 97–111, 119, 125
Hammond, Antony   57–8, 65, 69
Hawks   51
  falcon   47, 102
  sparrowhawk   71
Hemminges, John   128
Henry VII   52, 54
Henry VIII   20–2, 52–4, 62, 64
Heywood, Jasper, *Troas*   104–7
Heywood, Thomas   60
Hobbes, Thomas   3, 126
Holinshed, Raphael, *First and Second Volumes of Chronicles*   53, 113–15, 117
Holmes, Oliver Wendell   8
Horses   60, 69–71
Hounds   45–7, 51
House   23, 28, 30, 34, 39, 41, 45, 47, 50, 51, 61, 77, 86, 88, 90–4, 109, 129, 132, 133, 135
  ruins   81, 86–90
Household   46, 52, 54, 91, 112
Hunt, hunting   47–8, 51

Imagination and imagining   19, 21, 32, 39, 47–50, 62, 66, 69, 83, 85, 94, 99, 109, 125
Industry   17, 43, 46, 49–51, 76, 77, 91, 99, 140
Ingram, William   32–3

Interest   19, 20, 21, 24, 26–38, 79, 82, 86–90, 94, 96, 121, 123, 126, 127, 130, 131, 139
Ioppolo, Grace   125, 127

James I   18, 39–42, 111, 112, 118, 120, 125, 127
Jenkins, Harold   103–4
Jetzheit   138
Johnson v Smythe (1586)   77
Joint stock company   96
Jones, John   62
Jonson, Ben   18, 97–8, 112, 123, 125, 128–41
  Alchemist, The   18, 129–39
  Bartholomew Fair   130, 131
  Catiline   131, 132
  'Conversations'   130
  Epicoene   129
  'Ode to Himself'   130
  'To the Memory of my Beloved'   140
  'To Penshurst'   138

Kahn, Victoria   126
Kempe, William   40
King Lear   18, 20, 54, 75, 112–27, 130
King's Men, the   112, 128–35
Kreitner, Roy   127

Labour   6, 10, 39, 135, 137
Lambarde, William   39, 107–11
Law of Fraudulent Conveyance   36, 127
Law merchant   95
Leggatt, Alexander   65
Leinwand, Theodor   33
Lesser, Zachary   129–34
Levett v Hawes (1599)   73–6, 83, 126
Lindley, David   138
Lodge, Thomas   101
Loewenstein, Joseph   96, 97, 98, 100, 102, 118
London   53–69, 129–30, 133
Lord Chamberlain, the   112
Lull, Janis   66

Magistrates, Mirrour for 113
Magnificent Ambersons, The (1942) 60
Malice 87–8
Malynes, Gerard 95, 99, 133
Manners family, the 46
Manningham, John 64–8, 109, 132
Market, the 4–11, 141–2
Marlowe, Christopher and Thomas Nashe, *Dido Queene of Carthage* 100, 102–6
Marriage 74–6, 88, 91, 93
Marriage settlements 72–3, 76
Martin Guerre 2–3
Marx, Marxism 1, 3–4, 16, 33
Masque
 Jonsonian 123, 125
 in *The Tempest* 136–7
Maus, Katharine Eisaman 108
McAuley, Gay 92
McGill University *Making Publics* project 10–11
McMillin, Scott 60–1
Measure for Measure 93
Media 5, 56, 57, 65
Merchant Adventurers 118–19
Merchant of Venice, The 17, 71, 81, 82, 84–90, 91, 96, 126
Merchants of the Staple 119
Midsummer Night's Dream A 14, 63, 68–9, 93
Mildmay, Sir Anthony 22–3, 114
Miles, Robert 27–37
Milton, John 126
Monopoly 17, 41, 96, 97–8, 100–1, 109
More, Sir Thomas 17, 53–4, 107
 History of Richard III 17, 44, 53, 55–60, 107
 Utopia 44, 62
Munday, Antony 60

Natural love 40, 73, 126–7
Nebuchadnezzar's tree 23, 85
Negligence 63
New Historicism 1–11, 33, 38, 109, 141
Newton, Thomas 104

Norton, Thomas and Sackville, Thomas *Gorbuduc* 117
Nudum pactum 120–7

Occupy, occupation 12–13, 14–15, 17, 19, 20, 29, 31, 34, 35–7, 40–1, 47–8, 65–7, 69, 72–3, 79, 82, 97, 102, 126, 128–9
Orgel, Stephen 106, 109
Owners 16, 19–42, 87, 89, 90, 92, 94, 97, 102, 114, 127, 129, 135–6, 138, 140
Ownership 3, 19–42, 44, 49, 53, 71, 76, 81, 82, 86, 90–2, 94, 96, 102, 105, 120, 123, 125, 127, 128, 133, 138

Palmer, V. V. 127
Participation 23, 37, 64, 66, 67, 72
Parts 40, 48–50, 57–61, 63, 65, 66, 68–70, 72, 74, 83–5, 89, 91, 93, 95, 96, 112, 122, 127, 132, 133
 see also the woman's part
Partner 48–9, 59–60, 69
Partnership 26, 27, 34 60, 65, 72, 75, 76, 77, 83, 88, 90, 93, 95, 96, 112, 127, 130, 133
Party, parties 36, 37, 40, 55, 59–60, 74, 76, 77, 131, 135
 see also third party
Passion 125–7
Patents 39, 41, 95, 101, 112
Patronage 13, 14, 30, 40, 41
Patterson, Annabel 10
Peele, George, *The Battle of Alcazar* 70
Pembroke's Men 61
Perform, performance 10, 13–15, 17–18, 23–4, 33, 36–7, 39, 48–9, 51, 63–70, 72, 79, 81–6, 91–3, 98
Pericles 130
Phenomenology 81
 the phenomenological reduction 122
Phillips, Augustus 40, 108
Playhouse *see* Blackfriars, Globe, Theatre
Pleasure 43–51

Plot   66–7, 72, 75, 79–81
Plowden, Edmund   44
Popham, Sir John   106, 108
Possession   19–21, 24, 25, 28–31, 33, 34, 37–8, 40, 53, 81–3, 96, 100, 106, 113–14, 121, 128, 132, 136, 139, 140
  dispossession   83–5, 91
  quiet possession   37, 39–41, 43
  possessive authorship   96, 97
  repossessive authorship   140
Prendergast, Christopher   4, 11
Principality   80
Print   97, 109, 129, 134, 141
Private, privacy   114, 120, 126, 141
Privity   79–80, 135
  limitation   73–4
  path to   20, 23, 40
  privy   79–80, 126, 129
Privy, the   135
Privy Council   13, 24, 39, 87
Producers, The (1968)   29
Profit   14, 21, 24–37, 44–8, 51, 58–62, 64, 65, 69, 91, 95, 96, 121, 129, 136, 141
Promise   73–5, 79, 82, 120–7
  assumpsit   126
Property   4, 16, 17, 20, 22, 24–8, 31, 32, 34, 35, 38, 40, 43, 45–9, 53, 70–1 75, 81–3, 85–7, 89, 92, 94, 96, 100, 102, 113–14, 115, 121, 123, 126–7, 138, 140
  base   83, 91
  creation by industry   43, 49, 77, 99
  intellectual   34, 36, 100
  literary   100, 109, 140
  relations   2, 82, 89
  rights   3, 17 , 27, 28, 37, 86
  special property in theatre   43, 47–9, 53, 78, 83, 94, 124, 138, 140
  law   25, 37
Psychoanalysis, psychoanalytical theory   1–3
Public   7, 10, 11, 13, 18, 21, 24, 27, 30, 42, 57, 67, 119, 125–6
Public domain   140
Public good   24, 25, 38, 44, 58, 140
Public order   62

Public sphere   13, 18, 125–6, 130
  nascent   109
Publication   10, 13, 32, 65, 96, 113, 119, 129, 132, 134, 139
Pye, Christopher   5

Quia emptores terrarum (18 Edw.1 1290)   19

Readers   102, 105
  readership   105–7
Red Lion playhouse   27
Reservation   121–2
Richard II   15, 107–11
Richard II   39, 108, 107–11
Richard III   12, 17, 20, 52–5
Richard III   53, 55, 56, 65–71, 72, 78, 79, 80, 93, 106, 129, 138
Righter, Anne   98
Roman Catholicism   53
Rose playhouse   13, 61
Rutland, Earls of   46
Rutter, Carol Chillington   33

Sacks, D.H.   73, 101
Satisfaction   35, 70–1, 72, 83, 85, 89, 90, 93, 102, 105, 131, 137
Schenck v United States (1919)   8
Schlueter, Karl   81
Seneca, Lucius Annaeus   100–2, 104–7
  De Beneficiis   101
  Troades   104–7
Service   14, 20, 30, 40, 46, 49, 51, 62, 79, 80, 88, 91, 101, 107
Shakespeare, John   119, 122, 140
Shershow, Scott Cutler   33
Silence   82, 93, 115, 117, 123–4
Simpson, A. W.   73
Sinfield, Alan   108
Sir Thomas More   17, 54, 61–4
Slade v Morley (1602)   73
Societas   95
Spectator   17, 60, 64, 67, 69, 83–5, 89–90, 93, 114, 115, 122, 125, 129, 134, 135
  spectatorship   42, 64, 65–9, 71, 72, 82–3, 85, 90, 93, 112, 123, 125

Spenser, Edmund, *The Faerie Queene* 101, 102, 113–15
St German, Christopher, *Second Dialogue of Doctor and Student* 20, 120–7
Stature of Monopolies 97
Statute of Uses (1 Ric 3, c. 1) 20, 52
  (27 Hen 8, c. 10) 21
Strange's Men 61
Stranger, strangers 74, 76, 79, 80, 82, 86, 112–27
Structuration theory 12–17
Swine 48

Taming of the Shrew, The 12, 17, 43–51, 68, 76, 78, 84, 88, 115, 121
Taylor, Gary 61, 124
Tempest, The 18, 128–39
Theatre playhouse 13, 14, 16, 17, 19, 24, 25–41, 53, 61, 67–8, 79, 85–7, 91, 98–100
Things of pleasure 43–51
  materia voluptatis 44
Third party 20, 23, 70, 72–3, 77, 79, 82, 83, 88, 93, 112, 126, 128, 138
  see also parts
Thompson, Ann 103, 138
  and Taylor, Neil 103
Tilney, Edmund 60
Time 126
  duration 66–8, 86–7, 90, 92, 94, 96, 126
  unity of 135–9
Tripartite indenture 34, 40, 130, 133
Troilus and Cressida 47

True Chronicle History of King Leir and His Three Daughters, The 113–15
True Tragedie of Richard III, The (anon.) 70
True Tragedy of Richard Duke of York, The 61, 102
Trust, trusteeship 20, 21, 34, 35, 40, 72, 82, 88, 89, 91, 121–2, 124
Twelfth Night 62
Two Gentlemen of Verona, The 71, 78–84, 85, 86, 88

Use, the 19–41, 75, 77, 78, 81, 82, 120–4, 136, 139, 140
  execution of 23, 139
  see also Statute of Uses
Usurpation 55, 68

Virgil 100

Wagers and bets 51, 69
Waste 82, 87–8, 91
Waster 92
Wells, Stanley 124
Wilson, Luke 73, 131, 133
Winter's Tale, The 130, 131, 138
Woman's part, the 7, 23, 68, 73, 75, 78, 83, 89–93
Wool 118–22, 140
World 80–6, 90–2
Wright, Thomas, *The Passion of the Minde in General* 126

Yachnin, Paul 9–10, 16